ROOTS OF VIOLENCE
IN BLACK PHILADELPHIA
1860–1900

ROOTS OF VIOLENCE IN BLACK PHILADELPHIA 1860–1900

Roger Lane

Harvard University Press
Cambridge, Massachusetts, and London, England

LIBRARY OF CONGRESS CATALOGING IN PUBLICATION DATA

Lane, Roger.
    Roots of violence in Black Philadelphia, 1860–1900.

    Bibliography: p.
    Includes index.
    1. Afro-Americans—Pennsylvania—Philadelphia—Social
conditions.   2. Afro-American criminals—Pennsylvania—
Philadelphia—History—19th century.   3. Afro-Americans—
Employment—Pennsylvania—Philadelphia—History—19th
century.   4. Philadelphia (Pa.)—Race relations.
5. Philadelphia (Pa.)—Economic conditions.
6. Philadelphia (Pa.)—Social conditions.
7. Violence—Pennsylvania—Philadelphia—History—
19th century.   I. Title.
F158.9.N4L35 1986   364.2'08996073074811   85-13929
ISBN 0-674-77990-8 (alk. paper) (cloth)
ISBN 0-674-77978-9 (paper)

To Alfred Baker Lewis

ACKNOWLEDGMENTS

A NUMBER of people contributed to this project, and several of them were essential to it.

Ward Childs and his staff at the Philadelphia City Archives were as helpful as always in guiding me and my research assistants through the city's extensive collection of criminal records. Henry Williams once again supplied data collected by the Philadelphia Social History project. Peter Parker provided ideas as well as materials from the varied manuscript and other resources of the Historical Society of Pennsylvania.

Research funds were provided in part by Robert M. Collins, in honor of his father, Benjamin R. Collins.

Cristin Carnell, Mark Gerstein, Claudia Gutwirth, Paul Kelly, Tracy Kosman, Alfred Skerpan, and especially David Babbitt spent many hours in many places collecting data as research assistants.

Several scholars were critically important to the work in progress. Mark Haller contributed his special expertise concerning the operations of the criminal underworld; Allen Steinberg shared his knowledge of Philadelphia's criminal justice and court system; and Harry Sillcox was an invaluable guide to the substance and sources of the city's black history. Paul Jefferson and Eric Monkkonen, in addition, gave the full manuscript an intelligent and searching reading.

I would like also to thank the editors at Harvard University Press: Aida Donald for her criticism, Virginia LaPlante for her demanding job of editing, and Elizabeth Suttell for her compassion and support.

Violet Brown and, once again, Adeline Taraborelli typed the manuscript through several stages with their usual efficiency and good humor.

Finally, my wife, Marjorie Merklin, contributed encouragement at every stage, with significant help toward the end from our daughter Joanna Lewis Lane.

CONTENTS

INTRODUCTION

THIS HISTORY is ambitious beyond its necessary limits of time and place. Although based largely on the experience of a minority population, in a single city, over a period of less than half a century, it attempts to understand a much wider and more timely problem. That problem is the rise of criminal and, especially, violently criminal behavior in the United States over the past generation, and the fact that this rise has involved the Afro-American population more than any other. One aspect of this problem, the one most evident to fearful whites, is that blacks are disproportionately likely to engage in criminal activity of many kinds. The other more important aspect is that blacks are far more likely than whites to be victimized by theft and violence directly, and that the indirect effects of criminality have contributed strongly to the cycle of discrimination, poverty, and powerlessness that has narrowed the horizons of millions.

The origins and consequences of this cycle are illumined by joining two lines of historical inquiry that until now have been separate: Afro-American history and the history of criminal behavior. The key link between the two is the urban-industrial revolution, which affected the lives of whites and blacks in different ways. These differences help not only to explain long-term trends in criminal activity but also the often painful history of the black experience in American cities.

Despite contemporary concerns about the possible connection between race and criminality, the history of crime has ignored almost wholly the Afro-American population of the United States. During the 1960s there was often a distinctly racial edge to fears about rising rates of burglary, armed robbery, and homicide. But such rises were occurring at the same time in much of the world. Local explanations thus had limited value. A condition so widespread could not be understood fundamentally in terms of the changing racial composition of our inner cities any more than in terms of the size and composition of a given police force. The search for understanding turned back to the previous century and to places where blacks were so small a proportion of the population that the issue of racial difference was irrelevant. It revealed that the black experience in this country was not centrally important to long-term trends in illicit or violent behavior and was far from typical.

Until recently, the conventional wisdom was that rising crime was associated simply with the growth of cities, especially the rapid growth that marked the onset of the industrial revolution in the nineteenth century. Both Americans and Europeans who lived through this process feared the disruptive effects of the new economic order, and their fears found powerful expression among early sociologists, who explained anti-social behavior of all sorts as resulting from the depersonalization, anomie, and loss of communal life which allegedly affected those living in cities. While such theories have the advantage of explaining criminality in terms of a universal rather than a purely local perspective, they do not stand up.[1]

A more complex relation exists between social change, urban growth, and crime. Such nineteenth century "offenses against public order" as drunkenness, gambling, and prostitution fluctuated more often in response to changing public policies than to changing behavior, with arrests going up as a result not of increasing disorder but of higher standards of public behavior. Serious crimes of violence against the person typically decreased, notably murder, the most serious and best recorded of all these crimes. The same decrease was apparent in such property crimes as larceny and burglary. Although crimes against property usually tended to increase in times of hardship and decrease in times of prosperity, while crimes of violence reacted to the economic cycle in precisely the opposite way, these short-term fluctuations only masked the fact that both types of crime were decreasing over the longer term, often sharply so. The downward trend began typically sometime toward the middle of the nineteenth century. It continued for a long time, in most places until the middle of the twentieth century. Only recently has the incidence of crime begun to increase again, most clearly from about 1960. The typical pattern, then, has been a long U-curve rather than a simple line running parallel to urban growth and development.[2]

This U-curve in criminality has proved a nearly universal pattern, apparent in virtually every jurisdiction studied, including whole states, such as Massachusetts, small cities, such as Oakland, and all of the major metropolitan areas of the United States, as well as other cities as far apart as London, Stockholm, and Sidney. The American share of such a worldwide pattern cannot be explained in terms of the unique historical experience of our black population. This point is reinforced by turning from the shape of long-term trends in criminality to their causes. Although no single cause has been found for the U-curve phenomenon, it is associated somehow with the urban-industrial revolution. The timing of that complex process, in terms of its earliest impact on the behavior of large numbers of people, its full maturity, and its final giving way to the post-industrial era, coincide closely with the downturn, bottom, and upturn of the U-curve of criminality. The experience of American blacks is unique in part precisely because they were not merely bypassed but systematically excluded from the urban-industrial revolution, and this exclusion had important effects not only on criminal behavior but also, through criminal behavior on family life, racial leadership, and urban culture in general.

Unlike the dominant white population, urban blacks in America did not go through a cycle that started with a downturn in criminal or violent behavior after the Civil War. Their rates, instead, went up throughout the later nineteenth century, with only short-term interruptions, and they have continued upward through the twentieth. This uniquely rising curve contrasts sharply with the experience of those native-born whites and immigrants who lived through the same time but never in quite the same city. More directly, the process of tracing the importance and nature of black criminality, and placing it within a broader political and economic framework, contributes to a fuller understanding of the Afro-American experience itself.

An old tradition going back to W. E. B. Du Bois approached the black experience in terms of its problems or areas of social concern, notably criminal behavior and family structure. A more recent approach has stressed areas of black success such as the preservation of community and culture under slavery or the extension of this achievement after freedom into the urban present. The emphasis on a distinctive and valuable Afro-American tradition has had important results. But it has not confronted the troubling issues raised by criminal violence as a growing part of the black experience that corrodes and weakens other elements of the culture. This book returns to the older tradition, not to celebrate or even to describe the whole of the Afro-American experience, but rather to analyze the nature and effects of the unique problem of criminality.[3]

For over a century observers have offered different explanations for problems affecting the free black population. These have ranged from its innate or racial inferiority, to the persistence of African "barbarism," to the psychologically crippling heritage of slavery, to the handicap of a simple rural tradition in an increasingly complicated urban world, and finally to the cumulative effect of poverty and discrimination. Each of these explanations in some way improved on its predecessor. Yet each

one gave way before studies that exploded the concept of racial superiority, demonstrated the sophistication of African tribal society, and
showed the vitality and resilience of Afro-Americans in the slave and
rural South. Now even the last explanation does not quite work.

Poverty and *discrimination* are vague cover words that explain no
unique experience, no concrete historical process or condition. Social
and economic discrimination in the nineteenth century city certainly
helped create a cycle of criminal and, ultimately, violent behavior among
blacks, but neither poverty nor discrimination in itself is sufficient to
explain criminal behavior. Many individual victims of both poverty and
discrimination manage to live within the law, and group responses to
these problems also differ widely. Neither Hispanic nor Oriental immigrants, for example, have in recent years been arrested for violent
crime nearly as often as blacks, although these two newly arrived groups
are as poor, or poorer, in many areas of the country. Afro-Americans
as of the early 1970s were three times more likely than Hispanics to be
arrested for violent crimes in New York City, although they had higher
average incomes. The gap was even wider between blacks and Chicanos
in California, with blacks proportionally 4.9 times more likely to be
arrested for homicide, and 6.6 times for armed robbery. As these figures
suggest, not only the levels but the patterns of crime—such as the
relative ethnic or racial involvement in the several kinds of offenses
against public order, persons, and property—show characteristic variations. Afro-Americans, who comprise little more than one-tenth of
the population, have over the past fifteen years or so accounted for
about half of the recorded homicides in the United States, and nearly
three-fifths of the armed robberies. This fact can be explained by black
culture, which was the product of a peculiar and bitter history. That
history began with slavery and, for most blacks, continued under other
forms of agricultural dependence; but the patterns of criminality were
most strongly formed under the conditions of formal freedom, in the
city.[4]

There is no better place to trace the development of the black criminal
subculture than in Philadelphia. The period between about 1850 and
1870 was the turning-point when the U-curve of crime began its downward dip for the population as a whole. This trend is well-documented
in Philadelphia. Census data, though of often dubious reliability concerning blacks, provide ample background. A wealth of studies offer
more sheer information about this city than about any other. Most
important, Philadelphia was the subject of Du Bois's 1897 account of
the Negro population, then the largest and most established of any in
the urban north.[5]

These histories, together with contemporary criminal records and the newspapers, both black and white, explain what happened during the critical years when blacks emerged from rural slavery and began, for the first time as full citizens, to create an urban culture. Their culture was distinctive from the first and continued to develop patterns of its own. Its specifically criminal patterns derived from the black economic experience, which differed from the white and produced a distinctive social psychology. As a result, many blacks had a different experience with the line between legal and illegal activities.

The urban foundations of this disparity began in the post–Civil War era when the dominant population enjoyed unprecedented prosperity and personal security. The whites' new experiences of school and work served to regiment their behavior in ways that resulted in a marked decline in interpersonal violence. The period began hopefully for urban blacks as well. All of them won formal gains in status, and many had the skills needed to benefit fully from an expanding economy. But only a few were able to make real occupational gains. The great majority of blacks were explicitly denied the opportunity to participate in the new age of industry and thus they continued to live lives filled with insecurity and tension, without benefit of the economic and behavioral changes experienced by their white neighbors. The promise of elective politics also proved illusory. Despite able leadership, Afro-Americans experienced political failure and abandonment at every level, which served to strengthen rather than break their cycle of dependence and frustration.

Economic discrimination and political failure had important consequences for social behavior. As members of the minority group were tempted into various kinds of crime, the gap widened between black and white involvement in many illicit activities. Some of these activities proved profitable, but most did not. All contributed to a rising rate of black homicide. Vice, theft, and violence combined to weaken the structure of the family, and they posed special problems for the emergent but vulnerable business and professional elite.

The criminal subculture that flourished in the later nineteenth century has had long-term effects on crime rates in general and on homicide rates in particular. Many of the distinctive criminal patterns evident in the post–Civil War era are still apparent late in the twentieth century. During the intervening years the gap between white and black rates of violence in general continued to grow in direct reflection of the different political and economic experiences of the two groups. Partly as a result of this long history of criminal behavior, millions of urban Afro-Americans are now less ready to participate in the dominant economy, and are noticeably more different from their dominant neighbors, than were their predecessors, who were originally shut out of the urban industrial revolution several generations ago.

Political   diversity   Black/White
                                    Criminality

+

Economic experience

· 1 ·
A TALE OF TWO CITIES

NINETEENTH CENTURY AMERICANS generally believed in progress. To live in any great city during the years between 1860 and 1900 was, for most, to justify that belief in experience. This was the classic period of urban-industrial growth, which created the physical city that exists today. Most of all it was a time of great prosperity, of a rise in the level of living, which saw the creation or expansion of all of the institutions—schools, police forces, hospitals, ball teams, and zoos—which are now associated with "civilization." Philadelphia shared that prosperity and that process in a way that seems from a distance as orderly and predictable as the streetcar lines that helped to define it.

The city's black minority, living through the same period, not only shared in some of these advantages but celebrated the most important gains of Afro-American history. The Civil War brought the chance to fight slavery directly. The Thirteenth Amendent to the Constitution freed the slaves. The Fourteenth Amendment promised all the benefits of full citizenship, and the Fifteenth specifically guaranteed the right to vote. The next several decades brought other, if less dramatic, gains and opened other opportunities.

But few blacks were in fact able, or allowed, to use these new opportunities. The memory of victories won during the 1860s obscured the fact that in fundamental ways the later nineteenth century was for freedmen a frustrating period of economic losses. Far from orderly and predictable, the life of Philadelphia's blacks was full of uncertainties, of unclear lines and half-hidden traps. A number of professionals and entrepreneurs were able to transcend these problems and establish moderately successful careers. But with these few exceptions, all blacks experienced insecurities and contradictions that reinforced their realization that the economic rules and roles followed by the great majority were irrelevant to their own condition.

That the majority was not much concerned about this situation reflects, in part, the fact that the minority was still a small one (see map). As of 1860, the census counted 20,630 black people in the city, or 3.7 percent of the total population. By 1900 the official number had reached 62,613, or 4.8 percent, a population still not visible enough to dampen the prevailing optimism. But no matter how overlooked by the city's whites, Philadelphia's blacks were already numerous and strong enough to have developed distinctive institutions of their own. Even less noticed was the fact that, while others had changed to meet the imperatives of a new Age of Industry, they retained their older and thus increasingly distinctive patterns of behavior.

WHITE PHILADELPHIA

By the end of the nineteenth century the words *orderly* and *predictable* could be used to describe not only the growth of the industrial city but the behavior of most of its people. Over a million Philadelphians by then went daily to work or to school, to ball games or to theaters, much more easily and peacefully than would have been possible two or three generations earlier. The achievement of order on this scale took place on two levels, one public and external, the other private and internal.

Only the national habit of optimism—certainly not the experience of the immediate past or a hard look at the immediate future—could have led any Philadelphian in 1860 to imagine the political and social order that would follow later in the century. Yet some of its economic basis was already in place. The city had long been a textile center; more recently it had begun to turn to heavy industry as well, its Baldwin Locomotives having led the railroad boom of the preceding twenty years. Although New York had by then taken its place as the nations's biggest city and its leader in national finance, Philadelphia was still a busy port and the economic capital of the coal-and-iron Keystone State.[1]

In 1860, all of this was threatened by the growing hostility between North and South. The city's conservative leadership had not endorsed the economic policies dictated by southern Democrats during the 1850s, but they were frightened even more by the possibility that the election of Abraham Lincoln as a Republican President might drive the South into secession. Most of the major northern cities voted against Lincoln in the fall, because the business community everywhere feared the loss of southern cotton and consumers. Philadelphia in particular had close social as well as mercantile links below the Mason-Dixon Line, which made it especially sensitive to southern fears about the future.[2]

The local leadership watched helplessly while the national house divided, and it was equally unable to put its own house in order. The

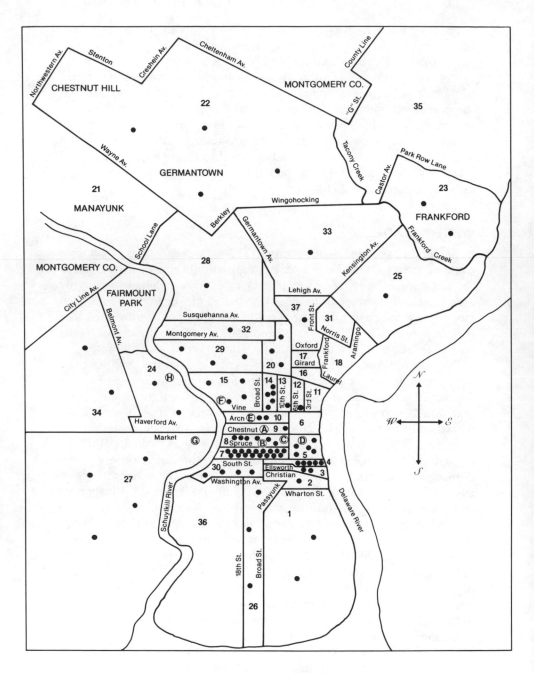

Wards of Philadelphia with black population in 1890 (one dot to every 500 black residents). (A) City Hall, (B) Academy of Music, (C) Walnut Street Theater, (D) Independence Hall, (E) Free Library, (F) Art Museum, (G) University of Pennsylvania, (H) Zoo.

previous thirty years had been marked, as in all big American cities, by riot, rout, and tumult over a variety of unsettled and unsettling issues. The 1830s nationally were a time of depression and violent protests. The 1840s were even more turbulent, marked by a kaleidoscopic series of clashes in which Irish immigrants "hunted the nigs" in their little enclaves, nativist bigots attacked Catholic churches, and displaced workingmen resisted the new industrial technology. Local authorities were often forced to call in state and even federal troops. In Philadelphia the sense of official helplessness contributed to the consolidation of city and county, in 1854, in order to set up a corps of professional policemen—a move already made, for the same reasons, in Boston and New York.

In its early years the police force was hardly irresistible. The newmade officers were often overmatched in confronting either youthful street gangs, volunteer fire-fighting companies (formed it often seemed to set fires and fight each other), or well-armed bands of toughs or river pirates like the famous Schuylkill Rangers. Pocket revolvers, made available by Samuel Colt and his imitators, joined with such lesser technological advances as slingshots and brass knuckles to help push the murder rate in Philadelphia to the highest recorded levels of the century. Every city experienced somewhat different levels of group violence as the result of its own peculiar ethnic and geographical mix, the strength of its institutions, and the nature of its politics. One official measure was provided in the spring of 1860 by a visiting delegation from the newly "opened" island of Japan. At the end of their eastern tour the Japanese left a cash tip to each of the police escorts which had followed them, the amount proportioned to the amount of thuggery from which the visitors thought they had been protected. The *Public Ledger* noted, somewhat wryly, that Philadelphia ranked just behind New York. But in any case there was no city, with the possible exception of Boston, whose local authorities were fully in control of its own streets on the eve of the Civil War.[3]

The war itself ironically helped ease this situation by narrowing ethnic differences and stabilizing the city's politics. Although still divided about the place of blacks in the city and the nation, the great majority of Philadelphians were supporters of the federal union. Catholic-Protestant divisions were eased as young men of all persuasions volunteered to die. And Pennsylvania industry was one of the winners to emerge from four years of fighting. Most Philadelphia businessmen were sure that Republican policies were responsible for continued prosperity throughout the postwar period. Politically, northern Democrats learned to accept the consequences of southern defeat and to confine their differences to the electoral process. Locally and nationally, the result was a stable two-party system, with the Republicans generally dominant.

Lincoln Steffens, writing shortly after the end of the century, char-acterized the long period of Republican rule in Philadelphia as a time when the city was both "Corrupt and Contented." His sketch has since become the official portrait of that era in municipal politics. The system encouraged honest and even honorable men to serve as mayors, in the knowledge that they could or would do little to upset the actual ma-chinery of government. That machinery was based on the corruption of the electoral process and fueled by chicanery at every level, from the privileges granted to corporations at the highest level to others given to gamblers and madams at the lowest. Reformers never stopped com-plaining, and they won one highly publicized victory in the municipal elections of 1881. But most citizens remained content so long as they got the basic urban services. In fact, the city's sewers flowed, its schools expanded, and its public transport grew to meet demand.[4]

Most important, the city government won the battle for the streets. In the beginning, urban police in America must have seemed like rival street gangs to their opponents. Whether quasi-official, like the fire companies, or fully official guardians of the peace, like the police, they were all made up of young men from the working classes, ready for violence, often hired at election time to protect or attack at the polls. Each group was given the job of curbing undesirables. The Rangers kept blacks east of Broad Street after dark; the volunteer fire companies, depending on their ethnic makeup, made things hot for Irishmen or Orangemen in the neighborhoods they dominated; the police were sup-posed to arrest tramps, beggars, or drunks who caused complaint. In the earliest years the official police were in fact distinguished by their vulnerability. They walked alone, while others traveled in packs. Vir-tually everywhere the men on the beat resisted the move to put them into uniform, in part because a distinctive outfit would make them easier targets for abuse and assault.[5]

In 1860 Philadelphia Mayor Alexander Henry succeeded in ordering the men into uniform blue. Over the next ten years the force continued to develop, adding a river and harbor service, a detective branch, and new layers of administration. But there was little increase in its real strength until the election of 1871, when in the course of replacing a Democratic with a Republican administration, the city during October experienced the last of its great race riots. The ability of white gangs in those riots to range about the racially mixed downtown wards at will, savagely injuring several black men and killing four, was a dramatic demonstration that the police force was neither ready nor able to do what it had been created for. Within the month the city council au-thorized an increase from 600 to 1000 men. One of the champions of this increase, William S. Stokley, was elected mayor—the first in a long, unbroken line of Republican ascendants and in some respects the hard rock upon which the succession was built.[6]

"Martinet" Stokley was a strict believer in public order, if not in law. As councilman, he had led the movement earlier in that year to abolish the dashing and belligerent fire companies in favor of a less colorful but more efficient force of professional firemen. He was fully aware that the October riots were directed against blacks in part because they were Republicans, and also that a police force capable of guaranteeing Afro-Americans access to the polls was capable of guaranteeing Republican successes in a variety of other ways.[7]

The openly partisan use of police to prevent political cheating by one side and to protect it by the other was then a continuing feature of local elections. The practice was denounced by reformers, newspapers, and the political "outs." But many of these groups swallowed their criticisms when the same kind of police muscle was mustered in defense not of the political but of the more fundamental economic status quo. Unlike the popular uprisings of the mid-nineteenth century, which had generally taken the form of ethnic or intergroup riot, it was the strike, the direct confrontation between labor and capital, which most frightened the middle classes in the decades after the Civil War. The most threatening strike of all occurred in the summer of 1877, when wage cuts and layoffs on the Baltimore and Ohio system spread into Pennsylvania and westward. Mobs battled police and troopers in several cities. Much of Pittsburgh was set afire, and Philadelphia sent its own regiments across the state to help. But in Philadelphia itself—headquarters of both the Philadelphia and Reading and the giant Pennsylvania Railroad systems—Mayor Stokley held the line. He promptly and illegally banned all public meetings, and his police beat down all attempts to attack railroad yards and terminals. From that time on the police department's annual reports took special pride in the fact that the force was able to keep the peace, protecting anti-union workers and company property whenever a major strike broke out.[8]

After ten years as mayor, the Martinet was retired to a job as Director of Public Safety, where he and his successors continued the job of keeping the force loyal and battle-ready. The war for the streets had by then been won decisively. Though the great confrontations, such as that in 1877, drew the most attention, the victory of the police was even more important in terms of the routines of city living. Down through 1870 every fire had been an occasion for a small riot, with officers afraid to make arrests on the scene. As late as the spring of that year it was not uncommon for a raiding party to be repulsed by small-arms fire when attempting to crack down on a gambling house. By the middle of the 1870s, when the fire companies had been abolished and the Rangers broken up, such incidents were rare. By the middle of the 1880s they had become almost unimaginable. The city's thoroughfares and alleys were of course never fully quieted. Firecrackers, fights, and the sound of pistol shots remained as much a part of the street scene as cobblestones and horse manure, but they had a greater tendency to fade at the approach of heavy boots. The police in Philadelphia and elsewhere had in effect established a practical monopoly on the use of collective force.[9]

The newly effective power of local authority was part of an important larger pattern. The atmosphere of public tranquility, the ability to walk the streets in safety, was for the well-established one of the benefits of the Gilded Age that enabled full enjoyment of the others, the matured or civilized aspects of urban life as it still exists. But the public order that served as the foundation of these benefits was complemented and in large part enabled by an important change in private behavior, which resulted from economic conditions.

This was the era in which structural steel, high-rise construction, and elevators transformed the look of downtown city buildings. Electric lights, telephones, and typewriters transformed the nature of the work inside these buildings, as the scriveners of an earlier day were replaced by a white-collar army in which ambitious young men served as noncoms and women as privates. Transport within and from the downtown area was revolutionized by lines of street railways, drawn first by horses and then in the 1890s by electric engines, which were often elevated above ground or even carried in tunnels below.

For Philadelphians this was typically a time for the founding, building, and flourishing of urban institutions. The city's monumental city hall was over twenty years in construction following the laying of its cornerstone in 1874 squarely at the junction of Broad and Market. The Academy of Fine Arts reached the peak of its national prestige just as the University of Pennsylvania, moved to its present site across the Schuylkill, became a genuine institution of higher learning. The Art Museum was founded in 1877, the Free Library in 1891. The imperial lights of Broadway had not yet reached out to dim the luster of Philadelphia's own Walnut and Chestnut Street theaters, while the Academy of Music remained the country's largest hall. For those with more raffish tastes this was the heyday of vaudeville and of the kind of popular entertainment served up at Forepaugh's Museum or circus on Arch Street. The Philadelphia Phillies joined the National League in 1883, and the ballpark, opened a dozen years later, was reputedly "the best athletic ground in the world." All classes were able to enjoy the exotic beasts housed in America's first zoo, which opened in 1874 in the southwest corner of the city's giant Fairmount Park. Two years later the park served as the site of the Centennial Exposition, and visitors came from around the world to celebrate the wonders of the Industrial Age in honor of the nation's hundredth birthday.[10]

What made all of these things possible was the continued and unparalleled prosperity of city, state, and nation. Despite two major depressions in the early 1870s and middle 1890s, the thirty years between 1870 and 1900 encompassed the biggest increase in industrial productivity in our history. Pennsylvania's oil was the original basis of John D. Rockefeller's fortune, and its iron was the basis of Andrew Carnegie's. The Pennsylvania railroad, headquartered in Philadelphia, was the biggest corporation in the country. The port of Philadelphia remained second only to New York's, and by the 1890s Cramp's shipyard, along the Delaware, was second to none in its ability to furnish much of the world with steelclad warships. The textile business was the biggest in the city, and its hundreds of mills turned out more cloth and carpeting than any other in the United States. By the century's end there were thousands of manufactories in Philadelphia, making everything from wagons to watches.

All this activity meant not only fortunes for the few but a dramatic rise in real wages for many, a rise nationally that averaged about 35 percent over the thirty years from 1870 to 1900. The reigning social myth of the era was that the economic system offered a test of will and character, that anyone who worked hard and lived thriftily could make it up the ladder. In the real world the working class knew that the system was at least as much a lottery as a test, and even Horatio Alger admitted that success required luck as well as pluck. But it was true that, barring ill health, long layoffs, and other misfortunes outside of anyone's control, a skilled or even merely steady worker could improve his or her lot. The way in which tens of thousands did so was visible all over the city. Philadelphia, with its high proportion of skilled working people, was home to more building and loan associations than any other city. Nearly a quarter of all homes were then owned by their occupants, a higher percentage than in any other city, and miles of brick row houses helped save Philadelphia from the high-rise density that plagued New York.[11]

The effect of the new industrial order was also manifest in a change in behavior. People drank less, committed fewer crimes, and generally lived more sober and rational lives than they had earlier in the century. The best clue to this development is the changing rate of violent death in the city, notably suicide and murder. The official records dealing with these two causes of death are not entirely trustworthy. For suicide, the honesty and accuracy of reportage varies with every jurisdiction, and murder, too, is often a matter of legal definition, or of the justice system's willingness to pursue difficult questions about the deaths of often socially marginal people. Despite these problems, the changing patterns of both forms of violent death in nineteenth century Philadelphia were clear, and revealing.[12]

After several decades in which there was no real movement at all, the rate of suicide in Philadelphia increased steadily from about 5.5 per 100,000 inhabitants a year during 1869–1871 to 10.8 per 100,000 just thirty years later. Over the same period the rate of indictment for murder dropped from an annual average of 3.1 per 100,000 to 2.1. The figures indicate much about the habits and customs of thousands of ordinary people whose lives left little trace other than the way in which they left them. The falling murder rate occurred despite a growing legal sensitivity to violence, as shown by the fact that the justice system prosecuted cases in the later period that it would earlier have ignored. Perhaps more important, the drop in murders happened despite a steady growth in the number of handguns carried in the city.

In the nineteenth century even more than today, most homicides occurred as a result of otherwise routine quarrels, often among acquaintances, friends, relatives, or lovers. Such quarrels usually resulted in nothing more than angry words or gestures, perhaps a drunken shoving match. It is normally hard for one healthy adult to kill another with nothing more than fists, feet, teeth, or whatever otherwise innocent object, such as a chair or beer glass, comes readily to hand. Most murder cases in the nineteenth century involved no deadly weapons; guns of any sort figured in only about 25 percent of them, as compared to the modern figure of roughly 65 percent. Thus, the murder rate could not approach the levels of the late twentieth century so long as the business of fighting in barrooms and kitchens was a kind of lottery, with extremely long odds, in which only rarely did a swinging kick hit a weak heart or a falling head hit the bricks or barstool at a lethal angle. Handguns, as distinct from the huge and cumbersome single-shot pistols carried earlier by dragoons and duelists, were not developed until mid-century, and they remained for some time expensive and uncertain weapons, carried only by semiprofessional street fighters and police. Even with these limits, the existence of these little guns, easily hidden on the person, was largely responsible for a spurt in the murder rate during the 1850s, to 4.0 per 100,000. As time passed, revolvers got steadily more reliable and more widely available, making it simpler to translate a passing fit of murderous rage into the irrevocable fact of murder itself. But the homicide rate did not rise in tandem with these developments; instead it fell through the rest of the century. Though murder was becoming easier to do, less of it was being done.

The decline in the homicide rate is one clue to a significant change in mass behavior and in social psychology. As time went on, city dwellers in general were acting in more rational, less reckless, and more orderly fashion. The reason for the change was simply that the new economic order of the later nineteenth century demanded a shift in the way in which people worked, learned, and lived their lives in general. This shift affected the way in which people "socialized" their aggessions; leading them away from the kind of behavior that ends in homicide.

Homicide and suicide rates moved in different directions because they are different and even opposite ways of expressing aggressive emotions. Suicide is aggression directed inward, toward the self, while homicide is aggression directed outward or at others. Different people, and by extension different groups, typically develop different ways of expressing their anger. Some are allowed or encouraged to express themselves spontaneously in ways that seem natural, to go their own way, to behave reflexively and without calculation. Others learn to repress their anger, to cooperate, whatever their individual feelings, to behave and obey. The two patterns show up most vividly at the extremes. People who commit suicide are typically careful, obedient, and sensitive to their environments. In contrast, people who commit homicide are those who, when pushed to the limit, tend to lash out recklessly.

By and large certain groups, despite many individual exceptions, are socialized to behave mostly in one way or the other. In the middle of the twentieth century lower-class people tended to behave recklessly, at the extremes homicidally, and middle-class people tended to behave carefully, at the extremes suicidally. The highest homicide rates among white Philadelphians in the nineteenth century were achieved by Italians, Irish, the native-born, Germans, and East Europeans, in that order. For suicide, as measured by the national census of 1890, the ranking was neatly reversed: those born in Eastern Europe were the most suicidal, and those born in Italy were the least. The psychological differences involved are even more significant when used not to show differences between groups at a fixed date but to illumine changes in the social psychology of an entire society over time.

In the older traditional economy, characterized by small farms in the countryside and crafts and commerce in the city, the line between "living" and "working" was often blurred, sometimes deliberately. However hard people worked, it was typically at their own pace, without supervision. The long seasonal calendar was important, but not the hourly clock. Farmers, shopkeepers, and cobblers answered only to themselves and were free to interrupt the day to drink, fight, joke, or gossip together. But the newer kinds of work in factory and office were much more jealous. Both blue- and white-collar workers worked under supervision, with an eye on the time, often in unremitting and repetitive jobs. They had to learn to endure long stretches of boredom and frustration without complaining outwardly. They had to learn that, in such places, orderly and predictable behavior was in the long run rewarded and impulsive behavior was punished. They had to learn, in short, what most of us still learn in school. Around 1870, at the very time when the rate of suicide began to move up and murder down, factory and bureaucratic employment in the United States began to rise dramatically. And it was in the same years that for the first time large numbers of young people began to graduate from the nation's new public school systems and go on to work in these factories and offices. The most important instruction that these new schools gave was not in literacy. Americans had always learned somehow the rudiments of reading and writing, whether at home or as apprentices, singly or in small groups. What differed now was that they learned in big, heavily disciplined classrooms, where they were taught to sit still, take turns, hold their water, mind the teacher, and listen for the bell. All of this was perfect training for the new kinds of work into which most of them would graduate. And like the work itself, the training was precisely the kind that would tend, over time, to raise the proportion of suicides among them and reduce the risks of homicide.

This process was going on over a much wider area than Philadelphia. At any given time only a minority of the city's adult population had been born in it. The behavior of the majority was shaped not only by the experience of living there but also by the earlier experience of living elsewhere—in the valley of the Ohio or the Rhine, in Richmond, Turnersville, or Ballyferrit. While the new economic order manifested itself most sharply in a great industrial metropolis, it was making itself felt all over the western world. And so was the orderly and predictable behavior that it demanded.

BLACK PHILADELPHIA

Philadelphia's blacks meanwhile lived in a very different city. Those who were alive at the time of the urban-industrial revolution did not truly live through it. The end of slavery raised high hopes, but for most blacks it did not bring any real material gain. In fact, the heavy weight of white hostility and discrimination meant that the period was as often marked by retreat as advance. And if the white world was one of increasing order and predictability, the black world was not. Legally, socially, and economically it was a world of varying degrees of discrimination, full of unpleasant surprises and dead ends, which had important consequences for social behavior.[13]

By 1860 an uneven but fully sanctioned system of discrimination had been built in Pennsylvania and all but a handful of the other free states.

After 1860 the official status of Afro-Americans at the national level was defined in terms of the Thirteenth, Fourteenth, and Fifteenth Amendments to the Constitution. The first of these amendments was unequivocal, and in the generation after the Civil War the formerly slave states learned to live with black freedom. Acceptance was eased by the fact that the freedmen remained in a distinctly subordinate position, as continued white intransigence blocked the full potential of the other two amendments. In Pennsylvania, however, the Fifteenth Amendment was made fully effective over time, and the Fourteenth largely so.

The war had, meanwhile, pushed the government into officially calling for black soldiers, a call that many young male Philadelphians accepted eagerly, although they were made to serve in segregated units. Shortly afterward, the city's street railway companies were forced to abandon the formal rules that segregated passengers by color, although not the less formal practice of all-white hiring in uniformed positions. The state did not allow blacks the right to vote, forbidden in its 1838 constitution, until required to do so by the Fifteenth Amendment. But after a brief period of violent resistance in the streets of Philadelphia, the right was fully accepted.[14]

Other legal victories were less clear-cut and slower to come. In 1874, in a case involving the ejection of a black man from a theater, the Pennsylvania Supreme Court ruled that the injured party might sue for damages. In 1887 this decision was supplemented by a state law which made it a criminal offense for restaurants, hotels, and other places of public accommodation to discriminate. In a matter of equal or greater importance the state in 1881 forbade discrimination in the assignment of pupils to its public schools. These laws were important, but they nowhere ended the problem of prejudice. Headwaiters, for example, had no trouble in discouraging unwanted "colored trade" by means short of criminal refusal. And the issue of school admissions and transfers was in Philadelphia a highly complicated and political business, which had familiar results. Most black youngsters went to schools that were segregated de facto, and their admission to white ones, such as the Thaddeus Stevens Grammar School, was sometimes the signal for riot.[15]

The city itself continued in several areas officially to separate black from white. No one apparently challenged its right to maintain entirely separate colored departments, one for each sex, in the House of Refuge, a juvenile reformatory. The same system prevailed in the charity wards of the House of Correction and in the Blockley Almshouse. The state's own Eastern Penitentiary and the County Jail in Moyamensing were never officially segregated in this fashion. Although they were supposed to separate their inmates in a more radical way through solitary confinement, so that no two convicts of whatever color could be in contact with each other, this system was largely inoperative as a result of overcrowding or the convicts' ingenuity. And although inmates learned a number of things, neither place—unlike the House of Refuge—officially conducted a school, the sort of sensitive institution in which it was often thought necessary to draw the color line.[16]

Official segregation in such marginal places continued because those directly affected had no power and perhaps no wish to object, while neither black nor white opponents of racial prejudice wanted to draw attention to it in these dismal circumstances. Some things had improved: the right to vote had at least the potential to bring change, and the legal victories of the 1880s were of symbolic importance. But the remaining vestiges of legal discrimination scarcely mattered in comparison with the greater burden of social and economic prejudice.

Social prejudice covers a multitude of white attitudes and behavior in a number of difficult interracial settings. The variety of attitudes and settings alike makes it much harder to generalize about the social treatment of black Philadelphians, as compared to their legal and economic treatment, or to find any clear sense of direction—either progress or retrogression—among its convoluted irrationalities.

The word *prejudice* scarcely conveys the intensity of hatred that whites directed, often violently, against the Afro-American population of Philadelphia. Some of this violence may be explained in terms of the nearly universal tendency of young men to join gangs in defense of their turf. Most intergroup violence was conducted within rather than across racial lines. The Schuylkill Rangers ran out rival white gangs in much the same way that they treated blacks. Yet there were real differences between the ways in which young white men fought each other and the ways in which they attacked across the color line.

Since before the Civil War the business of "hunting the nigs" had often been aggressive rather than defensive, not so much a question of protecting white neighborhoods as of invading and even destroying black ones. Gang members, in dealing with other whites, acted much like territorial fish or certain species of belligerent mammals: they ignored most passersby and were aroused only by others much like themselves, namely sexually mature young males who offered a threat or at least the possibility of a good fight. During antiblack riots, in contrast, gang members beat women as well as men. And it was not uncommon for small bands to attack aged, inoffensive black men found alone.[17]

At the extreme, such behavior was abnormal, even pathological. For example, Leonard White, twenty-six years old, was arrested in March, 1890 when bystanders called police to a scene in which six or eight youths, including White, were swarming over one elderly black man, a stranger to all of them. The young man was hardly doing battle for the integrity of the neighborhood, being himself a visitor from Baltimore. A two-year sentence for felonious assault, picked up for a prior similar offense, had not taught him to curb his hatreds. And it seems that nothing could, as against all self-interest and under the heaviest restraint, he repeatedly attempted to strike and bite at any black face in reach, even when it belonged to a policeman at the station house or the turnkey assigned to bring food and water to his cell.[18]

But individual madness does not fully explain the situation. A couple of White's companions were brought in that day and the next, and they behaved as rationally as any two toughs caught up by a heavier force of bluecoats. The problem was precisely that they, along with the innumerable others involved in similar incidents over the years, were reasonably representative of the city's working-class youths, and believed that they were winning points and prestige by their actions.

It is often impossible to tell just what set off any given eruption. It may have been the breach of some unwritten rule governing who was "allowed" to walk, talk, or dress in a given fashion, or to be in a given place at a certain hour. Or, as with White, the impulse to violence may have been triggered by a stimulus as simple as color itself, vented on the first black to appear. For Afro-Americans at the time, then, constant uncertainty was simply a condition of existence. The three black men who stopped at Crossin's Tavern in the small hours of May 25, 1880, presumably expected to get the three beers that they ordered. But they could not have been astonished by a refusal. And at some level they must have allowed for their actual reception, a savage beating by Crossin, his bartender, and every Irish patron in the place.[19]

One generally provocative trigger for these brawls was a uniform, any uniform, which suggested power or authority. It was murderously dangerous for a black man to wear a watchman's cap, unthinkable for one to serve as conductor on a streetcar, with the right to admit or throw out passengers. Above all, in the early 1860s, the prospect of black men in blue uniforms, under arms, was more than many whites could bear.[20]

In Philadelphia, as nationally, there was a passionate debate about using Afro-Americans to fight the Civil War. Opponents cited the horrors visited on the white population of Santo Domingo following the successful slave revolution of 1798 and propped up these fading memories with fresher ones from India's Sepoy Rebellion of 1857. But a more immediate set of fears overcame the resistance of local officials when in July 1863 General Robert E. Lee invaded the Commonwealth of Pennsylvania. The need for men of any color prompted the federal government to institute the first national draft, and the state and city followed by allowing separate colored regiments to recruit and train around Philadelphia. But in addition to other disabilities, these black troopers, who eventually amounted to several thousand, were not allowed to parade or otherwise join in official celebrations, during or even after the war, for fear that the sight would incite the majority.[21]

Black veterans, however, could not be shut out of these activities indefinitely. In 1869 a special company, the Grey Invincibles, was formed within the state militia. These men and others, like their white counterparts, got together on Decoration Day to march in honor of their dead. But unlike the white regiments, they often had to run a gauntlet of mocking bystanders. The line of march was too long for the police to control it, and the men were often followed by stones and pistol shots, and in 1880 a crowd even pressed inside the gates of the little Mount Lebanon Cemetery where several hundred "colored" casualties were segregated. The fact that no one was ever killed in the course of these parades—pistol shots were thought scarcely more serious than firecrackers—was due largely to the fact that no one really wanted to take on several hundred armed and angry men. But at times bayonets were fixed and ready, and there were casualties of various ages and colors. Several people were shot and stabbed in the 1880 incident, and nearby saloons were broken up by excited hecklers and veterans.[22]

But the troubles about Mount Lebanon were not repeated. Such scenes faded as the city got more orderly, and in excited times the proportion of shouts and firecrackers rose at the expense of flying lead and stones. The smaller black-white affrays also died down in number and intensity, as over time fewer blacks were killed by gangs of whites. The election riot of 1871 was the last time that the interiors of private homes were consistently violated. By the 1890s, although a black man in a largely black district might still be assaulted on his own doorstep by a passing white stranger, the district itself was safe from invasion. Although no one could count on being fully safe at night in white neighborhoods—certainly not in unfamiliar saloons—white violence was measurably on the decline.[23]

The less dramatic forms of social discrimination nevertheless remained strong, and even more than white violence, they remained inconsistent, unpredictable, and inescapable. Social discrimination was inescapable for urban blacks everywhere in the nineteenth century for the fundamental reason that virtually all were in constant contact with the far larger white city. Philadelphia as late as 1900 still had the largest black population of any city north of the Mason-Dixon line, as the census counted 62,613 Afro-American residents, just ahead of New York's 60,666 and trailing only Washington's 86,702, Baltimore's 79,739, and New Orleans' 77,714. But even Philadelphia could not support a "ghetto," as its black housing was not always segregated by household, court, or alley, certainly not by street or block (see map). The largest concentration was located in the Seventh Ward, bounded east and west by Seventh and Twenty-fifth streets, north and south by Spruce and South, with somewhat smaller numbers in the Eighth Ward to the north, the Fourth Ward to the south, and the Fifth Ward to the east. The social center of the population was at the corner of Seventh and Lombard streets. As of about 1890 such local landmarks as Gil Ball's saloon, the political meetinghouse at Liberty Hall, the James B. Forten School, the historic African Methodist Episcopal building known as "Mother" Bethel Church, the philanthropic Starr Kitchens, and the College Settlement were all located within a block of this corner, while the Church of the Crucifixion, the Institute for Colored Youth, and the Nineteenth District Police Station were not much farther away. But even here at its heart the district was shared with other ethnic groups, both immigrant and long established. No one ward in the city had a black majority, and conversely no ward was wholly white.[24]

The maps that locate the minority population in those years, with their symbolic black dots, in fact look something like the impact of a badly loaded shotgun. The reason for this pattern—an irregular central cluster with a number of smaller scatters—was fundamentally economic. From this perspective, as Du Bois put it, the main function of urban blacks was to serve as "purveyors to the rich." Among legitimate occupations, the women overwhelmingly worked as domestics, launderers, and the like. After unskilled labor, the other largest occupational category among the men was also personal service, as servants, waiters, coachmen, and messengers. Among Philadelphians generally the most important determinant of residence was the location of work. For blacks this meant clustering in the often unmapped alleys and streets behind the elegant town houses of Spruce and Locust Streets, and in a number of less concentrated areas. It also meant closeness to the wharfs, hotels, and warehouses where casual labor was needed. White hostility kept blacks out of some neighborhoods, except as live-in servants, and as the minority grew, it tended to push west along a relatively narrow strip bounded by Locust Street on one side and Bainbridge on the other. This pattern necessarily involved blacks constantly with their employers, on the one hand, and, on the other, with groups of immigrants who dotted the same neighborhoods.[25]

In some cases there were clear unwritten rules that governed relations between the races. Undertakers, for example, with virtually no exceptions, dealt with the bodies of their own. The situation with barbers had a more complex consistency. A white person never cut black hair, but a black might serve a clientele of either race so long as he did it exclusively and no given razor or pair of scissors was used on both.[26]

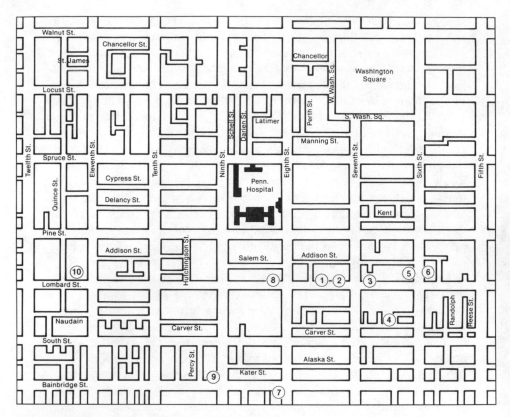

The Heart of black Philadelphia circa 1890. (1) Gil Ball's Saloon, (2) Liberty Hall, (3) Starr Kitchens, (4) College Settlement, (5) James B. Forten School, (6) Mother Bethel Church, (7) Church of the Crucifixion, (8) Nineteenth District Police Station, (9) Institute for Colored Youth, (10) Matthew S. Quay Club.

Most of the other situations encountered in a quasi-segregated society were not so clear-cut. Here, as elsewhere, blacks lived in a world full of contradiction and uncertainty. There were no signs to show which hotels, restaurants, and saloons tolerated Afro-American patronage and which did not; the only test was experience, often painful. More important, although treatment of blacks varied by class, age, and institution, there was no identifiable white group or organization—elite or working-class, Catholic or Quaker, child or adult—which could be counted on to behave consistently.

Most black Christians went to either Baptist or A.M.E. churches with no white members. A significant minority, however, perhaps as many as one-third, belonged to mostly white denominations, and this choice created a highly complex institutional situation. In a few cases white Episcopal pastors or vestrymen served largely black congregations, although never the reverse. Presbyterians, although less segregated at the higher or General Assembly level, usually maintained separate churches for each race. Among Protestants generally the tendency was to suggest the separation of Sunday schools or whole congregations when the Afro-American membership grew big enough to allow it. In the 1880s an A.M.E. bishop, invited to the dedication of a nearby white Methodist chapel, was required to sit in a special section toward the back.[27]

Clergymen typically joined together in annual convocations, conferences, or synods, at which their universalist doctrines clashed with the local mores in ways that required a variety of ad hoc or ambiguous solutions. When the Methodist Annual Conference met in Philadelphia, in 1884, there were some forty-five blacks among the several hundred delegates in attendance. All of the black delegates were invited to the all-male reception held at the Academy of Music, but no local black laymen. Conversely, the blacks in town held their own welcome for the forty-five delegates at Liberty Hall, on Lombard Street, at a function attended by several prominent white men, not all of them politicians. In general, such arrangements held throughout the period, although the tendency was toward more rather than less segregation at the local or congregational level.[28]

The Catholic situation was more paradoxical. On the one hand absolutely no black priests were ordained anywhere in the United States until 1891, and none at all in Pennsylvania through the nineteenth century. The American hierarchy was notoriously an "Irish closed shop," and the Irish, ethnic backbone of the whole institution, were the most fiercely racist of contemporary immigrant groups. The Philadelphia Archdiocese did sponsor two segregated institutions. One was the Mary Magdelene Society, organized in the city in the 1890s in partial response to the fact that the Protestant Magdelene Society refused to treat colored prostitutes. The Mary Drexel Home for Colored Orphans, located just outside the city, was founded in an era when no orphanage anywhere mixed children from both races. One church, St. Peter Clavers, on Lombard Street, was intended to serve black needs, and a national association of Catholics was named for this first missionary to black Africa. At the same time, however, the several hundred black communicants of Philadelphia, most of them immigrants from the French or Spanish West Indies, were scattered in many churches across the city. Roman Catholicism was the only Christian denomination with a truly universal reach, and the only one to conceive of the whole Afro-American world as a potential missionary field. Even the skeptic Du Bois joined more active Protestants in seeing the tradition of equal treatment among Catholics as having a unique potential for encouraging rapprochement with the immigrant working classes.[29]

The position of the Quakers was even more paradoxical. Up through the Civil War no group approached the record of the Society of Friends in helping blacks both nationally and locally. The Friends were the first to attack slavery, and before the war a number worked with Robert Purvis, William Still, and other black Philadelphians in various abolition societies, as well as in the Underground Railroad for fugitive slaves. Quakers were also the first to organize schools for Afro-American children, although the earliest of these were restricted to the primary grades. The Institute for Colored Youth, founded in Philadelphia in 1842, attracted young people from all over the country and produced a heavy share of the city's black leaders throughout the century. Smaller foundations were continued, such as the Home for Colored Orphans and the Home for Destitute Colored Children, also founded before the war. At the same time, once the fight for freedom had been won, the level of Quaker concern tended to recede.[30]

The Society of Friends was never large, and in the nineteenth century, having long since lost its missionary impulse and accepted its minority status, it had no interest in seeking new members, especially among blacks. The Friends of Philadelphia in particular, weakened by doctrinal splits and declining membership in the city proper, were no longer as active in secular philanthropy as they had been in the past. As a result, while the city's black population grew, the Quaker institutions did not, either in size or in number. After the war most of their Afro-American primary schools disappeared as public education expanded. In those remaining white and sometimes black teachers cooperated uneasily in teaching segregated black children. In the 1860s there were some squabbles over salary and over whether leadership should be black or white. The Friends saw no more of value in contemporary black culture than did other whites, and their schools were definitely Quaker, teaching

Quaker ideals, stressing quiet order, and ignoring fripperies such as instruction in music or in art. It is impossible to read the reports of the orphans' school, for example, without being impressed, on the one hand, with the genuine concern that it witnessed and, on the other, wondering about the future of its graduates, youngsters without place or heritage, with no real contact with the black community and no welcome in the white. Fannie Jackson Coppin, principal of the Institute for Colored Youth, finally won the battle over music. But black teachers did not mingle easily with white, and the boards of the Quaker institutions of any kind were not open to any but members. The quasi-closed "family" character of the Society precluded any genuine openness toward the city's black population, and by century's end relations were more correct than easy.[31]

The position of other members of Philadelphia's white elite was much the same. Republican leaders denounced the excesses of this most violent period in the history of southern racism, and citizens of both parties joined in efforts to curb the milder local symptoms of the same disease. An event such as the 1871 election riots united them all. Several judges defied majority opinion in extending or protecting basic constitutional rights, as in cases involving streetcars and other places of public accommodation. Members of the bar rallied to make sure that potentially inflammatory black-white murder cases did not result in legal lynchings. Within a few years of the Civil War the leading journals made a ritual of condemning blatant forms of discrimination, citing cases of black achievement, and including accounts of black Masons, Baptists, or Republicans alongside white. The city's largest paper, the *Public Ledger,* never reprinted the Rastus, 'coon, and razor jokes sometimes found even in its black counterparts and disdained the mocking style adopted by many others when reporting events among the "dusky damsels" and "dark Lotharios" in "Little Africa." The city never lacked for charitable clergymen, kindly mistresses, protective patrons. But among upper-class Philadelphians, to be "a friend to the colored race" did not imply anything like full acceptance or easy relations.

Philadelphia's black elite was also a tightly closed group, a society hard to penetrate by outsiders. Certainly no whites were familiar within this private circle. Conversely, none of its members moved with ease among their white acquainances.

Through the years, as with legal status, there was some improvement. In the early 1860s no one but a handful of Quakers or other abolitionists ever appeared on public occasions in the company of blacks. Mutual contact increased considerably during the 1870s and 1880s. But many Afro-American leaders found that unselective admittance of whites into their own circle could prove painful. In 1886 a white reporter, after visiting an amateur production of *The Mikado,* wrote a satirical account of the performance and the audience both, emphasizing the precise color and occupational status of everyone mentioned. A year later an open production of Richard III by a largely professional all-black cast drew a white audience that was curious at best, mocking at worst.[32]

Whites in general accepted certain aspects of Afro-American culture, but they were not so ready to accept achievement in forms or areas that they were used to claiming as their own. Thus, the Fisk Jubilee singers were always popular in Philadelphia, but the artist Henry Tanner fled the city in the 1880s to practice painting in Paris. In 1890, Reverend Ira Yeocum's wife, an Oberlin graduate, was not allowed to join the Philadelphia Musical Academy, despite her light or "quadroon" coloration. And in 1897 Paul Lawrence Dunbar read his early poems to an all-black audience.[33]

Du Bois himself, the elegant graduate of Harvard and Berlin, was surely the best qualified man of his generation to cross the barrier, and yet his account of the problems suggests bitter personal experience. A white "friend" in private would not greet a black man on the street; a white might freely call on a black but then be shocked at a reversal; a meeting "open to the public" was in fact not so. The only possibility for genuine intercourse in a relationship other than that of master to servant was in the strictly formal involvement of professional or other work in common.[34]

A small number of elite blacks and whites served together on the boards of just two of the dozen or so social agencies which, by the 1890s, dealt exclusively with blacks. Those with a mixed or all-white clientele had all-white boards. Those who ran Philadelphia's charities used the degree of social fellowship in their activities as the basis for choosing to discriminate or no. Thus the soup kitchens served black and white alike, as did the Society for the Protection of Children from Cruelty, whereas the Young Men's Christian Association drew the color line, as did orphanages, schools and the Country Week Association, which brought urban youngsters out into the fresh air in the summertime.[35]

Matters were somewhat easier among working professionals. A number of clergymen met occasionally on a footing of formal equality. In 1876 the Pennsylvania Supreme Court unanimously waived the residence requirement for John Lewis of Yale, the first black man admitted to the bar in Philadelphia. William Still's daughter, Dr. Caroline Anderson, who in 1878 was the third black graduate of the Philadelphia Women's Medical College, was called on to serve as the treasurer of her alumni association. There was great resistance to allowing Nathan Mossell to enter the University of Pennsylvania's Medical School, but at his graduation in 1882 the ceremonies were interrupted by an unusual and prolonged applause; he was admitted immediately to the staff at Pennsylvania Hospital, though not to the County Medical Association. Black lawyers, in spite of Lewis, were in general less numerous and secure than black doctors. None worked for a white firm, although George Mitchell and John A. Sparks both served their apprenticeships with Rhoades, Woodruff, Hopper, and McCollin, apparently at the invitation of the municipal reformer Clinton Woodruff, and A. F. Murray studied with former District Attorney George A. Graham.[36]

The opportunities for professional training in Philadelphia were greater than those for undergraduate education. The need for white acceptance made the city's black elite very conscious of the progress made by young men and women in the white colleges: at one gathering in 1890 the host offered a toast to "the hope of the race: Du Bois and Morgan at Harvard, Boucher at Yale, Cook at Cornell"—names clearly familiar to everyone present. But the total was still small. The Afro-American graduates of Philadelphia's own institutions made up an inverted pyramid. By the end of the century roughly twenty blacks from all over the country had earned degrees from the University of Pennsylvania's medical and dental schools, less than half a dozen from the law school, and one had earned a doctorate in religion. A much smaller handful had gone to the university's undergraduate college, and none to the socially exclusive DeLancey Street School. No black had ever gone to the Quaker colleges, Haverford and Swarthmore, and certainly none to Bryn Mawr, whose president, M. Carey Thomas, was an ardent champion of Anglo-Saxon superiority and especially hostile to "our . . . semi-civilized American negroes." The reason for this inversion of the usual educational pyramid was simply that whites could not comfortably accept black classmates into the undergraduate world of the late nineteenth century, with its network of social clubs, literary societies, balls, teas, and games. Professional training, on the other hand, was impersonal enough to allow the acceptance of merit on its own.[37]

Genuinely free and informal contact between the races was thus restricted, on the white side especially, to the lower, working, and lower middle classes. There is a paradox here. Working-class whites had no sense of *noblesse oblige* toward Afro-Americans as a group. Many were violently colorophobic; others were at least ambivalent. But shared activity was common, as was friendship and even love.[38]

Accounts of routine life among ordinary or inarticulate people are much rarer than those provided by the archives, books, and private papers that deal with the elite. But such accounts do exist, and a number of contemporary sources deal explicitly with black life and with the relations between the races. The most important are the newspapers, not only the Afro-American weeklies but the regular daily press. Some of the white papers published explicit social commentary about race relations; all of them offered descriptive accounts of street scenes, games, and dances. The most revealing material is often inadvertent, the result of reporting, for example, about the disasters which typically filled the pages of the *Inquirer* or the *Public Ledger:* boiler explosions, train wrecks, and stabbings. Accounts of violence, especially murder, are rich sources of social history. An inquest, or trial, is like a sudden flash of light which illumines a number of surrounding events and conditions that would otherwise have gone unnoted. The fact that Afro-Americans routinely attended the Cloakmaker's Ball, for example, is revealed only when the routine is interrupted by a fight on the way home. One learns that red peppers in the shoes ward off the cold only when a killer prepares for a long flight in February.[39]

This kind of evidence, which cuts across all groups and classes, tends to reveal more about the behavior of habitual criminals than of clergymen. But for black-white relations this bias is appropriate. Parts of the criminal underworld in fact comprised the most racially integrated milieu in late nineteenth century America, as gamblers and other criminals crossed the color line more easily than most. The customers of many brothels, too, were less racially fastidious than those who went to beauty shops.

Next to criminals, children of different races found it easiest to get along. Housing patterns were not tightly segregated, streets and alleys were open to all, and youngsters have always been less reluctant than adults about invading neighbors' yards and kitchens. Most newspaper accounts of mutual play involved boys rather than girls, partly as a result of the fact that boys play active competitive games, open to any who dare, and they tend to admire the gifts of boldness, strength, and speed. Black or white, boys were more often likely than girls to catch a reporter's eye when playing soldiers on the Fourth or skylarking around parades or firemen. And they were much more likely to fall out of trees or run into streetcars.[40]

These boyish activities could be violent, even dangerous. One measure of the increasing insistence on order late in the century was that the adult authorities cracked down more and more upon unruly juvenile behavior. This meant not only arrests for playing cards or baseball on Sunday, when the neighbors complained, but homicide indictments of twelve-, eleven-, and even ten-year-old children when a swinging broomstick or a violent tag somehow killed a fragile playmate. This increasing strictness makes it especially significant that when Chester Elsie, a black fourteen-year-old, fatally stabbed his twelve-year-old white neighbor Frank Dougherty in the spring of 1899, no action was taken, despite the interracial character of the incident. The coroner's jury concluded that the two were close friends, boys will be boys, and accidents will happen.[41]

There were even uglier ways for boys to be boys which reflected less harmony among them. Not all fights were among friends, and words like nigger were even handier than bricks and had the especially delightful quality of driving grown men to distraction. It was the youthful inmates themselves who insisted that the House of Refuge be divided into separate white and colored wings. In this case, and again in the case of the city's public baths, boys could draw the line more sharply than their elders.[42]

Philadelphia's first public baths were built in the summer of 1870 and were operated by Alaska Street Mission in an effort to provide the masses with the benefits of soap and towels. The water itself was provided by the Delaware, which flowed through the wooden slats of two enclosures—one sixteen feet square for whites, the other twelve feet square for blacks—which were open to men and women on alternate days. In time the city took over and expanded this modest operation, adding enough new baths at different locations so that people of either sex could use them on any summer's day. At the same time it lifted the color bar and added another: after six o'clock, at the workday's end, the men's baths were reserved for adults only. The formal rules were informally sabotaged during the daytime by picket lines of white boys, "themselves far from ordinarily clean," who organized to drive off any black youngsters who tried to approach. Once the evening hour was reached, the workingmen, black and white, soaped down in company and normally without incident.[43]

These workingmen shared a good deal more than the river. Most of the popular masculine pastimes were sometimes enjoyed by both races together. Of the team sports that were becoming widely popular in the postwar era, only baseball was played by workingmen or professionals. Afro-American ballplayers were officially excluded from the National League shortly after its founding, and local teams, both amateur and professional, were organized along racial lines. Yet there were often games between black and white ballclubs, and the best local amateurs shared fields and other facilities, especially in the earlier years. Carl Bolivar, a local black historian, observed that "baseball did wonders in the way of levelling prejudice."[44]

The situation was similar in other sports. Before the 1890s, when heightened discrimination drove many from the business, black men were counted among the leading jockeys across the country, and whites and blacks together crossed the Delaware on Sundays to watch the races at the Jersey tracks. Above all, boxing, the most proletarian of sports, enjoyed a long tradition of men from both races meeting together in front of mixed crowds without incident. Although the city held separate white and colored amateur championships in the 1890s, enthusiasts dropped into both to check out moves or footwork and to place bets. Among Philadelphia's professionals it was common for black men to serve whites as seconds in the ring, or vice versa, taking the critical and intimate role of doctor, strategist, and spiritual advisor.[45]

The most popular form of recreation in the nineteenth century city was, however, drinking. The consumption of alcohol was higher then per capita than it is today, especially among men. And a significant number of whites and a majority of blacks who drank in public did so in company with men of other races. In a city that was roughly 95 percent white, where three to five thousand saloons and speakeasies catered to over a million inhabitants, the majority of these establishments rarely had to deal with the issue of black patronage. But relatively few of these places were owned by blacks, and even fewer served an all-black clientele. When Du Bois set a squad of students to watching the saloons on a Saturday night and counting heads, in order to measure the extent of the drinking problem, they recorded that every place they visited in the Seventh Ward was patronized by both races, sometimes in virtually equal numbers and at the minimum in ratios of three or four to one either way.[46]

This pattern was common in much of the city. Blacks and whites not only sat down together but mixed in groups that roamed the streets, bar-hopping through their neighborhoods. And whether drinking together or close by, both groups did almost all of the things that men tend to do when drinking. Mostly, in order to get into the papers, they had fights; the association between assault and alcohol was strong. But stories about these fights—when it is possible to find an "issue" at all— show the variety of other shared activities. With the significant exception of pure racial prejudice, these men fought over the same range of issues that provoked them in all-white or all-black situations. Up to the point of hostilities they had been playing cards, talking politics, making bets, or, classically, arguing about whose turn it was to pay for the drinks. Doubtless the racial line helped to clarify the sides when a quarrel between two men erupted into a general melee. But peacemakers from either group might break into a racially homogeneous affray, and a black man might protest, and as a result die, when a black pickpocket tried to roll a white colleague.[47]

The range of soberer relations was considerable. Afro-American men and women served as landlords, employers, and supervisors of whites; black policemen killed white youths as well as vice versa; men and women of both races told fortunes and performed abortions for the other. Such close contact inevitably bred close personal bonds.

One of these bonds was revealed in June 1880 when a black woman, Mary Dorsey, of 1033 Locust Street, was given three months in the House of Correction for running a "disorderly house," or brothel. This interruption in the household's routine brought her untended daughter Nellie to the attention of the Society for the Protection of Children from Cruelty. The Society had been responsible for passing and then enforcing a law against "harboring a minor for immoral purposes," and its interest in this case may have been heightened by the fact that Nellie, an adopted child of twelve years old, was a pretty girl by all accounts, graceful, blue-eyed and blond. In Dorsey's absence, Nellie was taken from the house and placed in the West Philadelphia Industrial School of the Immaculate Conception. On her release in September, Dorsey sued the Society for Nellie's return. She had taken the child as a foundling after several white neighbors had refused. Even the almhouse had turned Nellie down on the grounds that she was "too beautiful" to admit, as virtually all of the infants given to it died within months. The Society did not dispute that the girl had been well cared for, sent to school and indeed to Sunday school, and was healthy and devoted to her mother. Yet Dorsey could not promise the judge that she would not go back to the only profession she knew. His decision, with the consent of all parties, was that Nellie should stay at the Catholic School until her majority, while Dorsey contributed to her support and otherwise enjoyed her rights as a mother.[48]

The more usual forms of interracial love were adult and heterosexual. When Du Bois dealt with the issue of intermarriage in 1897, marriage between the races was illegal in most states, and it was an especially difficult situation in a decade marked by the highest number of lynchings in American history, many of them prominently featured in the Philadelphia papers and involving supposed violations of interracial sexual taboos. Yet there were 33 of these unions in the Seventh Ward alone, which Du Bois projected to 150 for the city as a whole. Contrary to the prevailing impression, most of the people involved were what he called members of the "honest servant class" rather than "immoral persons." In fact, he refused to count several cases of "cohabitation" that tended to "savor more of prostitution than of marriage." The effect of this criterion, however, was to rule out a number of people who were regarded as "married" by themselves, the newspapers, and the law. Marriage between the races was thus much more common than Du Bois indicated, or if not marriage, at least the relations and sentiments then thought to surround it.[49]

Passion may be immeasurable, but the daily papers of the nineteenth century surely encouraged a belief that murder, or suicide, was its most genuine expression. And while they preferred to feature people of some social standing who killed themselves, spouses, lovers, or rivals, they found a number of more ordinary examples among blacks and whites in Philadelphia. One of these involved a young woman named Emma Grant and a white man, Henry Wilson, who had been "courting" her for some time. Wilson, who had recently been fired from his job as a bartender in a black-owned saloon, called on Grant early in the evening of September 17, 1888, and invited her into the back yard of the house on Minsker Street where she worked for a white woman. The nature of her job was never specified, but it may be deduced from the later testimony of two white male visitors to the household, both of whom insisted that they had been there only for a matter of minutes, collecting bills or chatting on the doorstep, despite the fact they had brought in some beer in a bucket and left articles of clothing in the parlor. When the two men, the hostess, and a black domestic heard a pistol firing three times, they rushed into the yard to find Grant and Wilson lying side by side. She died at once; he, having bungled the end of his life almost as badly as the rest of it, hung on for several more months in a cell at Moyamensing.[50]

The amount of serious or fatal violence among mixed couples in Philadelphia indicates that these affairs were both common and difficult. The most obvious of external pressures never occurred in Philadelphia during the postwar era. There had been one prewar riot, in 1849, sparked by white resentment of a mixed marriage. And in an incident in 1890, a gang of men were ready to attack a Chinese laundryman thought, wrongly, to have married a young white employee. Despite the lack of such episodes involving black and white couples, social discrimination in other forms haunted their lives. Though third parties rarely practiced violence on these people, they often practiced it on each other, and on outsiders. In the first six months of 1881, two of the nine homicide trials or inquests in the city involved legally married interracial couples. In the five years from 1895 to 1899 members of this group, which Du Bois estimated at less than one-tenth of one percent of the population, were involved in over two percent of its adult murders. One incident is especially revealing of the complexities of interracial living. The killer was a man named Thomas Grobes, son of a white woman, husband of another, but socially labeled black. The victim was his best friend, Horace Hopkins, shot in Grobes's kitchen at 3 A.M. at the end of a long and drunken party. The third man present, a young white letter carrier, testified that the bullet was probably meant for him, as Grobes objected, on racial grounds, to his courtship of the daughter of the house. The affair, like interracial coupling in general, was simply an extreme example of ordinary race relations. Contact was far more usual than commonly believed. It was also full of unpredictable possibilities and tensions.[51]

Whereas legal segregation was fading in importance, and social prejudice occurred only on occasion and unpredictably, it was economic discrimination that dominated the shape of life among Philadelphia's Afro-Americans. The city's black population, which had always been clustered around the bottom of the economic ladder, remained there as of 1860. Over the next forty years the general rise in productivity affected everyone in the society and helped reduce the absolute level of misery. But despite better opportunities for the tiny class of black professionals, persistent hostility and prejudice prevented the great majority from making any occupational gains. In several areas blacks were in fact barred from or lost ground in jobs that had earlier been open. Most important, the black working class was effectively denied entry into those new jobs, blue collar and white, created by the urban-industrial revolution of the late nineteenth century. By 1900 Philadelphia's blacks as a group were still clustered at the bottom, wedged in more tightly than ever and relatively worse off, in comparison with their white neighbors, than they had been when slavery still ruled in the South.[52]

The two groups that made the most gains during this era were doctors, both mainstream and homeopathic, and lawyers. Philadelphia's blacks were served in the early 1860s by Dr. James Wilson. He was succeeded in 1864 by Dr. David Rossell, a young man trained in Germany, who maintained a considerable practice among German immigrants as well as his fellow Afro-Americans. Rossell was joined in 1870 by Dr. E. C. Howard, educated at the Harvard Medical School. By the early 1880s, after Nathan Mossell's graduation from the University of Pennsylvania, there were five trained physicians in the city; by 1885, eight; and by the late 1890s, fourteen, plus three dentists. Lawyers were slower in getting established. John Lewis was the first, in 1876, and his death in 1891 left young Theophilus Minton the only practicing black attorney in town. Eight or nine more joined Minton later in the decade. Even if only a minority made a living from their knowledge, the rise was impressive.[53]

The number of secular journalists, too, which had been nonexistent in 1860, expanded through the 1870s into the 1890s. Aside from those who worked for the A.M.E.'s *Christian Recorder* or other denominational organs, the typical pattern for a black journalist was to start with a "colored" column of religious and social news for a white paper; the Sunday *Mirror* and then the *Mercury* used this device to build circulation with Afro-American readers. The next step was to write for an out-of-town paper or, better, start a weekly in Philadelphia itself. Several of these weeklies failed, and not even Christopher Perry, who founded the still successful *Tribune* in 1883, could make a living out of journalism alone. But by the 1890s he and perhaps a dozen other men and women were contributing regularly to both black and white papers.[54]

Thanks largely to the Institute for Colored Youth, the only non-primary school staffed mostly by blacks, Philadelphia throughout the later nineteenth century was able to export teachers to places all over the country. Opportunities in the city itself as of the 1890s were limited to the forty or so who taught in the handful of public and Quaker private schools for Afro-American children. No black was allowed, for any time, to teach mixed or all-white classes.[55]

The clergy furnished the bulk of black professionals. Unlike the others, these professionals were not always highly educated, and their ranks late in the century included near-illiterates as well as men with university training. Their growth in numbers roughly paralleled that of their potential congregants, with 80–100 pastors serving a population of about 60,000 in the late 1890s.[56]

As a group, the various professionals were growing quite quickly. Although their absolute numbers were tiny, never accounting for as much as one percent of the adult population, they were rising fast enough either to provide better service for their mostly all-black clientele or to make some inroads among their white competitors. This was not so true, however, among the entrepreneurs, small businessmen in legitimate occupations, who shared the role of leadership.

In a few cases segregation provided these people with a future as assured as the growth of the Afro-American population itself. By far the largest group of black entrepreneurs were the barbers and beauticians who dealt with black patrons only. These people operated several dozen shops in the 1890s. They were followed in importance by the undertakers, cemetery owners, and real estate dealers, each of those groups having fewer than five shops. All of the other businesses were open to all customers in varying degrees, although white patronage was shrinking over time.[57]

The commonest neighborhood enterprises were restaurants and cigar or grocery stores, which were often shaky little places, and contemporary leaders continually complained about the lack of racial solidarity, entrepreneurial interest, and business skill, which left blacks to buy life's necessities from white shopkeepers rather than from their own. The little places tended to fail for internal reasons. Not so, however, with those black entrepreneurs who served the general public, specifically caterers, barbers, tailors, and upholsterers. Their ominous pattern of failure had external causes.[58] The most important of these businesses in Philadelphia was catering, which by 1860 had been virtually a black monopoly for over two generations. The Golden Age, however, when the leading black caterers "ruled the fashionable world," was beginning to fade as early as the 1870s, perhaps with the death in 1876 of Thomas J. Dorsey, their most noted representative. The growing prestige of French cuisine, the competition of white hotels having a larger capital, and the growth of a new middle class insecure in dealing with service of any kind combined to make the catering business progressively more precarious. By the 1890s only a few dozen people still carried on the old tradition in some fashion, and only thirteen or fourteen did so successfully.[59]

The same pattern was found among all of the other small firms that served mostly white patrons. Here again Philadelphia was archetypal, in that the end of the nineteenth century marked a general decline in these enterprises, only partly balanced by the success of those blacks who dealt with a wholly segregated clientele. The decline resulted in part from the growing size of the Afro-American population, which got more segregated residentially as its numbers swelled. Just as the potential black market grew, whites found it less natural or comfortable to visit black areas. This demographic development was reinforced by two others. One was the worsening white racism all over the country; the other, in response, was the growing ideology of black separatism and solidarity among the leaders.[60]

The whole class of Afro-American entrepreneurs had thus grown very little by the century's end, although a black journalist had noted in 1885 that "Philadelphia contains more successful men of business than any other city we know of." The total is in fact hard to establish. The census of 1900 put the number of black "owners and executives" at one and one-half percent of the working population, or from 300 to 500 people. But the census is an often inaccurate guide to the occupational structure among Afro-Americans. An 1899 survey by Atlanta University, which defined "businessman" as someone with goods to sell or an investment of five hundred dollars, put the number at just 45. Du Bois's own hazy tally of legitimate businesses was closer to 200, or somewhat larger than the whole number of professionals. Both groups together then constituted an elite of less than two percent of Philadelphia's adult Afro-Americans.[61]

The social and other activities of this class make it easy to forget how small it was, and how fragile its economic base. Visitors from out of town conceded that Philadelphia boasted "the greatest number of educated and refined colored people of any city in the United States." None of its own papers, save the *Christian Recorder,* survived the era, but the Afro-American press in New York featured a regular weekly "Letter from the Quaker City." A number of correspondents wrote these columns over the years, reporting on politics and gossip, church, lodge, and society events. All of them were educated men and women, and most of them were masters of that nineteenth century style, common to both black and white journalists, which varied the most repetitive of stories with consciously arch variations, so that one young couple "Bows Before Hymen's Altar," while another "Solves Cupid's Puzzle by Making One Out of Two."[62]

Late in 1883, an ebullient young man, Charles A. Minnie, began a weekly contribution to the New York *Globe*. Like his counterparts in Boston and New Orleans, he describes a richly patterned social life, in which his fellow Philadelphians do dramatic readings and hold poetry or song contests at private parties. The churches put on plays and run benefit "star concerts" at the Academy of Music. He himself goes to formal balls, catered weddings, and bachelor dinners. And then, to open his letter of November 17, he takes "great pleasure in informing the citizens of Philadelphia and vicinity of his appointment as salesman in Browning's Clothing Store, Ninth and Chestnut."

Minnie is exultant, even obsessed, and his next several letters amount to a kind of sermon on the Horatio Alger virtues. "We believe that if a number of our young men were to acquire a thorough business education they would find no difficulty in gaining admission into many of the mercantile houses of this city." He himself won the job on only the second try. Others are also making it in the white world: "Kate Carter is an example of what a little energy will do. She is employed as a clerk at Frank Siddall's office and in full view of the entire community." There are other similar examples: engravers, bricklayers, messengers, and clerks. His own work goes well, his co-workers are friendly, and "the moral is plain: Young Men, Get Trades!"

The week before Christmas, Minnie is fired. The weather has been warm, sales have been slow, and "his people"—the account is written in the third person—are even slower to come by in the expected numbers. He protests that four weeks is hardly enough in which to show his stuff: the protest is in vain. A couple of weeks later his byline disappears from the *Globe*.

This painful story is unusual only in that Minnie was given the illusion of opportunity; it was his friend, Kate Carter, who had a truly exceptional position. As late as 1900 only one percent of the city's black labor force had been able to win jobs as clerks or salespeople, and the overwhelming majority of them worked for the government or for black employers. This Philadelphia story was only one chapter in the annals of a nearly universal discrimination. The telephone, typewriter, and department store together created an enormous new pool of jobs that

had never existed before, but everywhere Afro-Americans were excluded from them.[63]

This systematic denial of white collars to black people resulted not
from any lack of qualifications but from open prejudice. The census
indicates that impressive gains in literacy were made between 1860 and
1900, as the proportion of those unable to read and write was cut from
nearly half of all adults to not much more than ten percent. The contemporary black press, with its vivid letters and other amateur contri-
butions, showed that mastery of the language was spread far wider than
the opportunity to use it on the job. Whatever their problems, Philadelphia's schools turned out far more educated blacks than its employers
would hire. Afro-American politicians in the 1880s pushed to get the
city and state to adopt a system of civil service and, beyond that, a plan
for hiring in order of merit, confident that any fair method would improve the chances of their constituents. John Wanamaker's Department
Store was hailed for hiring a few token blacks. When Wanamaker heard
a white woman complain, he was said to have answered that there were
no "niggers" in his place, only men and women of different colors. But
other businessmen were not so open or so strong-minded. Du Bois cited
a long list of wasted talents, including a man with a degree in mechanical
engineering working as a waiter, a graduate of the select High School
for Girls doing menial labor, and a woman fresh out of a business college
unable to find a secretarial job anywhere in the city.[64]

These failures were only part of a larger pattern. The most important
fact about the structure of black opportunity, both blue collar and white,
was that it was almost wholly unaffected by the contemporary industrial
revolution. While it was often possible for the white majority to drive
Afro-American competitors out of established trades and preindustrial
occupations, it was much easier to keep them out of new ones from the
beginning. As a result, the next most important fact about black employment in this period was that roughly 90 percent of the urban black
population everywhere worked with their hands, "below the white-collar
line," in jobs that required virtually no skills at all. This was true in
Philadelphia in 1860, and despite the great gains made by other groups,
it was still true in 1900.[65]

The census figures suggest that slightly over 15 percent of all black
males were skilled workmen as of 1860, although the barbers, who
accounted for about a third of this group, far outnumbered workers in
the more prestigious building trades. Over the next decades black skilled
workers declined slightly in proportion to the whole male workforce.
By 1900 the leader of a newly formed black union declared that the
situation in Philadelphia was worse than in the South.[66]

In southern cities before the Civil War and to a lesser extent in the North, free blacks had enjoyed a monopoly of some trades. In the South especially native whites wanted to own land rather than to work in cities, and everywhere the American dream was to leave wage labor to others and go into some kind of profit-making enterprise oneself. Many of the more prosperous immigrants, too, headed straight west. Thus, the demand for construction was often filled by black freedmen, many of whom had learned carpentry, plastering, masonry, and other skills that were still largely unknown to the Irish peasants crowding into the eastern seaports.

The black position had begun to erode, however, well before the war, and that erosion continued through the later nineteenth century. A greater number hung on in the South than in the North, especially in the traditional, preindustrial crafts, simply because there had been more of them to begin with and less competition from white immigrants. But entry into the newer trades, such as boilermaking, tool-and-die cutting, and railway engineering, ranged from difficult to impossible. In fact, industrial work generally, whatever the level of skill, was closed to all but whites.[67]

The American labor movement as a national phenomenon dated from this postwar era, when for the first time countrywide conventions or associations aspired to speak for the whole of the working class and represented several different local or international unions. None of the leading spokesmen for this movement at the national level denied that Afro-American workingmen were potential brothers and deserved an equal chance in the marketplace. But these principles had little effect in practice, and union hostility was a major and perhaps the fundamental reason for the exclusion of blacks from the factories and skilled trades.

It was not yet clear what a union ought to be—whether a kind of fraternity, a political pressure group, a reform association, an expression of universal brotherhood, or a vehicle for ensuring a monopoly of certain skills. Some of these models, notably the fraternal and the monopolist, implied the exclusion of anyone definable as different. Those who wanted to work through the political system, rewarding friends and punishing enemies, found it hard to deal with black leaders who were tied, it seemed irrevocably, to that Republican party which had freed the slaves and given them the vote. Timidity suggested that to include black members would be to lose an uncertain number of hostile whites.

Each of the national labor organizations faced these problems in turn. None of them had any power to dictate membership policy to the various groups they brought loosely together. The National Labor Union, a kind of reform convention of the late 1860s and early 1870s, dealt with the issue of black union membership simply by ignoring it. The Knights of Labor, which originated in 1869 as a secret fraternal association, took a relatively strong stand on equal admission, but black members joined in numbers only on the eve of the sharp decline that began in 1886. The American Federation of Labor, which broke with the Knights in 1885, was always made up mostly of elite craft unions. Some of the building trades admitted a few black members or set up separate Jim Crow locals, but others were rigidly and constitutionally all-white. The most important labor organizations outside of the Federation were made up of men who worked for the railroads, the largest employers in the country, and the Brotherhoods of Railway Firemen, Engineers, and other skilled workingmen were also lily-white.[68]

The great majority of the workforce still belonged to no unions at all in this period, but employers often cited labor hostility as the reason for their own failure to hire Afro-Americans for any but the worst of jobs. Most were themselves unwilling, like the owners of department stores, to put blacks in positions that involved contact with customers, such as salespeople or streetcar conductors. Again the stated reason was not black incapacity but white prejudice. It was argued that to use blacks almost anywhere was to invite labor trouble ranging from constant friction to mass walkout. Among Philadelphia's manufactories only Midvale Steel chose to defy the conventional wisdom on this point. At the suggestion of the efficiency expert Frederick R. Taylor, Midvale broke from the tradition of hiring ethnic gangs under foremen from their own group, and in this fashion the company had integrated several hundred blacks into its workforce by the 1890s. But Midvale remained unique among the corporations in the modern industrial sector of the city's economy. Baldwin Locomotive turned out a thousand railroad engines a year, and Cramp's shipyard turned out several thousand tons of vessels, wholly without black input of any kind.[69]

Employers sometimes tried to break the pattern, as when in 1898 the Philadelphia and West Chester Street Car Company hired two black motormen—not conductors—to run its new electric trains. The experiment lasted only as long as a two-week strike by the other workers. More fundamentally, racial prejudice created a situation that capitalists could manipulate to their advantage, as several labor leaders understood. Businessmen were fond of reminding white workers that there was a great pool of "lusty fellows" out there, "some with shoulders twice as broad" as theirs, all willing to work for low wages in return for the break and traditionally "tractable" as a result of their heritage of slavery. The threat was usually enough to keep the whites in line. When it was not, black strikebreakers could be hired or, in smaller places, imported by the trainload. The Philadelphia press was full of such stories, featuring bloody firefights between white miners and state troops, all of them object lessons for the parties involved.[70]

For blacks the situation was a classic catch-22. Many leaders believed that the long-term future lay in cooperation with the labor movement. But in practice virtually every occupational gain in the period, city by city, was won when black scabs replaced white strikers. This was a risky business at best; employers were not notably loyal to imported workers once a strike was settled. And win or lose, any confrontation only worsened the relations between Afro-Americans and organized labor.[71]

In Philadelphia a typical drama was played out in the summer of 1890. That August, against a background of stories about Russian pogroms and an expected influx of Jewish immigrants, the city's largely Russian-Jewish cloakmakers struck the major firms. The movement sputtered quietly for a couple of weeks until the 16th, when the Philadelphia *Inquirer,* under the front-page headline "A RADICAL CHANGE," carried a surprising announcement by one of the partners in Blum Brothers, the leading spokesman for the manufacturers. "The places of the striking Russians will be filled by the employment of colored people." He explained that he had earlier been contacted by the Reverend B. W. Christian of Shiloh Baptist Church and by Common Councilman Christopher Perry, publisher of the Philadelphia *Tribune,* who had urged him to hire black seamstresses. Now the time seemed ripe. Although some of the newcomers might take a while to break in, just as the Russians had, "within a month we expect that from 1500 to 1600 colored persons will be at work for the different manufacturers."[72]

This announcement was variously received with "excitement" and "dismay." Four days later it was reported that Christian had some 100 black women and girls at work in his own home and church and was looking for more room. The following week he rented a building at the corner of Twelfth and Locust, big enough to house 180 workers. Blum announced the same day that the strike was over and the workers back. When asked about the black pieceworkers, he expressed an airy confidence that there was plenty of business for all. In fact, a number of cloakmakers were still holding out and only drifted back over the next several weeks, saying that "though they have nothing against the colored race as a race they hold them in the same light all union men hold those who take their places in a strike." Christian himself held out only until mid-October, when a delegation from his church convinced him that he was out of the clothing business and needed to get back to the Gospels.[73]

The defeat was typical. As a result of union organization generally, blacks were virtually excluded from the garment industry of the North. And in Philadelphia in this period no strikebreaking effort ever successfully breached the wall erected by white hostility and prejudice. The vast majority of black men and women thus remained in the two worst categories in the occupational lexicon: "domestic and personal service" and "unskilled labor."[74]

The working experience of the black woman differed from the white in three important ways. First, married or single, a far greater proportion of black women worked for wages rather than as unpaid housewives. Among blacks, there was no tradition that to take any outside work was somehow shameful in itself, and the majority of adults took whatever they could get, two or three times as many as white women as of 1900. Second, a greater proportion of black women distinguished themselves in those learned occupations available to them. For example, Dr. Caroline Anderson ran a dispensary for the Berean Church, Fannie Coppin served as head of the Institute for Colored Youth, and Mrs. N. F. Mossell and Florence Lewis wrote for both white papers and black. Third and most important, however, over 90 percent of legitimately employed black women worked as servants, waitresses, launderers, and cooks.[75]

Among black men, the same domestic and personal service ranked second only to unskilled labor. The common denominator for both groups was low wages. While Philadelphia's masons earned about $20 a week in the later nineteenth century, as did the more skilled factory hands, a stevedore at 20 cents an hour was hard-pressed to make $10, even given full employment. Du Bois figured that less than a third of the black *families* in the Seventh Ward made that much weekly, although the women and children contributed more than in white families. Roughly 90 percent of the whole black group failed to make enough to meet the "minimum adequacy budget" of $643 yearly for a family of five.[76]

Beyond this poverty, the worst thing about unskilled labor was its insecurity. Everyone in this category, which included porters, janitors, longshoremen, and common laborers, was by definition interchangeable with anyone else of the same strength and sex. And the jobs just came and went with the course of the seasons and the economic cycle.

The real objection to domestic service was not the level of wages. Two to four dollars a week in the 1890s, plus room and board, allowed female servants to take home as much as factory hands, perhaps as much as schoolteachers, and to eat better as well. But the work was degrading and unpleasant on account of its irregular hours and demands, the built-in uncertainty of having always to answer to the whims of other people. For blacks this kind of insecurity was heightened by a change in fashion that threatened their jobs increasingly in the later 1880s and 1890s. Rich Philadelphians, in an age of rampant Anglophilia, felt the need to "upgrade" domestic service, which meant in effect to adopt contemporary

British standards. The easiest way to do so was simply to replace Afro-Americans with foreign whites, a movement that cost the jobs of a number of relatively skilled coachmen, cooks, and butlers in the city's better neighborhoods.[77]

There was ironic cruelty in the fact that urban blacks never had a secure hold even on the lowest rungs of the metaphorical job ladder. Each successive wave of immigrants—German, Irish, Italian, and Jewish—was granted a broader range of choices, and each, collectively, moved past the blacks. But there were always laggards, and the boats kept coming and unloading fresh newcomers. By the early 1890s the worst slums of Philadelphia, in the river wards along the Delaware, were more heavily peopled by refugees from southern and eastern Europe than from the southeast United States. And while many of these people would someday move up and out, at any given moment they were eager to challenge blacks for work of any kind.[78]

One object of the labor movement was to ensure some sort of job security, but the unskilled were by nature hard to organize. The Hod Carriers Union did bring black and white together beginning in the 1880s. But that was the only interracial union with any continuous existence. In many northern cities blacks had been driven off the docks and out of longshore work entirely as early as the Civil War, largely by Irish competitors. But the length of Philadelphia's shoreline, spread out along its two big rivers, prevented any body of men, in either a union or an ethnic group, from establishing a monopoly. Black workingmen and white thus seem to have worked together in every sense, and men of all colors fought on both sides of the sometimes bloody and always futile efforts to establish the International Longshoremen's Association.[79]

Even when available, however, stevedoring was, like other labor, uncertain work, dangerous, seasonal, and sporadic. There were always cold months, when nothing moved out of the icebound Great Lakes ports. Twenty cents an hour was earned only for working, not for the hours spent waiting and watching for ships to arrive. In the best of times unskilled laborers generally worked fewer weeks than skilled. Some spent the winters back in Maryland or Virginia, where if the weather was not warmer, fatwood was cheaper than coal and food was easier to find on the farm. For those without that kind of refuge or with families to care for, there were always times when, as Richard R. Wright, the black economist, put it starkly, "outside charity must help or . . . crime must be resorted to."[80]

Charity of several kinds was an important, even essential part of life among the urban poor. The city itself provided an almshouse for the

most desperately sick and helpless. Like all of the public welfare institutions—with their meals of "walkaway rice" and their management
too often in the hands of sexual tyrants, bullies, and thieves—the almshouse was never an attractive place. But the advance in general prosperity and, with it, in community benevolence led to the multiplication
of private agencies of all sorts.[81]

The oldest of the private alternatives specifically for blacks were the
Quaker Home for Colored Orphans and the Home for Destitute Colored
Children. The earliest records from these places were fundraising appeals filled with painful accounts of death among the tubercular "little
scholars" they had taken off the streets. Death was a much less frequent
visitor toward the century's end, and candid photographs show healthy
and cheerful children at play, in dramatic contrast to the grim formality
of such alternatives as the public House of Refuge. At the other end of
the life cycle there was the Home for Aged and Infirm Colored People,
a model institution established with a quarter-million dollar gift from
Philadelphia's richest black man, the lumber dealer Stephen Smith.
Several black churches sought to provide relief for their communicants
and housing for their elderly. About a fifth of all Philadelphians got
their medical care for free. For blacks in particular Dr. Mossell founded
the Frederick Douglass Memorial Hospital and Training School in 1895.
The number of places that provided free meals, baths, clothing, and
shelter on an emergency basis was growing continually.[82]

All of this was important; none of it was enough. Several dozen old
people and young did get what was by contemporary standards the best
in institutional care. Poverty did not grow worse absolutely; blacks as
well as whites enjoyed the benefits of the great surge in the late century
economy, and as real wages rose, the necessities of life grew relatively
cheaper. The level of public health improved, and the worst of housing
moved aboveground, out of the waterlogged cellars of the prewar period.
The combination of public and private charity provided a rising level of
protection from absolute misery, and as time went on, there were no
more stories, as there had been in 1860, of black Philadelphians literally
starving to death in their own homes. But there was no relative improvement. The mass of black working people were still condemned to
common labor, with little chance for an escape, deprived not only of
the most obvious benefits of the new economic order but, for better and
worse, of the changes in social psychology wrought by both public schooling
and by factory or bureaucratic work.[83]

The great age of city-building, then, set different social and economic
patterns for Philadelphia's racial majority and minority. Ambitious blacks,
those driven from better jobs or trained in skills they had no chance to

use, must have felt deeply the contrast between their own insecurities and the increasingly orderly, predictable, and prosperous lives of the white majority all around them. While the wider city was growing more peaceable and less violent as the century progressed, their own neighborhoods were not. And to many of them, looking for collective or individual opportunity, it seemed that somewhere between charity and crime there was politics.

· 2 ·
RACIAL AND URBAN POLITICS

POLITICS was promise of many kinds in the era of the Civil War and after. The new-won right to vote opened novel opportunities everywhere for blacks, whose leaders were aware of what was happening in the South and other places as well as at home. The relative size of Philadelphia's black population and its role as a Republican voting bloc in a largely Republican city, state, and nation potentially gave it more strategic leverage than any other black population in the urban North. Some tried to use this leverage to win power and dignity for the race as a whole; theirs was a politics of race. Others tried to win personal security and advancement through the many forms of aid and patronage turned out by the machinery of party and of government; theirs was the politics of Philadelphia. Both were symbolized in the careers of Octavius V. Catto and Gilbert A. ("Gil") Ball.

Professor Catto, of the Institute of Colored Youth, was the driving force behind Pennsylvania's Equal Rights League and the most active local leader in the fight for black suffrage. On election Tuesday, October 10, 1871, a little more than a year after that right was won, he was murdered in an attempt to keep him and his fellows from exercising it. Gangs of white men, mostly Irish Democrats, had begun harassing blacks on the preceding Sunday. The violence escalated on Monday. Next morning, with some encouragement from the police, the gangs became a mob, the electoral process broke down in several of the river wards, and by late afternoon, with Isaac Chase already axed and Jacob Gordon shot to death, the state militia got ready to mobilize. Catto, a major in the militia, was returning home to get his uniform and had reached the sidewalk in front of his home at 814 South Street when a young man with a bandaged head rushed up and fired a pistol once into his back and again into his chest. The dying man collapsed into the arms of a police officer, while his assailant escaped into a nearby tavern and out the back.[1]

The scene climaxed what turned out to be the last of the city's major race riots, but as no one yet knew that, official Philadelphia was frightened and outraged. A mass meeting was held on Friday the 13th, under the auspices of the city's leading citizens. At Catto's funeral, 5000 people, black and white, crowded into the Race Street Armory to view the body, and the procession itself, which included one infantry brigade, three regiments, eight other military detachments, and 125 carriages, took three hours to move down Broad Street, packed with spectators on both sides, to the little Mount Lebanon Cemetery where the rites were held.[2]

Gil Ball's life was less dramatic, and his death less tragically symbolic. Ball died in bed, nearly twenty years after Catto, of apparent heart failure. No one had ever honored him officially; he had never led a crusade or even a movement, never held public office or made a published address. Yet half a century later, old-time ward leaders recalled Gil Ball's place at the very center of early black politics in the city. And human memory being short, his funeral in December 1890 was called "the largest . . . for a colored man ever held in Philadelphia." There was no Broad Street procession, but Lombard was blocked off for hours.[3]

The neighborhood had lost a politician of a very different school from Catto's. Like "Bose" Cobb in Boston, "Mush-Mouth" Johnson in Chicago, or "Starlight" Boyd in Cleveland, Ball ran the kind of place a man could go to, black or white, and have a drink, meet a woman, make a deal, or find a game. The saloon was also a kind of dance hall and place of assignation with some claim to respectability; his political clubhouse up the street catered to a rougher trade.[4]

Ball's politics and Catto's were built on different but by no means incompatible principles. Both were Republicans, interested in mobilizing and using the black population to maximum advantage, outside the regular elective process as well as inside. Full participation in politics might bring status and recognition as well as favorable legislation. It might equally bring patronage, or access not only to government service but to a host of other jobs, on projects ranging from the streetcar system to the construction of City Hall.

Catto and Ball also shared the fact that they died young—the first at thirty-one, the second at forty. While each enjoyed some success during his lifetime, their fellows and co-workers were unable to win what either man had promised. The politics of race was directed toward collective solutions to black problems, and ultimately to the nation as a whole; the politics of Philadelphia, in its concern with more private gains, was more parochial. But while local affairs sometimes seemed to have little to do with national, the two in fact were linked. What happened in Washington and to the freedman in the South was critically important to what happened closer to home. And by century's end, as the larger promises were punctured and the hope of freedom gave way to the reality of dependence, it was impossible to hold onto the gains once made in Philadelphia. The failure had long-term consequences in terms not only of losing power itself but also of encouraging patterns of criminal behavior.

THE POLITICS OF RACE

Catto's politics was the politics of race, or the organized pursuit of greater equality, opportunity, and recognition for the race as a whole. These goals were considerably older and more fundamental than the right to vote. In the northern states, in fact, the heroic age may have been the time before the Civil War when blacks and their few white allies worked for abolition and in such movements as the Underground Railroad, against often violent resistance. Many Philadelphians who had been involved in these activities went on to fight the war itself, and other battles. But during the late 1860s there was a shift in active political leadership as it passed to the generation led by Catto and away from the two chief veterans of the prewar era, Robert Purvis and William Still.

Partial surrender to a rising generation was easy for Purvis, who was consistently above criticism and, once freedom was won, somewhat above the battle. Born in 1810, his father a slaveowner from Charleston, Purvis was largely white in ancestry and appearance, one of the rare people who could freely "choose" his color. He chose black. Educated at Amherst College and given enough of a fortune to qualify him for the most enviable of occupations, that of a "gentleman" freed of the need to work for a living, he settled in Philadelphia. During a time when the city's small and isolated black population needed leadership, Purvis helped supply it, lining up white allies, sheltering fugitives, facing white mobs, and at times sitting up all night with a rifle across his knees. For three decades after the Civil War until his death in 1898, he grew into the role as one of Philadelphia's leading citizens, always available to lend his advice or person on critical or ceremonial occasions. But he was never, in these later years, involved in the day-to-day business of elective politics or community leadership.[5]

His friend and associate, William Still, was another story. If Purvis was an aristocrat, Still was a Horatio Alger hero. Born in 1820, he had come to Philadelphia as a penniless youth and worked at a variety of jobs until he found his talent as an entrepreneur. He, too, was involved in abolitionism and the Underground Railroad. During the war he got an appointment as supplier to the black troops at Camp William Penn. He afterward dabbled in real estate, traded in whatever was available, and finally settled into the coal and ice business. By the 1870s he was one of the two or three richest black men in the city. Much of his money went to philanthrophies. He succeeded the Reverend Stephen Smith as president and principal angel of the Home for Aged and Infirm Colored People, supported the ailing abolitionist Sojourner Truth in her last years, founded a black branch of the Young Men's Christian Association, and helped a variety of local and national causes until his death in 1902. But while he shared with Purvis a distaste for postwar city politics, he differed from him in his talent for drawing controversy.[6]

Still had gotten into a characteristic squabble before the war. An Ellen Wells stopped at his house on a tour designed, she claimed, to raise money to buy her children out of slavery in Kentucky. Still, who believed that she was a fraud, wrote a letter accusing her of being a prostitute as well. Wells got wind of the letter and sued for criminal libel. Attractive and articulate—she was "almost white in appearance"—she had little trouble at the 1860 trial in painting Still as an ungallant penny-pinching villain. The whole affair cost him $100 in damages, ten days in jail, and considerable goodwill.[7]

A few years later Still found himself again under an attack that seriously hurt his reputation among the city's younger black leaders. Next to slavery itself, the issue involved was the most emotional one ever to affect the blacks of Philadelphia. In 1858 the city had begun to grant charters to a number of horse-drawn streetcar companies; eventually there were nineteen of them. Most of these companies refused to carry blacks at all, although some eventually put on special cars for them— every fifth or tenth, for those who could wait—or allowed blacks to sit on open platforms exposed to the weather. When the war came, however, these concessions were seen as inadequate. The Emancipation Proclamation and then the call for black troops made the political and social future of the Afro-American a central issue for the nation as a whole. The blacks themselves were by then aroused to the potential in what was no longer just a "white man's war." In Philadelphia they were required daily to witness the spectacle of men in the uniform of their country denied the right to ride in cars officially chartered by the city, and of women and children forced to walk miles to visit soldiers in the hospital. What had been an annoying practical problem became an intensely symbolic one as well. At this juncture Still chose to appeal to the conscience of the white majority, while another younger group chose to appeal directly to the indignation of the blacks and, among other tactics, to take the streetcar issue to the streets.[8]

The situation was in several ways ironic. Still had first raised the issue in 1859 in a newspaper article, and he kept it alive with a letter widely reprinted in the foreign press. As leader of an elite black civic association, he had petitioned the railway companies for service in the early 1860s. And it was he who arranged an indignation meeting at Concert Hall on January 15, 1865, at which an impressive committee of white civic leaders began the process of petitioning the state itself for a change in policy. There was a logic in going to the state through such men as the Baldwins, Wetherills, Biddles, and McKims who made up the Concert Hall Committee. They had the vote, and the blacks did not. But at that point in history others demanded a more active role.[9]

Ever since passage of the hated Fugitive Slave Act of 1850, blacks in Philadelphia and elsewhere had organized to oppose it bodily as well as verbally. When petitions and attorneys failed, it was sometimes possible to storm a jail or courthouse and rescue a fellow black consigned for shipment back South. In March 1860 a court hearing over the status of an alleged fugitive developed into a contest, with cheering whites packing the room to prevent any attempt at rescue, and a black crowd in the streets fighting police and constables in a vain effort to get at the condemned man's carriage. None of the ten men arrested for riot in this episode belonged to the small group of black leaders who had led the abolition fight. Still and Purvis perhaps kept out of such activities because of their long association with Quakers and the pacifist William Lloyd Garrison.[10]

The war itself, once the call for black troops had gone out in 1863, gave ordinary blacks a further chance to join directly in the fight for freedom. It is not clear how many local men signed up, since the eleven regiments that trained outside the city drew recruits from a wider ara. But the census of 1860 counted 2415 black males in the city between the ages of nineteen and thirty-five, and roughly 8600 men passed through Camp William Penn and were credited to Pennsylvania's quota, or twice as many as from any other free state. Although they were granted only $10 for signing up—white men got $300—and were otherwise severely treated, toward war's end it was worth a man's life in Cross Alley to refuse enlistment.[11]

It was in this excited atmosphere that the national Equal Rights League was founded in October 1864. Its purposes, radical by contemporary standards, were stated simply in its title. Its membership was all black. Its strongest chapter was in Philadelphia, where Catto was a member and integration of the streetcars was now the leading issue. And the League appealed to a wide constituency by encouraging the often spontaneous effort to challenge the car companies by simply defying the rules.[12]

The tactics were simple. Women, sometimes pregnant, mingled with white crowds, climbed into streetcars, and had to be ejected. Clergymen in collars did the same. Black men sometimes gathered at stops and rushed to fill the cars before anyone else could enter. As the major speaker at a meeting of the Union League Association in January 1865, Catto urged men "to vindicate their manhood, and no longer suffer defenseless women and children to be assaulted or insulted by ruffianly conductors and drivers."[13]

A few white allies enlisted in this battle. Some Quakers had already begun to boycott the streetcar companies, and other passengers objected to the more outrageous scenes, as when a zealous conductor locked the doors in order to take two women to be "whitewashed" at the depot. But only two of the city's seven daily papers took up the cause. Although the Reverend William Alston was thrown off a car while carrying a sick child in convulsions, the Protestant ministry had apparently exhausted its moral concern in a concurrent controversy over operating the lines on Sunday. Grand juries ignored attempts to indict conductors for assault. An appeal to Alexander Henry, the Republican mayor of the city, was met with the remark that he would not want his wife and daughters to ride with "them" either. The police were more than willing to back up conductors with clubs, often to the music of white passengers' applause.[14]

Civil suits were a little more successful, beginning in 1865. In the key case an old woman testified to injuries received when the conductor called on two other passengers to throw her out on her way home from doing church work with wounded soldiers. Judge Joseph Allinson, then, had finally heard enough. His directed charge to the jury was a perfect summation of the case as seen by the white elite. "The logic of events over the past four years has in many respects cleared our vision and corrected our judgment," he confessed, and a people who had rallied to fight for their country "should not be denied the rights common to humanity."[15]

But the loss of this suit and others was not enough, at $50 apiece, to sway the streetcar companies. Their argument that letting a black minority aboard would lose them white patrons was confirmed when the Frankford and Southwark tried it for a month. Their stand was reinforced in 1867 when the Pennsylvania Supreme Court upheld the legality of segregation. The sporadic demonstrations on the cars themselves were fought to a standoff, with the satisfactions of direct action balanced by the constant threat of racial riot. Sometimes a carload of young men returning from graduation at the all-black Lincoln University, for example, could cow a driver into silence. More often such cars were sidetracked, abandoned, or even lifted off the tracks by helpful white crowds.

The Equal Rights League, like the Concert Hall Committee, could see that, whatever happened on the streets of Philadelphia, the matter would have to be settled in the capitol at Harrisburg.[16]

Left to their own inclination, Pennsylvania's state legislators would doubtless have echoed something like the sentiments of Mayor Henry. The state had voted for the Thirteenth Amendment, abolishing slavery, by only a 60–40 margin. A bill to abolish railroad segregation had died in 1865. But in subsequent years, especially in matters affecting black rights, the politics of the state reflected the politics of the nation. In 1867 the Republicans in Congress were just beginning to take charge of Reconstruction in the South, moving to block off control by ex-Confederates and hold onto the area with the aid of newly freed black voters. In that same year the Commonwealth of Pennsylvania finally voted to end discrimination on its streetcars. It was a victory that the winners recognized had little to do with "love to the Lord and thy neighbor."[17]

The fact that victory was won on the ground and with the allies first chosen by Still and other leading members of the Social, Civil, and Statistical Association was not enough to win them points with the younger militants. In the final months a rumor got around that Still had been ready to abandon the interests of all black riders in favor of concessions to a few as rich and well-connected as himself. Clues to the origins of this story appear in the published attitudes of the Concert Hall Committee. Working-class patrons of the streetcars—richer men rode carriages—had apparently complained that black folks smelled bad. The Concert Hall group did not concede this directly, but its own literature was equally preoccupied with the issue, implying that it was simply a case of the pot maligning the kettle: their opponents were "those who do not use cologne water, but who patronize whiskey and onions, which can be noted a rod off." The committee also noted characteristically that, once given the right, blacks "resort to the cars sparingly, and when not in clean clothes voluntarily take their old places on the forward platform." Somehow this odor of condescension, picked up from his white associates, was hard for William Still to shake. A mass meeting was held at which he and his friends were denounced as "base enemies of our race." Still's reply was rambling and defensive, a long complaint about the younger generation's failure to appreciate hard work and success, its impatience, and its irreverence. To make the generational symbolism complete, the only person he named as an accuser was Jacob White, Jr., son of an old friend, newly appointed head of the Roberts Vaux School, and the classmate, teammate, and best friend of Octavius V. Catto.[18]

During the late 1860s it was the Equal Rights League and not the older groups that drew the most attention among blacks. Catto's own position was enhanced in 1867 when the League's first president, Jasper Wright, and vice president, Joshua Giddings, went South, where the Radical Republicans in Congress, having seized oversight of the Reconstruction process, had opened unparalleled opportunities for able black men. In their absence Catto became the central figure in the state League and then secretary to the national. When in 1869 President Ulysses S. Grant appointed another League member, Professor E. D. Bassett, as Minister to Haiti—the highest diplomatic post ever given to an Afro-American citizen—another opportunity was opened. Bassett had been Catto's superior as principal of the Institute for Colored Youth. When he left, the Quaker board appointed the younger man to head his alma mater, a position that made him ex officio a spokesman for Philadelphia's black elite.[19]

These years were promising ones for this charismatic man and his cause. Catto himself cut a dashing figure, capable of running up a clothing bill of $113.50 in just two months, at a time when his salary as principal was less than $1000 a year. A poetic and highly eligible bachelor, he was often seen in company with Caroline LeCount, another leading activist. He was a founder of the Pythian Baseball Club, one of the city's first and, black or white, its best. The club was important for reasons well beyond its ranking among the pioneers in the newly popular national pastime: the roster of its first four teams amounts to a kind of roll call of the leading black politicians, educators, and lawyers of the next thirty years. Catto was the shortstop and captain; Still, a disgruntled contributor. Still, that spring, wrote a letter resigning as a sponsor: after describing the way in which he had amassed his money, he noted, "Our kin in the South, famishing for knowledge, have claims so great and pressing that I feel bound to give of my means in this direction . . . in preference to giving for frivolous amusements." Club Secretary Jacob White, Jr., who had felt his lash before, replied that he would accept the resignation only after Still's dollar in dues was paid up; otherwise, "neither the acquisition nor the disposition of your means is of interest to us as an organization."[20]

Catto's local ascendency was, however, dominated by events in the South. Literate blacks everywhere were part of a cosmopolitan class. Their own histories and family connections typically bound them with others up and down the country. Their newspapers kept them informed not only of national developments but of critical events in every state and city where activity was strong. And the most exciting news in the history of racial politics was coming out of the Old Confederacy. Those officers of the Pennsylvania Equal Rights League who followed Union troops into the defeated South were only two of many. Ex-slaves every-where were being mobilized to seek education and other forms of eco-nomic and social advantage through the exercise of political power. The result was still unclear, for southern whites were fighting back at several levels—voting when allowed, appealing to other whites on the basis of their common race, and riding at night with the Ku Klux Klan or other groups devoted to maintaining their supremacy. The Republican Con-gress, having grasped the political potential in black support, maintained troops at several places in the South to aid beleaguered local forces. The Fourteenth and Fifteenth Amendments were intended to shore up this black-Republican alliance with constitutional guarantees.[21]

From the perspective of Philadelphia, these events were both exciting and frustrating. At a time when black Louisianians and Mississippians were electing their fellows to statewide offices and even the Senate of the United States, the Afro-American residents of Pennsylvania, far from the action, still had no right to vote at all. Neither Catto's eloquence nor the varied activities of the Equal Rights League could mask the fact that the state was one of the last in the North to override its own constitution and ratify the Fifteenth Amendment. The first attempt to do so, in 1868, was defeated in the state House of Representatives by a margin of 68 to 14. Soon, however, the Commonwealth's Republicans came to see what passage might mean for the party countrywide. Local blacks, too, were more concerned with the national than the statewide implications of the measure. Upon final passage in 1870, when it seemed that millions of their fellows everywhere would now be guaranteed a share in power, Philadelphia's leaders recognized Tuesday, April 26, as a special day of celebration. The Union League Club gave Catto a com-memorative silk banner, and a huge procession wound its way to Hor-ticultural Hall for speeches by Catto, Frederick Douglass, Purvis, and distinguished whites. The usual stones and pistol shots that followed the parade were perhaps shrugged off as losing gestures.[22]

After all this, the first election locally was an anticlimax. The year 1870 was an off-year, with no races of importance and no black can-didates on the ballot. The city was Democratic, under the administration of Mayor Daniel Fox, and there was no way to change it. Although there were more blacks in Philadelphia than in any other city of the North, their potential influence was still insignificant in comparison with that of the rural millions of the South. Relatively few turned out to vote. There was some trouble in the always fractious Fifth Ward, where the new voters were harassed and assaulted by Irish Democrats. The matter could have been handled by the local authorities, but in fact the police were actively involved in the effort to keep black voters from the polls. The United States Marshal responded by calling in the marines, citing the federal Force Act just enacted with the South in mind, and events proceeded in relative quiet.[23]

In these years the fortunes of Catto's beloved Pythians mirrored what was happening to his race. The ball club had been founded in an era when the Equal Rights League was beginning to assert local leadership. In its early years it shared the facilities of the all-white Philadelphia Athletics, whose captain, Harry Hayhurst, umpired its more important games. Relations were then good, and there was the chance they might grow better. Jacob White wrote a warm note to congratulate the other club on its claim to a "national" championship, but Catto had designs of his own. The skill of the Pythians, he noted in the spring of 1867, was attracting "considerable interest, and not a little anxiety, among the white fraternity." A true championship would have matched both blacks and whites together, but the matter was never settled on the diamond. Despite support from Hayhurst and others, the Pythians and other Afro-American teams were excluded in 1869 from the Pennsylvania Convention of Baseball Clubs, one of the first formal moves in a campaign that eventually barred blacks from the professional leagues.[24]

Although Catto was still a young man, and the future for himself and his fellows looked far better than it had a decade earlier, there was nothing locally now that could recapture the emotional intensity of the streetcar fight, or of the earlier war years when he had led the entire male graduating class of the Institute for Colored Youth up to Harrisburg to enlist. In the city itself there was nothing of importance left for him to do, and he may have been looking for a job in Washington and the chance to make an impact on the wider national stage. Perhaps he and his contemporaries could sense that black power in the South was beginning to slip as President Grant and the Congress tired of fighting what was in effect a continued civil war against southern white guerillas.[25]

The turning point may be assigned as conveniently to the year of Catto's death as to any other. On election day in 1871 there was still hope and much activity, but the chance for genuine revolution in the status of Afro-Americans was gone. Where gains had been greatest, so had losses, as southern whites returned to power wherever federal support was withdrawn. By 1877 the pattern was complete. Although by no means powerless and in many areas still able to vote and hold office, the majority of southern rural blacks had been reduced to the partial citizenship that fit their economic dependence. The federal Civil Rights Act of 1875, essentially forbidding segregation, was passed only after removal of the provision for common schooling. The act was in any case evaded from the first. The United States Supreme Court began the process of emasculating the two great protective amendments, virtually nullifying the Fifteenth in the *Cruikshank* case of 1874, and in 1883 it struck down most of the Civil Rights Act as well.[26]

In Pennsylvania, as in the northern states generally, there were no such obvious reverses. When the Republican party convened in Philadelphia in 1872, the black vote was still thought important to success. One black orator, the ex-Philadelphian John R. Lynch of Mississippi, seconded the renomination of President Grant. Others, black and white, denounced the Ku Klux Klan, praised the antislavery record of Vice-President Henry Wilson, and defended the right of men and women to marry whomever they chose. The struggle for equal rights and recognition then continued, but victories came more slowly.[27]

Upon Catto's death, the Equal Rights League moved its headquarters out of town to Reading. In Philadelphia the orator Isaiah Wears joined William D. Forten in keeping the League in touch with the Republican party. But it was hard to maintain earlier levels of enthusiasm against the background of failures in the South.[28]

The chief issue for the black press was the continued state provision for separate schools, which in practice were primary schools, since no jurisdiction could afford separate grammar or high schools for the few blacks who qualified to attend them. But here there was some ambivalence, for even Philadelphia's all-black schools had a majority of white teachers, and white schools had no black teachers at all. One effect of desegregation might then be the loss of some of the best jobs enjoyed by black people in the city. The matter was settled first by a court case in rural Crawford County, where in 1881 a Judge of Common Pleas declared separate schooling in violation of the Fourteenth Amendment. The legislature followed this up by statute law. In practice, however, very little changed.[29]

The same outcome followed the effort to open public places such as restaurants and theaters. A black man sued successfully in 1874 when denied a theater seat. The legislature tardily responded in 1887 by providing for criminal fines in cases of such discrimination. But the fine in effect set a cap on damages. Experience with the federal act and with the Supreme Court's Civil Rights Act decision had by then shown that nothing dramatic need change with the law.[30]

The concern for a politics of race never died, and there were always occasions to call it out. The anniversaries of the Emancipation Proclamation and the Fifteenth Amendment were celebrated every year with sermons and parades, while men like Still and Purvis assumed their roles as elder statesmen, recognized by white and black alike. Forten and especially Wears seemed ready to succeed if not quite to replace them. There were the National Colored Congresses in the 1860s and the Afro-American League in the 1890s. Distinguished Philadelphians were involved in these and other racial causes throughout the period. But in terms of numbers and energy, the politics of race had given way, by the early 1870s, to the gritty and less dramatic politics of Philadelphia.[31]

THE POLITICS OF PHILADELPHIA

The politics of Philadelphia in the decades following the Civil War was potentially a means of black advancement along two routes. One route was to work for the rewards of patronage at all levels and by winning elective office. Winning office in turn might contribute to progress along the second route, toward power and independence, which in a local analogue to the politics of race might lead to the real improvement of conditions in black neighborhoods. But despite some movement along the first or narrower route, the city's blacks were almost wholly unable to make any broader gains along the second route.

The reason for this disappointment was not that the political machine had no use for black voters, because the dominant Republican faction was historically more dependent on black voters than any other party. The reason was only partly that the more educated members of the group had been indirectly bribed by offices and patronage. Though office was important to black men, their share, at somewhere between one-fifth and one-tenth of what their numbers and activities would warrant, was a continual source of complaint rather than complaisance. The primary reason for the failure to achieve black power was that the mass of black voters in Philadelphia, as in the Reconstruction South, had been bought off.[32]

The association between blacks and vote fraud dated to that first election in 1870. Banners in the downtown wards warned Democrats to beware of "Colored Repeaters," who would "Vote Early and Vote Often." Mayor Fox's police were stationed at the ferry to block off any black immigrants from Camden, and a carload from Baltimore was railroaded straight to county jail. But the occasion was more historic than memorable, as most new voters simply did not vote. Not until the next year, in Catto's last election and Gil Ball's first, did several thousand local blacks make their real debut in politics.[33]

The role in which they were cast, as mercenary infantry, would last for decades, even generations. Although a few men aspired to more, most were unable even to see across the muddy trenches that they manned.

Overblown military metaphors come easily to historians of nineteenth century politics, whose vocabulary is inherited from an era in which campaigns were described in terms of positions taken and defended, swords crossed, guns fired, flags run up or down. The trappings, emotions, and substance of political activity were all, indeed, as martial as the party organization could arrange. Bonfires were lit, bands played, and marches held as signs of competitive strength. In Philadelphia, Republican triumphs were hailed with a cannon shot from the roof of the headquarters at Eleventh and Chestnut. Most leaders after 1865 had been commissioned officers during the war and were expected periodically to rally the troops in terms of duty, honor, and country. The troops themselves served out of some combination of conviction and avarice. And the first person systematically to enlist black Philadelphians in the Republican cause, in his own 1871 campaign for district attorney, was a Colonel William B. Mann.[34]

Republicans could assume a prejudice in their favor. During the ceremony to mark passage of the Fifteenth Amendment Catto had noted plainly that the "black man knows on which side of the line to vote." But this preference could not in itself bring thousands of his less educated fellows to the polls. In Philadelphia, as in many cities, the franchise was restricted to taxpayers. The logistics of political organization began with the twenty-five cents needed to furnish a man with a poll tax receipt. Beyond that, the going price for a vote depended on a variety of market factors, the potential value and the predicted closeness of a given election. The Democratic offer to black voters in 1870 was a cynical ticket "Good for One Drink," worth a nickel or two. The more usual amount ranged from one dollar to ten and, in extraordinary cases, fifteen dollars a head, at a time when a dollar a day was thought to be an honest wage. Businessmen to whom the outcome of a local election could mean millions of dollars supplied these funds. Campaigns also hired men to guide new or illiterate voters to the polls, to provide them with ballots properly marked or "scratched," and to protect them against challenge and interference. And if significant numbers could indeed vote early and often, so much the better.[35]

Gil Ball played a familiar role in this operation. Politics always had room for a tough young man who could be counted on to show up at the polls with twenty others who would do what he told them. A talent for brawling could be parleyed into other opportunities. One favorite route to power led straight into saloonkeeping, where a man could be useful to the police and politicians on the one hand and to his people on the other. And Ball's Bar, at 720 Lombard Street, was in fact located not far from his political clubhouse and just down the block from the Nineteenth District Station House.

Ball's first known involvement in a brawl occurred in 1870, when at the age of twenty he knifed and was knifed by one Shadrach Davis in a barroom at Seventh and St. Mary's. Davis had apparently started the fight by accusing Ball of turning in his girl friend for a household theft.

The claim sounds right; it was common enough for a man in trouble to buy his freedom with information. And the years that followed were marked by the same cooperative but not fully easy relations with the authorities.[36]

Ball acquired the saloon itself later in the 1870s. It was a big two-story building with a restaurant and bar on the first floor, a piano, more intimate tables, and a number of female regulars on the second. Ball was an early supporter of Colonel Matthew S. Quay, a major power in the politics of the state, and he founded the Quay Club further up the street, where between elections and parade days the members played craps and faro. "Connections" presumably provided the capital and the protection necessary for all of this, but they were not enough to keep Ball himself entirely out of trouble. There was at least one arrest in the early 1880s for beating a woman, and another—this one clearly harassment—for assaulting a man. Often there was trouble at the bar, and in 1887 Ball's lieutenant at the Quay Club was gunned down by an angry gambler. But the fact that both establishments were so close to the station house generally helped to keep things quiet. Policemen often served as bouncers in protected places. Ball rang in the entire station house reserve force, for example, when "Four Kings" West and a delegation of New York City sporting men threatened to tear up the club.[37]

Although Ball's world was built on illegality and violence, his successes quickly bought him a kind of respectability. He was mentioned warily in columns of the black press usually reserved for outstanding members of the race. The white press recognized him as a "noted" or "stalwart" politician. When in 1884 Frederick A. Douglass married a white woman more than thirty years his junior, Gilbert A. Ball—together with Robert Purvis, the abolitionist Isaiah Wears, and two local office holders—was one of the leading black Philadelphians interviewed for the *Record*. And if the editor of the A.M.E. *Christian Recorder* perhaps winced at this choice of representatives, he reprinted the comments nonetheless. (Purvis and Wears, predictably, thought their old friends' match a private matter; the politicians, equally predictably, thought it impolitic; Gil Ball did not think anyone that old should get married at all.)[38]

All this recognition was not misplaced. Ball and others like him were in fact essential to any success enjoyed by local black Republicans and, beyond that, to the working of the party and of the city itself. The government of nineteenth century cities was a problem. Contemporaries tended to blame the machine, a corrupt organization dedicated to turning public business into private profit. But the problem was more apt to be the fundamentally unworkable structure of the government itself. Jacksonian Democracy had saddled big and complex cities with a system of organization based on the extreme diffusion of power, with a long array of officials elected from small and localized jurisdictions. Left to themselves, these parochial representatives could not cope with the problems of the city as a whole or mount anything as ambitious and necessary as a centralized police force, a gasworks, or an aqueduct. The function of the machine was thus to unite all these officials in the same party and give them some sort of common purpose, so that mayors, councillors, and other elected officers could act together. The real problem, perhaps more important than corruption, was that the party itself was a reflection of the government it tried to manage, organized from the bottom up, full of local sentiments and jealousies.[39]

The political machine was not itself a smoothly running mechanism, with a single purpose and direction. A better metaphor would be an "army" headed by uncertain commanders, trying to hold together a coalition of Italian condottieri or Chinese warlords. The skillful deployment of men and muscle by loyal noncoms like Ball was needed to hold the whole together, as well as to move it in any given direction.

Consider the logistics of putting out a unified slate of candidates for that critical October election of 1871. On a single day in June the Republican party held eighty-four separate conventions in the city's twenty-nine wards to nominate candidates for school directors, common and select councilmen, state senators and representatives, judges, and a mayor, district attorney, city commissioner, controller, treasurer, prothonotary, and coroner. Each of these conventions had been preceded by a primary election, organized by wards and precincts. The major conventions for city or countywide offices involved several hundred delegates and were conducted with all the trappings of selecting presidential candidates, such as temporary and permanent officers, credentials committees, challenges, and the threat of bolters. The coroner's convention, not untypically, turned into a riot and had to be adjourned. The rest were held together in large part by an army of doorkeepers and bullyboys, messengers and police. [40]

At the general election, held four months and innumerable rallies, parades, and bonfires later, the need for troops was even more elemental. The Democratic opposition was usually strong enough to elect at least one citywide official, in addition to a congressman and a number of local officers. Other forces, such as Sabbatarians, outraged taxpayers, and municipal reformers, sometimes sniped at both of the major parties. Every election was marked by challenges at the polls and was followed by court contests. None passed without gunfire. At least nine men were killed at the polls or conventions in Philadelphia between 1870 and 1900. And in every election, without exception, the biggest Republican margins were counted in Ball's Seventh Ward, the center of black settlement in Philadelphia.[41]

This faithful record, however, won limited rewards. During the first seven years of the Republican ascendency, from 1871 to 1878, no Afro-American was elected to office of any sort. The federal government rewarded a few distinguished men: Theophilus Minton was posted to the treasury, the lawyer John Stephen Durham followed Bassett to the ministry in Haiti, and John Smythe was given the same job in Liberia. Otherwise the national party offered blacks a handful of such jobs as watchmen or porter in the customs house or post office. The city government, too, found room for only a few turnkeys, messengers, and janitors to join the corps of teachers in its colored schools. Although the party had several hundred elective offices to fill, it was content to pay off its black troopers with drinks and dollars at election time and with the kind of intangible benefits that kept Ball in line. For other men, with other ambitions, this kind of wage was not enough.[42]

CHALLENGES, GAINS, AND CHOICES

The first black man to run for office in Philadelphia was Ulysses B. Vidal, an old associate of William Still, who bucked the Republican organization by running as an independent for school director in 1873, and for common council some three years later. He seems to have had some help from the Democratic opposition, but he earned no more than a couple of hundred votes. His experience served to underline the issue that black leaders would have to face regularly for the next several generations, not only in Philadelphia but all across the country. In the city specifically, as they began in the late 1870s to win public office and then to make breakthroughs in patronage, the offer of independent alternatives meant that they had to define their relationship to the regular Republican hierarchy, determining just how much they owed to the Grand Old Party and how far they dared to stray away from it.[43]

The question was simple in form but complex in substance. The Republican party, however disappointing its performance in those years, was symbolically and historically the party of freedom. For most blacks it was also, more immediately, the source of whatever little benefit was available in town. It represented, in short, both the politics of race and the politics of Philadelphia. Black leaders found it emotionally difficult to give aid and comfort to the white southerners and Irishmen who led the Democratic alternative; they were also aware of the thin line between goading an elephant and enraging it.

The 130 delegates to Philadelphia's first black protest movement had this clearly in mind when they met at Liberty Hall on February 2, 1877. Locally, this was the day when young Frank Kelly was arraigned for the murder of Octavius Catto, nearly six years earlier; nationally, Congress was still maneuvering over the disputed election between presidential candidates Samuel Tilden and Rutherford B. Hayes, which would decide the future of the southern states. Most of Philadelphia's black leaders did not attend the protest, including Ball, Purvis, Still, Wears, and Forten. The delegates were mostly younger men, some of them federal or city messengers or watchmen who aspired to something bigger. After denouncing the absentees, they noted that "our guidance, our right of franchise, under God, has been secured to us by the Republican Party," but they complained that they had suffered "ignominy, and sometimes persecution," on the party's behalf and had been "denied even a portion of the proportion and emolument of the party that we are entitled to."[44]

Such arguments were always based on the black contribution to continued Republican power. At the national level that power was being undercut by Hayes, the apparent President-Elect. During his campaign as the Republican candidate, Hayes had required black strength in the South. But after the election, he needed Democratic support in Congress to validate the credentials of his southern electors and was ready to cut a deal with the Democratic opposition to withdraw federal troops from the few remaining areas where they had shored up black Republicans. This was one of the final stages in abandoning the freedmen in the former Confederate States, but it had no immediate effect in Philadelphia, where the black vote was still critical to Republican victory. Black men in the city voted more regularly than white, in both senses, and with some 6500 or 7000 voters they accounted for over 10 per cent of the usual Republican total. Mayor Stokley, despite all of the legitimate and illegitimate resources at his disposal, won his 1877 reelection bid, just weeks after the Liberty Hall meeting, by a margin of only 64,884 to 62,129.[45]

The year 1878 marked a local breakthrough when two of the Liberty Hall delegates, F. J. R. Jones and James Needham, were officially nominated and elected to unpaid positions on the sectional school boards of the Seventh and Fifth Wards. Given the relative insignificance of these offices, which were the lowest in the party's gift, this historic first was no real cause for celebration. President Hayes, once installed, had gone through with his promise to withdraw the troops, but the impact of this move was still unclear. The impotence of black Philadelphians, by comparison to their brethren in the South, was obviously a sore point still. In case it were missed, the Georgia-bred manager of the A.M.E. Church, the Rev. Dr. H. M. Turner, hit it hard later that year. Although Turner had been in town only two years and was about to leave, he felt the need to make a few parting observations. "You may think your local matters are none of my business," he wrote in the *Christian Recorder*, "but think as you may I dare to tell you it is time you were getting more for your political services . . . with all of your speaking, organizing, parading the streets, ballyhooing, holding mass meetings, voting, and sometimes fighting, what do you get?" The list was shorter than the prologue: three menials in the post office—no letter-carriers or clerks—one clerk in the municipal tax office, and another in the customs house. Meanwhile, despite the school board election, two black teachers in the Roberts Vaux School of Jacob White, Jr., were replaced with white ones, making a total of 33 whites and only 11 blacks in the city's eleven colored schools.[46]

Both tensions and ambitions mounted when the nation prepared to elect a new President in 1880. The tenth anniversary of the Fifteenth Amendment was celebrated by a parade that was greeted with more than the usual number of cobblestones and pistol shots. Black voters retaliated on September 18, when over 15,000 local Democrats mounted the biggest demonstration in their history, with their top hats and banners posing irresistible targets as they marched through downtown neighborhoods. On election night, November 2, several blacks were in turn shot down in the Fifth Ward as they celebrated the Republican victory of James Garfield over Pennsylvania's own Winfield Scott Hancock.[47]

The city's black voters then found themselves entangled in one of the most complex mayoral elections in the history of Philadelphia. The background was set by an upper-class reformers' revolt against Mayor Stokley's regulars and "the ring" that had governed the city for years. Elite Philadelphians, like their counterparts elsewhere, were never really comfortable with local politics in the postwar era. As big property holders and taxpayers, they objected to waste and corruption; as men of principle, they complained about bribery and coercion at the polls; as aristocrats, they found it hard to deal with men like Stokley, who wore the unmistakably smoky smell of a lifetime spent fighting fires in the streets and dealing politics in back rooms. Organized into a variety of clubs, committees, leagues, and associations, upper-class Philadelphians tried persistently to win the voice to which they thought they were entitled.[48]

Reform leaders such as Rudolph Blankenburg were willing to work with the local Democrats, Independents, and any dissident Republicans who shared their distaste for the ring. Following some success in the fall or county elections of 1880, they organized a "Committee of One Hundred" to prepare for the mayoral contest, which, as a result of charter changes, would be held the following February. Though they enlisted some of the city's most prominent men and espoused a common set of principles, they could not agree on a candidate.

Meanwhile, the quiet Afro-American agitation for jobs and office, though largely ignored by the Republican regulars, did not go entirely unnoticed in other party circles. With the mayor coming under fire from several directions, a former Democrat, George de Benneville Keim, sensed an opportunity for himself. Early in the precampaign maneuverings he suggested to a number of black leaders that their resentment was well-founded. He promised, if nominated and elected on the Republican ticket, to give them even more than they had asked, namely jobs on the city's police force. The offer was a strong one; the police were not only Stokley's personal power base but a key to winning the often physical battle for command of the polls.[49]

With Keim and the One Hundred both attacking the ring from opposite angles, blacks saw an opportunity to win concessions. On December 9, accordingly, Alexander Davis called a special meeting at Liberty Hall to endorse Keim for mayor. The meeting went on to demand desegregation of the city's schools and to endorse a young Afro-American doctor, George Frisbie, for a seat in an upcoming special election for the state senate. The following night this maneuver drew unprecedented support from a dozen Democratic leaders of the Sixth Senatorial District. These Democrats, hopelessly outnumbered in the district but sensing opportunity amid Republican disarray, voted to endorse the Frisbie candidacy.[50]

The leaders of the One Hundred, while agreeing that Keim was no reformer, were unable to agree on any other champion. On December 20 they decided, instead, to go along with Stokley if he would endorse their list of demands. The black insurgents, however, remained in the field. Professor Richard Greener of Howard University, one of the first Afro-American graduates of Harvard Law School, returned to his native city specifically to endorse Keim's candidacy, which seemed to be gathering strength.[51]

Then the regulars rallied, with the full support of most of the black electorate. Frisbie withdrew his name from contention in the special senatorial election and eventually won only ten write-in votes, ranking him just ahead of President Garfield, King George III, and other scattered resisters to the great majority that Gil Ball and his troopers rang in for the official Republican choice. On January 10, in a test vote for a vacant place on the party's city committee, the ring carried seventeen wards, including all of those with substantial black populations, against just twelve for Keim's man. The next night Stokley won the Republican nomination and, with triumph at hand, explicitly repudiated the principles endorsed by the Committee of One Hundred.[52]

The next weeks were marked by a flurry of ticket-making, splitting, and scratching, and clambering in and out of strange beds. The Colored Citizens Club, comprising 150 men, endorsed Keim as an independent candidate. The Committee of One Hundred, after much maneuvering, eventually settled on a reform Democrat, Samuel King. When Keim withdrew, leaving the contest to King and Stokley, both sides appealed to the black vote. But the One Hundred had no real appeal. Although many among them had lent their names to the streetcar battle half a generation before, it would be an understatement to say that they lacked the common touch. Their alliance with the Democratic party was distasteful to most Afro-Americans. Their concerns about political morality and economy were far removed from and even hostile to the black demand for group recognition and patronage. And in the end, accumulated resentments among the white electorate decided the election. The black insurgents generally returned to the fold, as the Seventh Ward turned out its biggest Republican majority ever. But Samuel King managed narrowly to stagger through, beating Stokley and the ring in what was then and afterward hailed as a triumph of reform.[53]

The politics of King's administration, over the next three years, nevertheless produced some unanticipated benefits in terms of black patronage. Having tasted victory in February, the reformers wanted not only to consolidate but to advance. As part of this program they decided to ignore their repudiation by the voters of the Seventh Ward and to continue their efforts to win over the city's Afro-American electorate. The Committee of One Hundred began, characteristically, at the top, by adding Robert Purvis, who qualified on every count but color, to its roster of gentlemen. More important, on August 5, 1881, King made good on Keim's original promise by announcing that Alexander Davis and three other black men would be appointed to the police force; he then left town for Saratoga.[54]

This was a bold move, despite the flight that followed it. There were no black policemen at the time in any major northern city. Their debut, accordingly, was planned with care, and their selection was above reproach. In an era before any sort of civil service, when many officers were semiliterate at best, the four blacks chosen, although currently trapped in unskilled jobs, were characteristically overqualified. Alexander Davis, for example, born a slave, had graduated from nearby Lincoln University, worked as a schoolteacher, and founded a newspaper before leading one of the first revolts against Stokley. Charles Draper was a veteran of the United States Navy, and Lewis Carroll, for many years a turnkey, was an officer in the Grey Invincibles. Only Richard Caldwell had no experience beyond "laboring work" to offer.[55]

Neither the preparation nor the qualifications softened the impact of the move. Several policemen quit the force in protest. The new men were assigned to beats in or near black neighborhoods and immediately attracted crowds of spectators. Draper in particular, patrolling near the busy intersection of Eighth and Walnut, was dogged for days by an estimated thousand people, of every sex and color. The mood seems to have been more curious or mocking than outright hostile. Draper, presumably, had heard worse than "Ain't he sweet?" or "Is the thing alive?" All of this had been anticipated. The real issue, during the rest of King's administration, was how black voters would respond to his initiative. The matter was fought out in a series of unequal contests between men with different visions. On one side were those willing to consider at least some degree of independence, many of them older veterans of the politics of race. On the other side were those committed to the regular Republicans and their narrower version of the politics of Philadelphia.[56]

On August 22, three weeks after King's black appointments, Purvis, Still, and Jones called a meeting at Liberty Hall in appreciation of the mayor's courage. H. Price Williams and others struck another note by making a connection between the economic and political systems and urging black men to buy their own tax receipts and show frustration as well as gratitude at the polls: "then the factory doors will fly open." [57]

Eight days later a different group met at the same hall to test what the regular Republicans would offer. Their object was to demand that a black be nominated as city commissioner, a job that involved the oversight of local elections. The chairman, William Miller, suggested "it was time for the colored people to cease following, like sheep, the lead of a few scheming politicians and assert their own manhood," and he pointedly referred to Mayor King's bid for their attention. The next speaker then threw away the script. Representative Frank Givens, a veteran of the politics of North Carolina, called attention to the rows of empty benches in the front. He proceeded to lambast the absentees and organizers both. Black Philadelphians should be demanding nothing less than full proportional representation; their attitude was timid. Four police officers were a joke: "There are colored citizens with enough ability to sway and rule an empire"—but none of them, evidently, had gathered there that night.[58]

These remarks were not generally well taken, especially by the crowd in back. And when the next speaker, a federal magistrate from Washington, D.C., started off, "Being a stranger here, Mr. President," he got no further. Gil Ball, as a regular Republican and a native Philadelphian, had had enough of visiting southerners telling him what to do: "I . . . don't think a stranger knows anything about our affairs, and I don't think we should be called here to listen to a rambling talk that we don't agree with." It was time to get to the business of the meeting or, better yet, adjourn. The group then lamely recommended F. J. R. Jones, a watchman at the customs house, to the attention of his party. At a boisterous and badly split commissioner's convention the following

month, Jones got no votes, out of 686 cast, as his fellows continued to
vote as told.[59]

It was not quite regarded as heretical for a black man to desert the
Republican party. John P. Lewis from Yale Law School, still the only
black lawyer in town, was a lifelong Democrat, or as he put it, a man
dedicated to independent thinking and to the education of his people.
Still in 1874 had urged election of the independent, Alexander McClure,
over Stokley. H. P. Williams had run for commissioner in 1878 on the
Greenback-Labor ticket, and the Prohibitionists put up more black candidates for higher offices than any other party in the state. T. Thomas
Fortune, the leading black journalist in New York, continually urged
his readers to bargain, to pick and choose among the most advantageous
offers, to threaten the Republican party as well as to cajole it. But in
Philadelphia, while potential independents had the oratory, Gil Ball had
the voters.[60]

The Committee of One Hundred, as part of a campaign to elect a
reform governor, made a final appeal to the black electorate in the fall
of 1882. A number of old white abolitionists joined Blankenburg, Purvis,
and Still on the familiar dais at Liberty Hall to propose a series of
resolutions in favor of "Independent Republicanism." Their call was
drowned out. George Earle was ironically reminded of his younger days
when white mobs had invaded the same premises to drown out antislavery speakers. Robert Purvis was uniquely able to invoke a moment
of silence in the name of the absent but revered Quaker abolitionist
Lucretia Mott. In the hubbub, no one could bring the questions to a
vote.[61]

Mayor King, meanwhile, continued to name black officers to the
police force. On February 19, 1884, his bid for reelection was beaten
badly, as the Seventh Ward and others returned their usual majorities
for his Republican opponent, William Smith. King kept making new
appointments through his last lame weeks in office, however, bringing
the number of black officers to 35 out of a total of about 1400, a commitment too deep for any successor to disown. There was no political
point to all of this by then; perhaps there never had been. The mayor
had said all along that his only motive was a sense of justice. He never
again ran for any office but continued to work on behalf of the city's
blacks, winning recognition from former opponents and serving, over a
decade later, as the only white official of the new Frederick Douglass
Clinic.[62]

But the new mayor had the dramatic final word. Smith's first official
act was to call in Officer Lewis Carroll, one of King's four original
appointees, and fire him personally. The little flirt with insurgency was

over. Philadelphia's aspiring black politicians had learned thereafter to obey whatever orders they were given.[63]

A MODEST HIGH TIDE

The return of the Republican regulars in the mid-1880s meant for blacks an end to any hope of rapid progress. Political advancement became again a matter of obeying orders and waiting for rewards. There were no more breakthroughs, like King's police appointments. Gains were slow to come and incremental.

The next step up, after the two school directorships held since 1878, was election to the lower or "common" branch of the city council. Each of the city's roughly thirty wards was granted one common councillor for every 2000 taxable inhabitants, or usually four or five apiece. The proportionate black share of the seats was about three members as of 1870, seven or eight by 1900—even without counting their heavy commitment to the dominant party—but through the early 1880s they held no seats. In 1883 a black caucus had proposed the veteran abolitionist Levi Cromwell for one of the positions in the Seventh Ward, but at the Republican convention its members bowed to "Uncle Sammy" Williams, the organization's hand-picked Afro-American. Williams went down to defeat in the general election, but after that, and with insurgency defeated, the way was clear for black candidates. Jacob Purnell, with no fanfare, was duly nominated and elected to the common council from the Seventh Ward in 1884. Four years later he was succeeded by David Chester. When Chester died, George Wilson was elected to the vacant seat. In 1890 Wilson was joined by Stephen Gipson in his own Seventh Ward and by Constantin Hubert in the Fifth.[64]

By 1891, the city's blacks had elected three common councillors and five sectional school directors in the Fifth, Seventh, and Eighth Wards. In terms of patronage James Needham, a discount clerk in the tax office, and James G. Davis, head draughtsman in the Bureau of Gas, were the highest paid black city employees, at $1500 each. Councilman Gipson was a bail clerk at $1200, and so was F. J. R. Jones. Christopher Perry was an appointments clerk to the sheriff. Four other Afro-Americans worked as clerks in as many city departments, two as meter inspectors, seven as messengers. The city employed three black elementary school principals, about 20 teachers, 60 policemen, one fireman, eight public school janitors, and one page of councils. The Philadelphia correspondent of the New York *Age* furnished the list, with no apparent sense of irony, as a record for other cities to emulate. Although the numbers were not impressive, either absolutely or relative to the size and activity of the black electorate, the size of the legitimate black elite was smaller still, so that city and county employees made up a significant fraction of the white collar or stable salaried class.[65]

In 1885 the *Freeman* had commented that, despite the opportunities, politics "is not being entered except by those who have gained influence through methods which are repugnant to the better part of the city's colored inhabitants." Doubtless this applied to Ball. It was fashionable at the time to sneer at "professional politicians," or "office seekers," such as Jones, who had worked for the county as a sheriff's messenger, the federal government as a watchman, the police force as a special officer, the city as a messenger, and the sheriff again as a bail clerk. But in general the Philadelphia black elite was much less withdrawn and more political than the city's white aristocrats. Many of the city's leaders did not run for office only because, like Wears of the Seventeenth Ward, they lived in areas where the black vote was too thin to support them. In 1884 Andrew Stevens and Carl Bolivar founded the Citizens' Republican Club to give voice to these and others who wanted to be heard but held no office. The club was proud of the social standing of its members and of its strictly moral, businesslike approach. The rules forbade gambling or drinking in the clubhouse and vain expenses such as "uniforms, hall hire, printing, brass bands and the like."[66]

It was nearly impossible, after all, for a black man in the nineteenth century to isolate himself from the wider world of political change. Certainly none could rest complacent, as did so many white contemporaries, with the "natural" or God-given social order. There were times when even the most retiring had to close ranks and be counted, when some celebration or injustice demanded at least a signature or a conspicuous appearance at Liberty Hall. Of Philadelphia's rich and prominent blacks, only Colonel Joseph McKee and the West Indian Augustins and Dutreilles were habitually absent on these occasions. Men of the highest class, such as Purvis, Minton, and Durham, were continually involved in hard political and economic lobbying, working to get policemen promoted by the city or motormen hired by the railways. And whatever the credentials of the purely patronage appointees, such as Jones, the city's elected black officers were a fairly able and responsible group.[67]

The judgment is in part comparative, as the six Afro-Americans who served on the common council before 1900 stood up well in contrast to their spitball-throwing white colleagues, who shared a reputation for collective buffoonery. The councilor's office, usually the lowest available to aspiring whites, was the highest available to blacks, and they filled it with dignity. Purnell had a local reputation for oratory, as did the schoolteachers Gipson and Hubert. Chester was from the same elite Harrisburg family that sent a minister to Liberia. Stevens was a leading caterer and doyen of black society, while Perry, the last to take a seat, was founder and editor of the *Philadelphia Tribune*, a local institution by the time of his death in 1931.[68]

The members of the sectional school boards were equally distinguished. Three of the five were physicians: E. C. Howard of Harvard University, Henry Longfellow, and William Warrick, one of the first black athletes at the University of Pennsylvania. None of these men were approved by the Citizens' Municipal League, which endorsed "able" candidates for office, if only because they were considered too obedient to the regular Republicans. But from the viewpoint of their constituents the problem was not that they lacked ability, but power.[69]

Philadelphia's sectional school boards, which were composed of twelve men and, by the 1890s, women selected from each ward, did not set policy of any kind. That was the business of the Board of Education, composed of one man from each ward or section; no blacks reached that level until 1945. The sectional school boards could make minor contracts and building repairs to a limit of $100—a source of some corruption—but their real function was to dispense patronage. Acting under guidelines handed down from above, they "elected" the janitors, principals, and other teachers in each of the several primary or secondary schools in their wards. The two high schools, Central and Girls' High, were administered directly by the Board of Education.[70]

The whole system was flawed and chronically under attack. Three black concerns were voiced specifically from the late 1870s. First and worst, the public system separated black students from white; second, the black schools did not employ enough black teachers; and third, they did not prepare enough children to move on up, to compete successfully in the qualifying examinations for the high schools. The black directors could not by themselves make much difference. Although some progress was made in all three areas, the pace was slow, in part because the three objectives clashed with each other and in part because, in a test, the local boards themselves were virtually helpless.[71]

As of 1878, the year in which the first two directors were elected, there were only eleven black public school teachers in the city. Thirty-three instructors in the four legally colored schools were white. No more than two or three black children had ever been admitted to the high schools. The "proscribed schools" were the worst assignment in the system and drew its worst people. There could be no improvement until they were broken up or until the pupils were no longer humiliated by prejudiced instructors, "poor white girls and white men who can't find employment at anything else."[72]

Twenty years later the number of black directors had increased to five, and black teachers to twenty-five. Both gains were somewhat greater proportionally than the raw increase in the Afro-American population. But despite the legislation of 1881, integration at the primary and grammar levels remained a largely empty option. In 1897 Catto, Vaux, Hill, and Ramsey were still listed as colored schools. Individual parents who wanted to get their children out of these "wretched" places could apply for transfers, but officials and students at the white schools to which they applied objected, sometimes violently. Even more important, their departure created problems at the black schools left behind. Principals like Jacob White, Jr., struggled to hold on to his charges at Vaux because the number of teachers and the size of appropriations were based on average attendance. The first priority of a sectional school board was to protect and increase the number of jobs it elected.[73]

The problem of black impotence was illustrated by the James B. Forten School, in the fifth section, named after the abolitionist leader. In the late 1880s Forten was chronically in trouble, as a few Italian and Yiddish-speaking students crowded in among its blacks. None of its students even offered to take the high school exams. The more ambitious tried to transfer out; attendance was low, and discipline ragged. Some of the problems, parents suggested, arose from a boisterous barroom virtually next door, but a license court hearing turned into a lesson in practical politics when a number of school directors joined with trustees from nearby Bethel Church to testify in favor of the saloon. At the insistence of black voters, James Murray was elected principal in an effort to raise attendance and morale; the board may have found as well that the salary of $700–$800 a year was "not sufficient to secure a capable white man." Problems persisted, however, and in 1890 the Board of Education decided on the novel experiment of taking direct control and transforming Forten from a conventional primary-grammar school into an institute for manual and industrial training.[74]

The black voters were angry. Murray, the only one of the city's three black principals to head a school with a white teacher and white pupils, was to be fired. Moreover, an obvious stigma was involved. While manual training was not in itself objectionable—both the Institute for Colored Youth and the city had recently set up industrial schools or departments—this would be the first such training at the primary level, and it implied that the children at Forten were incapable of learning the conventional curriculum, even at the age of six. The sectional school board, largely white, was at first worried that in the name of some "Quaker Society experiment" it was losing control to the Board of Education. The majority were mollified when all of the staff except Murray were given jobs elsewhere. In 1891 Hannah A. Fox was installed as head of the reorganized school, at $1200 a year, and was given the rare luxury of an assistant principal, Agnes N. Fox, at $750. Murray got in a last gesture, during his final days, by approving 150 black pupil transfers: the whites in the outlying districts could worry about them.[75]

The goal of the new Forten administration: "that every boy will eventually become a first class cook, with the ability to make his own shirt," was never realized. The new school was little better than the old. Black literacy more generally continued to rise in the city, as did the tiny number of students qualifying for the high schools. But the Institute for Colored Youth throughout this period had a stronger record for preparing educated leadership than the Philadelphia public system as a whole.[76]

Five black school directors, spread out among thirty-one other men and women in three different sections, could do little. The six black common councillors, who numbered no more than three at any time, were even less effective. The great urban projects of the era—the public buildings, water system, and street railways—were beyond their power to affect at all. Presumably they had some voice in patronage, and a couple were able to win city jobs for themselves, but the number of blacks on the municipal payroll never got past one percent of the total.[77]

Several decades later, when Philadelphia's oldest black politicians were asked to recall these pioneering predecessors, they furnished names but no accomplishments, mentioning Purnell, Chester, Wilson, Perry, and Stevens in that order. "They were all organization men," the old-timers remembered—and they knew the type—but they had somehow forgotten the name, and the career, of Constantin Hubert.[78]

Hubert was the only black councillor in the nineteenth century to come from any ward other than the Seventh, Ball's bailiwick. A powerful speaker, he was known for his "constitutional disposition to kick within party lines." He was also the only black officeholder in the city to be active in the Afro-American League, a newly organized forerunner of the National Association for the Advancement of Colored People. And he began his term on council by submitting an ordinance demanding an end to racial discrimination in city employment.[79]

This was the first time that the council had been faced directly with the issue of race. The city solicitor managed to sidestep the question by ruling that, although Philadelphia city and county were coterminous, the council could not constitutionally legislate for the county. But Hubert by that time had reached past the politics of Philadelphia to the octogenarian Purvis and to black leaders not only in the city but across the state. These men helped to bring the issue to the state assembly in Harrisburg in 1891, as an Equal Rights Bill that would cover the Commonwealth of Pennsylvania as a whole. Hubert, by then president of the statewide Afro-American League, led the delegation that petitioned the assembly. The bill itself reached a second reading in the state house before a way was found to bury it.[80]

To the city's white Republican leadership all this was insurgency, if of a different sort from collusion with the Democrats. Hubert followed the equal rights challenge with an attempt to break the will of Stephen A. Girard, who had richly endowed a "college," or boarding school, for the education of "white male orphans" in the city; the provision was challenged as discriminatory. When the councillor's two-year term was up, he made further history as the first black incumbent to lose a general election, to a Democrat. His downfall was blamed on desertion by black voters, as Ball's troopers again did what they were told.[81]

POLITICAL RECESSION

The election of three councillors in 1890 represented the high-water mark of black elective politics in the nineteenth century and for decades to come. The same year witnessed, in the so-called Force Bill, the last serious effort in Congress to salvage the wider politics of race, to prevent the continuing erosion of black strength in the South. Symbolically and in part actually, the two developments are linked. National and local priorities met and clashed in the summer of 1890, the year of Ball's death. Ten years later they met again, when the Republican party convened in Philadelphia to embrace a very different vision from the one that had excited young Octavius V. Catto.

The story began in the mid-1880s, when a classic urban politician, Israel Durham, took command of Philadelphia's Seventh Ward. Eventually Durham came as close as anyone to ruling the city's Republican machine as a whole, but he never forgot his local roots: "What do I care who is President, so long as I can carry my ward?" In 1885 and again in 1890 Durham was elected one of Philadelphia's sixteen police magistrates. The fact that since 1874 the election had been held citywide was supposed to break the magistrates' link with specific neighborhoods. But they managed to beat this intention by swapping districts so that each could return to his home base. In the Seventh Ward a paternal magistrate, "always ready to oblige his friends," was in a strategic position to command the loyalties of noncoms like Ball.[82]

Another white Philadelphian, Boies Penrose, from the neighboring Eighth Ward, was meanwhile moving up through the politics of Harrisburg. The young state senator's district overlapped with Durham's. So in part did his interests and instincts. Durham was a gregarious personality, a theatergoer, sportsman, and one-time president of the Philadelphia Phillies. Penrose was a raffish glutton, an aristocrat with a taste for low life, a tireless visitor to the city's red light district, and reputedly the keeper of a black mistress. In later years, as a senior United States Senator, he would become the very symbol of corruption, but as a young man just out of Harvard College, he was thought to be an idealist. His territory, like Durham's, embraced much of Philadelphia's black district, and the black press gave him credit for pushing through the state's Public Accommodations Bill of 1887.[83]

First Penrose and later Durham were protégés of Matthew Quay, a long-time Republican power in state and national politics. Quay earned the title of "President-maker" by managing Benjamin Harrison's campaign of 1888, and within a year or two he was probably the strongest single party manager in the Senate of the United States. Through the next decade his working agreement with Penrose at the state level and with Durham at the city level gave the three men a commanding position in the affairs of Philadelphia. The troika could be embarrassed, and sometimes beaten, by other groups and coalitions. But they had the resources to absorb defeat, and generally they were as close to dominant as anyone in that bitterly factional era.[84]

It was thus no coincidence that Ball's formal political vehicle was named the Matthew S. Quay Club. This was the heyday of such clubs, with twelve to fifteen in the Seventh Ward alone, hundreds in the wider city. Their social function was to provide a place for the members to gather in private; their political function was to pass resolutions of condemnation or praise and to march in the mass parades that enlivened every big campaign. In a presidential year, the Republicans alone could turn out 25,000 men in uniform. And whatever its local reputation for riot, rout, and tumult, the Quay Club was, the *Freeman* insisted, the best-run club in the city.[85]

Ball himself was seriously set back in April 1890 when a panel of judges denied renewal of his liquor license. This was not a matter of partisan politics. The judges were never accused of corruption or petty maneuvering in such matters, and the Law and Order Society, which had brought the complaint about loose women and immoral behavior, was capable of embarrassing almost anyone, including the Academy of Music. But when the saloon closed down on June 1, Ball had nothing left but the Quay Club.[86]

Quay himself was at the time embroiled in a major congressional battle. Over the previous twenty years, especially since the withdrawal of federal troops under President Hayes, the number of black voters in the South had been steadily dropping as a result of white violence and intimidation. As a practical matter, most Republican politicians had given up on the situation. But many had not, and on June 26, 1890, Henry Cabot Lodge of Massachusetts introduced a bill in the House allowing for federal supervision of federal elections, in an attempt to protect black voters from harassment. The Democrats called it the "Force Bill" and summoned images of blue-clad troopers moving south once more. But it passed the House by a margin of six, mostly along party lines, and went on to the Senate.[87]

For Quay and other leading Republican senators the Force Bill necessitated an important choice of priorities, even identity. The protective McKinley Tariff, endorsed by the Republicans, was on the agenda of that session of Congress, and the Democrats were sure to fight it. In essence only one hard bill could be put through. Given the choice between industrial protection and civil rights, the senator from Pennsylvania moved to put off the Force Bill until December.[88]

Although Quay's allies insisted that postponement was not death, this move created a pained protest. The Philadelphia *Press* pictured the senator shaking hands with a southern colleague against a background of lynched and dying black men. Afro-American criticism was intense all over the nation, but most pointedly in Pennsylvania and in Philadelphia. The only break in a virtually united front was provided by the Matthew S. Quay Club, which sent the senator a resolution of endorsement and support.[89]

Although Gil Ball could never win the prestige enjoyed by the city's most distinguished blacks, he had grown into his role as a popular leader and black spokesman of a sort. He sold Fortune's papers in his saloon, and both the *Globe* and the *Freeman* mentioned him with a kind of respect. Although he took orders from the party, he was by no means subservient and was quite capable of raising a ruckus in public, as when he felt that he and a companion had been the victims of discrimination in being charged twenty cents for just two drinks and a beer at the fashionable Girard House. But any claim to respectable leadership was destroyed by his "highly disgusting show of loyalty" to Quay. The Force Bill, brought up on December 2, met with a filibuster. It died within a week. So, the next day, did Ball. The ex-saloonkeeper had got religion in his final weeks, and the Reverend C. C. Strum of the Union Baptist Church, accompanied by a choir, went to the funeral, held at home. So did the Knights Templars and representatives from sixteen other clubs and organizations. Politicians of every stripe paid their last respects to Ball, laid out with the official badge of the Matthew S. Quay Club across his chest. The senator sent a note but could not make it.[90]

The failure of the Force Bill was the coup de grace to the national civil rights effort. The following decade witnessed the nadir of the Afro-American experience under freedom. The South during the 1890s witnessed the highest number of lynchings in its history, the constitutional disenfranchisement of black voters in several of its states, and the establishment of a rigid legal color line across most social and public activities.[91]

Retrogression in Philadelphia was less dramatic. There was no absolute retreat in the number of schoolteachers, janitors, messengers, and clerks. The city's blacks never seriously bet wrong in local politics, to judge by the vote in critical elections. But loyalty to Quay, Penrose, and Durham brought no more gains after 1890. The five school directors never increased in number. No black replaced Hubert in the Fifth Ward. Wilson was retired in 1894. After Stevens's death in 1898, Perry hung on as the only black councilman in the city. Black politics by then had been reduced to its rudest essentials. No one of Ball's stature was able to succeed him, although a series of lesser men made sure that the troopers voted, or were voted, early and often, without question and with little reward.[92]

The general debasement of the electoral process during the 1890s resulted in part from the virtual death of the local Democratic opposition. The minority party had won a respectable share of citywide offices during the 1870s and 1880s and had consistently run up over 40 percent of the total vote. During the last decade of the century, however, a combination of local and national setbacks dropped that percentage into the 30s and even the low 20s. Whites in the richer wards, assured of Republican victories, no longer bothered to vote in number. The Republican totals swelled dramatically, and suspiciously, in the downtown wards, especially in the black precincts.[93]

One result of this increasing dominance by the Republican regulars was that the local reformers, organized as the Citizens' Municipal League, succeeded the Democrats as the effective opposition to the often badly divided Republican party. The Democrats had fought hard at the polls, and losing candidates had often sued for a recount. The Municipal Leaguers added another dimension by working around the calendar checking registrations house-to-house, absorbing whatever abuse was hurled at them. In the late 1890s municipal reform gathered strength all over the country, with Philadelphia leading the way. And the way itself led directly into the "malodorous" Seventh Ward.[94]

The pace of prosecution for vote fraud picked up in 1897 and 1898. Several offenders, black and white, were sent to prison. The most famous of these cases broke in 1899 when Deputy Coroner Samuel Salter, a white leader of the twelfth precinct, Seventh Ward, was arrested with eight of his lieutenants. When all nine men skipped bail amid clear signs of official aid and comfort, the Municipal League was outraged. Once more its earnest young lawyers and college students wound their way through the courts and alleys of the Fifth and Seventh Wards, sometimes showered with scalding water or lamp black. This time they were "looking for negroes of the lowest type," that is, the entire election board of the second precinct. All of them were allegedly living at one address as tenants of "Frenchie" Williams, president of the "Roody Doo Club," a colorful organization whose members were evidently hard to track.[95]

After a long search, warrants were finally served on Judge of Elections James Brown, Judge Herbert Rolles, and four others. Unlike Salter and his eight confederates, these six black men were left to take the fall; the party had provided no money for a flight and made no legal arrangements to save their bail bonds from default. The Municipal League, trying to get legal access to the voting lists, was determined to make theirs a test case, and the *Public Ledger* was happy to cooperate. Not only the League but the Law and Order Society, an anti-vice organization, was getting increasingly aggressive as the century wore out. And the *Ledger*, warming up to its new muckraking role, found that the connection between low life and politics, as illustrated by people like "Yellow Maggie" and places like the Roody-Doo Club, had something for all of them.[96]

The Republican National Convention arrived in town in June 1900, in the midst of several running stories about political protection for policy and prostitution in downtown Philadelphia. The party managers were looking forward to a new American century, fueled by prosperity and a bold new policy of imperialism in the Far East and the Caribbean. They were not interested in looking down into conditions in the Seventh Ward, or back toward the dead policy of encouraging freedmen in the south. The affair was a far cry from the last Republican Convention in Philadelphia in 1872. The party's colored delegates from the deep South states were asked directly whether they were in it only for the patronage, the federal jobs in river ports and post offices. No longer were they at the forefront of the wider racial cause. Most of them were denied hotel rooms, and many had trouble in public restaurants and were forced to board with local families. Charlie Warwick, the former mayor who had charge of official hospitality, provided a special subcommittee to entertain these "Mississippians," as they were known generically, and appointed two indignant white political enemies to run it.[97]

At the grand parade on June 18, the Citizens' Republican Club marched under its official banner, "We Believe in Education, Morality, and Equality under the Law." They were bunched toward the back, however, with the southerners and other colored organizations from around the country. The viewers had largely exhausted their applause on the cakewalkers, who led off.[98]

POLITICAL DEPENDENCE

The humiliation visited on Afro-American delegates to the Republican Convention of 1900 lasted no more than a week, but the black electorate in the host city was ignored and manipulated all year round. White politicians were not indifferent to black votes, but they had learned to buy them without making concessions to black issues or even offering much in the way of patronage. Potential black leaders, meanwhile, were forced to work within the narrow constraints imposed both by the inability of their potential following to look beyond a trooper's wages at the polls and by their own divisions and disunity. Even the relatively successful were unable to create any real constituency of their own. There was no "black vote," as a bloc, simply because there was no black "community"—just a mixed and often contentious population of "colored people," "Afro-Americans," or "Negroes," for whom only the white majority had a single, and contemptuous, name.

Among the most divisive local issues, even in adjoining wards, was the question of neighborhood, of Locust versus Lombard Street, or more important, of uptown versus downtown. In 1870 an argument over who should lead the figure at an uptown dance led to the killing of a downtown "Skinner," a thirty-two-year-old father of four, by a small group of uptown "Woodcocks," all of them also adult men. Two nights later, an enraged crowd of downtown men and women fell upon an uptown company of the Grey Invincibles, as they marched toward Sixth and Lombard, and created a riot in which a number of people were seriously injured and several hundred arrested.[99]

There was also the issue of geographical origin, of the West Indies versus the Mainland and, especially, the North versus the South. One local tempest broke after a celebration honoring Fanny Coppin's work as principal of the Institute for Colored Youth, when Hans Shedd, a quondam school director, complained that too many honors were going to "southerners." Coppin had come originally from New Orleans. She graduated from Oberlin in 1864, married a local minister, and in 1870 was named head of the Girls' Department; she succeeded Catto as sole principal on his assassination in 1871. The awards dinner, in 1890, was held in honor of her twentieth anniversary at the school.[100]

The whole spectrum of skin color, too, provided the black population as well as the white with reasons to distinguish, envy, and mistrust each other. The white press was frank about its prejudices. No extended reference to Purvis, for example, failed to mention the distinction of his British cousins, his "partly Moorish descent," and the lightness of his color. It was always easier to summon sympathy for victims of injustice by noting that he, or better she, was "extremely light" or "almost white in appearance." The black press and black spokesmen were not so openly "colorphobic," but the late nineteenth century was a time when blacks drew such distinctions more tightly than ever before or since. In Philadelphia specifically the relative whiteness of complexion was an important ingredient in marriage patterns, associations, social standing, and success.[101]

The church was also a source of group division as well as strength. Philadelphia was the birthplace of the first black churches in the United States, and the importance of these institutions and their successors all over the country would be hard to exaggerate. As a social, educational, and political force and as a source of group pride and individual consolation, the black church was far more important than its white counterparts. But each church was like a "tribal" organization, to use Du Bois's term, encompassing not the race as a whole but only a denomination or even a single congregation. The "black church" was an abstraction. In the real world Philadelphia was home to dozens of black churches, all of them in some sense competing for members and for resources.[102]

The problem of disunity, even within a given group or denomination, was illustrated by the *Christian Recorder* as compared with the Boston *Pilot*. The *Recorder,* based in Philadelphia, was the official organ of the African Methodist Episcopal Church in America; the *Pilot,* edited by laymen and published by the Archdiocese of Boston, was unofficially the leading Irish as well as Catholic newspaper in the country. The two were remarkably similar in form. Both weeklies, in addition to purely religious or pastoral material, published news from the old country, whether Ireland or the South, and featured poignant personals from people looking for relatives lost in migration. Their columns and editorials ranged over the relevant issues of the day, celebrating achievers within the group and denouncing enemies outside it. The *Pilot* was essentially Democratic; the *Recorder* its mirror image. But while the *Pilot* virtually never spoke ill of an Irishman and saved its invective for Protestant historians and British imperialists, the *Recorder* was apt to pick a fight with anyone. Black spokesmen were no more immune than white ones, and more space was devoted to criticizing A.M.E. Zion bishops than Catholic missionaries.[103]

Some of this difference simply reflected the nature of the two denominations. The Roman church had had centuries of experience in presenting only its cleanest linen to the outside world, while the A.M.E. was an open organization, perfectly willing to expose an episode of ballot-stuffing in the press. But the *Recorder*'s contentiousness had an economic basis as well. Like most black papers, religious and secular, it was in constant financial trouble, the result of its low rate of paying subscribers. The manager complained continually that far more people read the *Recorder* than paid for it and that it could not support itself. The result was that every other black journal which aspired to speak for the group as a whole—as virtually all of them did—was seen as competition for the pennies of its readers.[104]

Black editors, like white ones, nevertheless recognized that they had much in common, especially the politics of race, and in 1880 they organized a Colored Editors Association which brought together representatives from over fifty journals. The *Recorder* went faithfully to the conventions and typically found them occasions where "factionalism and inordinate ambition are rife and run riot with everything."[105]

The world of black journalism was in fact a Hobbesian jungle in which each was pitted against all. The *Star of Zion* was obviously in direct competition with the *Christian Recorder,* but even the "Quaker City" columns in the New York papers were a threat to the black journals from Philadelphia. In addition to the black columns in the white dailies, five weeklies, other than the *Recorder,* were published locally as of the late 1890s: the Baptist and Odd Fellows organs, a Germantown local, the *Standard Echo,* and the *Tribune.* At least four earlier competitors were the *Sentinel, Pilot, Spectator,* and *Independent.* Virtually all of the references to each other in these papers were contemptuous. The *Recorder* was sure that the *Tribune* would fail. T. "Turncoat" Fortune, editor of "our mouthy and rather meddlesome contemporary, the *Freeman,*" took a malicious delight in garbled newsprint and missed editions. And when the Philadelphia papers did reach Fortune's office, "they arouse our compassion by the aggravated development of their patented back disease."[106]

Price Williams, author of several columns and founder of at least two weeklies, was a favored target. Williams was a man of some local reputation who seems to have been into everything. He ran for city commissioner on the Greenback-Labor ticket in 1878, which did not bar him from a patronage job in the Stokley administration the next year, and in the early 1880s he spoke to both the regular Republicans and the independents. In 1880 he sued the *Recorder* unsuccessfully for libel. In 1884, although elected president of the Editors Association, he was jailed for failure to honor his paper's contracts. The *Freeman* described him as "an unscrupulous little demagogue . . . who hasn't the respect of three persons in the whole city."[107]

The real significance of Williams's story was that, like other editors, he was also ex officio a politician, when neither journalism nor elective office paid a living wage. The result was that the whole overlapping class of newspapermen and politicians were dependent on white pa-

tronage. Davis had found his way to the police through editing the
Spectator; Perry held a series of patronage jobs to keep his paper going;
Williams himself signed on as a station house turnkey, in charge of
feeding drunks and emptying their slop buckets. Given the limited opportunities available, all of these able and talented men were pitted
against each other for recognition and support.[108]

Philadelphia's black leaders managed to hold only a few major political meetings, in the course of forty years, without significant confusion
and dissent. Ambitions in the abstract ran high; there was always talk
about the possibilities in the State House and even the federal judiciary.
But it was only talk. During the critical years when blacks made their
painful move up from the first school directors to the first councillor,
the composite agenda for any series of meetings always began with
acrimony and ended with betrayal. The ritual opened with the denun-
ciation of absent members and continued through praise for the party,
demand for an office, and wrangling over who specifically should fill it.
The ritual always ended at the primary or general convention when the
nominee was jettisoned and the troopers voted as the party ordered.[109]

The problem was not lack of leadership—the city was all too full of
able and even charismatic men—but the leadership's inability to sustain
an independent politics of race, as against the increasingly dependent
politics of Philadelphia. Older activists such as Still and Purvis—successful businessman and gentleman respectively—had enjoyed some
genuine independence. But the economic facts of life in the postwar
city simply did not allow many men to succeed without enjoying favor-
itism at the hands of white Republicans. The overlap between journalists
and officeholders was most obvious because of its inhibiting effect on
the black press. Ball's personal charisma masked for a time his utter
dependence on white authority, but the loss of his saloon in the last
months of his life revealed it dramatically. Other quasi-legal or indeed
illegal entrepreneurs were at least equally indebted to shifting combinations of local politicos and policemen. The rising group of lawyers,
too, was heavily dependent on criminal business and needed the complex
patronage of judges, bailbondsmen, and other denizens of the magistrates' courts. The role of the Bethel Church trustees and the doctors
on the Fifth Sectional School Board, in the case of the saloon near the
Forten School, suggests that the Republican party had ways of reaching
even into the other professions. Its leverage over the black medical
establishment doubtless increased when the nurses' training program at
the Douglass Clinic was established with state funds. Whereas in the
more peaceable postwar city Catto's murder had been only the last echo
of an earlier and cruder era, the fate of the outspoken Hubert at the

polls remained a warning of what could happen under a more sophis-
ticated system of racial domination.[110]

Under these conditions there was no way in which leading blacks
could publicize issues dramatic enough to overcome the jealousies among
them and to unite them, across the lines of color, neighborhood, origin,
and class, with the dispossessed and often desperate stratum of blacks
beneath them. During the 1860s there had been issues with this kind of
potential, such as the fight against slavery, the war itself, and the streetcar battle. When given a chance in the South, the politics of race had
pulled thousands of new citizens together at the polls. But when that
hope died, there was nothing to replace it in the politics of Philadelphia.
Above all, unlike their Irish contemporaries in Philadelphia and elsewhere, Afro-Americans in the late nineteenth century were generally
unable to translate votes into jobs on a scale big enough to improve the
fortunes of the group as a whole. Instead, competition for the few
available places served to divide rather than unite them. Even Hubert's
Equal Rights Bill, opposed by the only practicing black lawyer in the
city, was frankly elitist in intent: "If a few are raised to a plane of higher
citizenship it will advance the rest of the race." When the issue was
reduced to whether any given man should run for office, the "rest of
the race" might be excused for thinking, like Ball: "Ah! The trouble is
this thing's set up for an individual, not for our people. There's cash in
it, you know that as well as I do."[111]

The right to vote was important in ways impossible to measure. Early
in the 1870s a brief debate took place at the polls when a white man
was challenged by a black to define the word *Nigger*. The confrontation
peaked when the black man noted quietly, "I've just voted, ain't I?
Well, you can do no more than that today, white as you are." And it
ended when, "looking very serious," he stepped up to add, "There's
another way I believe I'm just as good as you are . . ." at which his
opponent fled.[112]

Beyond these psychic satisfactions, black men did win some things at
the polls. Official patronage was important to the development of the
small salaried white-collar class and provided various kinds of help to
other leaders as well. But there was a price for this. At another level
politics helped to define and enable a large number of enterprises like
Gil Ball's, on or beyond the margins of legality, which had important
consequences for the population as a whole. And for most of the mercenary troopers, cut off from its more uplifting benefits and exposed to
its seamy underside, politics in Philadelphia must have seemed hard to
tell from crime.

· 3 ·
JUSTICE FOR ALL

WHATEVER the social, economic, and political differences between blacks and whites, all Philadelphians in the late nineteenth century were subject to the same laws and the same system of criminal justice. The records of police, courts, and prisons are important sources of information about the behavior of both races and the relations between them. Such records reveal that formal equality before the law did not, in most important respects, mask unequal treatment in practice.

The record on the books is at best, however, an uncertain guide to the reality in the streets. Some murderers, many burglars, and most drunks or gamblers are never arrested or, if arrested, not convicted. Collectively their misdeeds make up a "dark figure" of unknown or unknowable crimes that never get into the record at all. This makes it useless to try to establish absolute levels of criminal behavior simply by adding up the official statistics. One can only gauge trends or compare the records of one group with those of another from the same time and within the same jurisdiction.

And when the records are those of an unpopular minority, as in this case, they pose special questions of fairness and comparability. Since blacks had virtually no share in making the laws and very little in enforcing them, the official statistics could have been systematically biased because of either the nature of the criminal code or the means of its administration. Since the code expressed the ideals of the dominant group, it could have been part of an attempt to impose white middle-class values on others, the powerless in general and the blacks in particular. What the courts called "crime" might then have been seen, both by the labeled "criminal" and by the group to which he belonged, as an essentially blameless activity, even as a form of protest against the alien values embodied in the law. Even if in theory there were no opposition to these values, a prejudicial machinery of justice might have worked in practice to make blacks more liable than whites to arrest or conviction.

Yet neither situation applied to the actual administration of criminal justice in Philadelphia, at least with respect to offenses against persons and property. In cases of violence or theft, the frequency with which the city's working classes, black and white, turned to the courts shows that they did not resent but in fact embraced the fundamental legal attitudes toward those crimes that hurt them as individuals. And despite the general climate of discrimination, the city's courts typically lived up to the ideal of blind justice when dealing with people of different colors, as shown most fully in their handling of homicide in general and interracial murder in particular.

ADMINISTRATION OF THE CRIMINAL CODE

Urban justice in the nineteenth century was rooted in the same ideal of popular access to authority that marked urban politics. The criminal code that occupied most court time was a given, rarely affected by state legislation and almost never influenced by such distant institutions as the Supreme Court or the Constitution of the United States. On the whole, it was identical to the English common law, and criminal procedure, too, was still affected by the inherited tradition of private prosecution, where cases were brought not by paid officials but by aggrieved citizens. There was properly no "system" of justice. The administration of law was political only in that it resembled direct democracy; the law was not imposed on the populace, demanding conformity to rules set from above, so much as it reacted to individual complaints, dealing with injuries that one person committed to another.[1]

In treating crimes against property or persons, the code reflected common law and common sense by setting overlapping bounds within which the courts might sentence offenders. Simple larceny, the theft of something from a pocket, open room, or store, was less serious than burglary, theft that involves breaking and entering. Burglary in turn was more serious, because more frightening, when it happened in a private home than in a place of business, and when it happened in the night than in the day. Robbery was a broad category that involved force or the threat of force, such as using a forearm or weapon, and was a dangerous offense against both person and property. The seriousness of personal crimes progressed from attempted indecent assault to rape, or from simple through aggravated assault on to manslaughter and murder.[2]

The criminal process in Philadelphia, like the code, was much the same as in other cities in the period. An arrest was made, and a hearing held before a lay magistrate. Minor cases were decided summarily, whereupon habitual drunkards, vagrants, or streetwalkers were sent to jail or the House of Correction. Sometimes defendants were discharged on the ground that no serious case had been made, but the majority of them were held for bail or jailed for a further hearing. After that the case went to the district attorney, who might or might not draw up an indictment and pass it to the grand jury, which might or might not find a true bill and send it to court.

The criminal process was more complex than the criminal code, and it was a good deal messier in practice. Ideally, law enforcement should be swift, sure, and efficient, and in nineteenth century Philadelphia the operation of criminal justice did have the first of these virtues. For better and worse, it was swift. Normally a criminal case went to court, if at all, within a month of the arrest. Even the most important cases, such as murder, were usually conducted in a day or two from start to finish, sometimes in a single morning, with a verdict handed up within an hour of closing argument. And if the grand jury was in session, a burglar, caught red-handed on a Sunday morning, could, as the papers put it, be "railroaded" straight to prison by the following afternoon.[3]

But however quick in individual cases, criminal justice was neither sure nor efficient. It thus was incapable of systematic oppression of any given group, such as blacks. Each of its components—police and magistrates, the district attorney, judges and juries—operated so as to check and balance the others. The city charter, as amended in 1873, was designed to ensure that the several city magistrates, for example, were of different political parties, and either the voters or the party bosses managed to balance the politics of the police and the district attorney, for example, to guarantee that no one could make criminal policy without interference.

Certainly the police department did not dominate the process. Nineteenth century policemen got little of the respect and none of the prestige that their successors have enjoyed over the past generation. The men worked alone; it was difficult to summon help; and any arrest might be an invitation to a fight and later a lawsuit. Officers were routinely judged guilty of assault and sometimes of murder committed in the course of duty. Even an ardent partisan of Stokley's police force agreed that "courts are loath to admit, juries to believe, the testimony of policemen." The city had managed to do without them for most of the century, and by modern standards they continued to play a relatively modest role in law enforcement.[4]

The Philadelphia department was a little smaller, in proportion to the city's population, then its counterparts in Boston and New York, although it was bigger than Chicago's. Its regular detectives, who as late as the 1890s numbered only fifteen for a city of over a million, either served warrants or prowled the streets in search of criminals, usually pickpockets, on their own. The patrol force made tens of thousands of arrests each year, but most were for simple drunkenness, a matter that was treated as criminal in form only. Everywhere in the middle and late nineteenth century, the drive to clear the streets of drunkards was part of the demand for higher standards of public order. In practice, this drive often saved individuals from exposure or mugging, and if a night in the cells—the only real punishment—was a literally lousy experience for many, it was over in the morning. Other than making such arrests, patrolmen rarely acted on their own but rather responded to cries for help, breaking up fights and chasing thieves. And to a surprising extent, the police were bypassed entirely.[5]

Of all arrests reported in the Philadelphia *Public Ledger* and *Inquirer* for January 1880, over 40 percent, or 99 out of 242, had not been made by the police. And although both papers were presumably looking for the cases of most interest, only a minority of the 99 citizen arrests were for assault, a crime that the police did not normally handle. These lesser matters typically reached the courts when an abused wife or angry neighbor got a warrant from a magistrate and a constable to serve it. But in murder cases, too, the coroner or his deputy might make an arrest on the spot; a private watchman or angry storekeeper sometimes frog-walked a suspect straight to the bench; and citizens chased thieves and even killers, or broke into homes to rescue battered women from their husbands, and only then decided whether to call the police or bring in their captive directly.[6]

The magistrates who heard these cases rarely stopped them from proceeding further, but the district attorney dropped some, and the grand jury ignored a large number before the remaining cases went to court. Once there, the outcome—from a distance of one hundred years—was always in doubt. In following a given incident through the papers, one finds it hard to guess in advance how a jury might react to a defendant's manner and inflections. Judges were equally capricious, although over a period, statistically, the sentences made a rough moral sense. But this was the Victorian era, at the same time fiercely protective of private property and extravagantly sentimental. One young man drew time in jail for snatching and eating a pat of butter in the farmer's market. Another, an orphan appearing in the same court in the same month, broke down and cried when convicted for picking pockets, prompting the judge to suspend his sentence and the spectators to take up a collection.[7]

The end result of the criminal process was that only a minority of arrests in any category, whether as broad as larceny or as narrow as rape, resulted in conviction for those arrested. The percentage of convictions increased toward the end of the century, especially after 1896, when many minor cases were no longer heard at all. This had always been the goal of reformers, and grand juries repeatedly called for the elimination of formal trials and procedures for what they thought were trivial incidents, especially wife-beating, which accounted for about a fifth of all recorded crimes against the person. But the enforcement of law remained leaky and inefficient, basically because it was powered by individual complainants rather than representatives of the state, and these people wanted it that way.[8]

Each case was fundamentally brought by a victim, or "prosecutor." Only a determined prosecutor, with a strong sense of grievance, could carry it through the several steps to judgment. More cases of larceny than assault reached trial simply because people were more upset about the loss of their personal property than of their dignity, or perhaps of their teeth. The vast majority of thefts involved small amounts of money, household goods, or clothing. An assault case against a spouse or a neighbor was often treated as a kind of warning, or even as a punishment in itself since the accused, only a minority of whom made bail, spent some time in chilly cells awaiting hearings. Any case could be dropped once the two parties made a deal or the complainant decided that enough was enough.

Both the code and the process differed sharply, however, in dealing with two other kinds of offenses. One kind was regulatory infractions, such as breaking the law banning the sale of yellow oleomargarine. Since these crimes reflected not the common ethical sense of the society but the interests of various special groups, they were enforced only in response to political pressures. More important were the so-called "victimless crimes," officially defined as "offenses against public order," such as drunkenness or gambling. These were regarded as moral violations, but unlike the nearly universal prohibitions against ordinary theft and violence embodied in the code, these crimes often reflected only the particular morality of the legislative majority, in this case the native white Protestants. German immigrants did not believe, for example, that taking a beer on a Sunday should be a crime, just as Chinese did not share the dominant attitude toward gambling. Enforcement of these laws was also highly selective. Police departments often used these laws to harass political or other opponents, or people who had not arranged for immunity. The number of arrests for liquor or similar violations in a given year is thus not a direct clue to the real or comparative incidence of Sunday sales or drunkenness.

Despite these differences, although the system encouraged many kinds of abuse, systematic racial oppression was not one of them. The legal code on theft and violence embodied a simple set of widely shared values, applied equally to all groups. The legal process was in no way an engine of the upper or middle classes. Neither was it an engine of any political party. The factionalism of the era ensured that neither the police nor any other component of the system could act for long in concert, either to protect individual law-breakers or to prosecute whole classes. The process of law enforcement was instead largely a response to felt needs and pressures, especially in its earlier years, when "a large number of poor and working-class Philadelphians seized the criminal justice system and used it for their own purposes." The city's blacks emphatically belonged in that number, or as the *Public Ledger* put it, "the colored people love the law." That was one of the foundation stones, after all, of Israel Durham's power base as magistrate in the Seventh Ward. Blacks were often in court because, like their white neighbors, they often invoked the law against each other, or indeed anyone, when they felt that they had been wronged.[9]

COLOR-BLIND JUSTICE

"In human courts," W. E. B. Du Bois observed in the 1890s, "the rich always are favored somewhat at the expense of the poor . . . whites at the expense of Negroes." Or as others have recently warned, "Even the meaning of 'guilt' in a system run by and for white people was distorted for blacks." This has been true in many times and places. But there is no evidence of significant racial bias in Philadelphia's nineteenth-century court system, or indeed of those in any northern city in the same period. In terms of either the comparative likelihood of conviction or the severity of sentence for a given offense, the two indices that can be measured, justice was surprisingly color-blind.[10]

That there was bias elsewhere, in ways that never reached the books, is beyond doubt. This was true especially among policemen, who probably treated blacks more harshly than whites and sometimes made judgments on the basis of stereotypes. Black men were held for a time, on suspicion, simply because they were carrying bags full of chickens, or clothing, in strange neighborhoods. When a notably brutal murder occurred in 1897, a professional boxer was brought in for questioning simply because he was big, and black, and had a record. But this kind of discrimination, however real to those who felt it, had little impact on the court system. When no chickens were reported stolen, and when the big man showed that he had been at the Sharkey-McCormick fight, the suspects were released without booking, leaving no tracks in the official record.[11]

Systematic discrimination may be suspected when there are significant differences of any kind in the official record. If blacks had a higher ratio of convictions to arrests than whites, this might indicate a greater likelihood of guilt or, alternatively, bias on the part of judges and juries. If on the contrary their ratio of convictions was lower and blacks experienced many more arrests than convictions, it might indicate bias by police or prosecutors, who stopped blacks for trivial reasons or on little evidence. If after conviction black sentences were longer, treatment would have clearly been harsher than for whites, while if black sentences were shorter, perhaps blacks were being patronized, their crimes against other blacks not being taken seriously. But the Philadelphia records show no consistent differences of any kind. The issue is clearest with respect to the length of jail or prison sentences, the easiest matter to measure. Four studies dealing with various aspects of sentencing policy in nineteenth century Philadelphia—one of them also dealing with New York and Boston—agree that there were in general no appreciable differences in the sentences imposed on blacks and whites for the same offenses.[12]

There are two exceptions, which are either relatively trivial or tend to cancel each other out. From 1868 to 1900 larceny sentences for whites, which were originally slightly higher than for blacks, sank slowly until they were slightly lower. For example, in 1868–1870 white sentences averaged 1.03 years, black sentences .88, whereas by 1898–1900 the figures had sunk respectively to .69 and .75. Variations on this scale may be attributed to racial differences in the actual crimes committed, because larceny covers a considerable range of behavior. But there is no such easy explanation for the other exception in Philadelphia's sentencing for all offenses of all kinds in the mid-century years. White men averaged somewhat shorter terms than black, receiving 12.4 months on average, as compared to 14.8 for blacks, while black women were treated considerably more harshly than white, receiving sentences of 14.1 months, as compared to 8.5 for whites. These differences might perhaps be attributed to differing patterns of criminal behavior. The question remains, however, why legally black people who were listed, for descriptive purposes, as "Mulatto" in the jail records should have gotten substantially lighter sentences than any other group, with men averaging 10.2 months and women 3.2.[13]

With respect to the likelihood of conviction, or the ratio of conviction to arrest, the detective department in seven scattered years between 1877 and 1892 reported both the race of all suspects captured and the disposition of their cases. The combined record for property crimes, which are the bread and butter of the detective business, was: 1159 whites arrested and 619 convicted, or a rate of 53 percent, and 153 blacks arrested and 86 convicted, or a rate of 56 percent—only three points higher than whites.[14]

Beyond the official record, arrests were noted by race in the newspapers. For example, in 1870, 24 percent of whites and 17 percent of blacks arrested for personal and property crimes were convicted. In 1880, 40 percent of whites and 38 percent of blacks arrested for such crimes were convicted. In 1900, the balance was reversed, with 32 percent of whites and 41 percent of blacks convicted. Here again the pattern of differences was inconsistent and relatively slight.[15]

Finally, the most direct and significant evidence about justice, black and white, came from trials for murder and manslaughter. Homicide trials were the only ones in nineteenth century Philadelphia in which the race of both accused and victim was almost always noted in the press. These cases, especially those involving interracial incidents, furnished clues to black-white relations in general and presented the fullest and most dramatic tests of the city's legal system in operation. In treating cases of homicide, the justice system worked differently, in the late nineteenth century, from the way in which it works in the late twentieth. An unknowable but far smaller proportion of actual killings was brought to trial then than now. Fewer murders were reported, or labeled as homicide at the inquest stage, because of the inefficiency of the detective system. Little detecting was or could be done by the small squad of reward-hunters provided by the city. Only a few murder arrests were made by these official detectives. Most of them were experts only in spotting burglars or pickpockets, men who were in a position to make deals or split loot, but they had little time for the business of solving unprofitable mysteries. Less than half of those arrested for homicide were convicted of any offense, as compared with a late twentieth-century conviction rate approaching 90 percent.[16]

The record of successful prosecutions was held down for many reasons, the most important being the fact that the plea of self-defense was hard to counter. The typical case was the result of a fight, usually between two or more drunken men. Given conflicting memories and witnesses, juries often found it hard to tell just who had done what first and to whom, and they seized on an acquittal as the shortest way out of the fog of testimony.

The outcomes of all trials involving interracial killings in the years 1860–1901 shows that blacks were somewhat more likely to be convicted of killing whites than vice versa, in terms of both numbers of accused persons and numbers of episodes resulting in one or more nonaccidental deaths (see table). The number of accused persons was greater than the number of episodes because in several cases two or more people were

OUTCOME OF INTERRACIAL TRIALS BY RACE AND SEX OF ACCUSED AND
VICTIM, NUMBER OF EPISODES, AND NUMBER OF PERSONS, 1860–1901.[a]

Race (B,W) & sex (M,F) of accused/victim	Episodes		Individuals	
	Guilty	Not guilty	Guilty	Not guilty
BM/WM	10½	13½	14	18
BM/WF	3	7	3	4
BF/WM	0	3	0	4
BF/WF	0	2	0	2
Total	13½	25½	17	28
WM/BM	7⅔	18⅓	9	30
WM/BF	1	0	1	0
WF/BM	1	0	1	0
WF/BF	0	1	0	1
Total	9⅔	19⅓	11	31

a. Fractions represent split verdicts, in which, for example, one person was convicted
and another was not.

indicted following a fatal riot or brawl. The racial difference in convictions for killing the opposite race was wider in terms of number of
accused persons than of episodes. This disparity indicates that whites,
as the dominant race in the city, were far more likely to gang up on and
kill blacks in brawls or riots than vice versa. From the viewpoint of the
prosecution, all such cases involving multiple defendants or riotous situations were especially messy, regardless of the complexion of those
involved. The witnesses were more than usually liable to bias in favor
of one party or the other; even the best witnesses were confused; the
defendants often agreed to blame somebody else who had run off in the
excitement; and jurors were rarely persuaded to convict. Such episodes
explain why the number of white acquittals exceeded the number of
black. At the same time it obscures the opposite fact that in the majority
of cases, those simpler ones involving single defendants only and with
no brawl or riot in the background, juries were more likely to convict
whites of killing blacks than the other way around.[17]

The problem of convicting rioters is illustrated by one of the five
indictments that grew out of the election riot of 1871. This was the most
notorious white-black killing of the century, the one in which the bartender Frank Kelly was accused of the murder of Octavius V. Catto.
At the inquest on October 14 a number of witnesses had fingered young
Kelly as the slight man with the bandaged head who had fired the fatal

shots a few days before. But Kelly had skipped town by that time, and the Philadelphia authorities were apparently unable to catch up with him until he was arrested in Chicago nearly six years later. It did not escape notice among the city's Irish Democrats that the suspect was arraigned in the midst of an election campaign in which Mayor Stokley desperately needed black support against his strongest opponent to date. The trial was a long one by contemporary standards, running the last week of April and the first of May, and the testimony was difficult. The defendant was older and heavier by then, with a beard and no bandage. Blacks and whites appeared for both the prosecution and the defense, and several changed their inquest testimony in both directions. The eight Democrats and four Republicans on the jury decided unanimously not to convict. The prosecution was unwilling to give up, however, and Kelly was brought back the next month to answer for the killing of Isaac Chase in the same riots. This time the atmosphere was even heavier, as more surprise witnesses were brought, some were accused of tipping or coaching each other, and the judge ordered several arrests for intimidation. One member of the defense team was cited for contempt when he accused the district attorney's chief detective of suborning purjury. This time, on June 22, it took the jurors only twenty minutes to find Kelly innocent of murder, freeing him for extradition to Cincinnati on charges of vote fraud.[18]

Three other white men were accused of killing Isaac Chase and Jacob Gordon in the same riots, including Reddy Dever, who was tried fully eight years after the event. The killings themselves were clearly explicable in terms of racial prejudice. But the acquittals were not; they reflected rather the inherent difficulty in winning unanimous verdicts, beyond a reasonable doubt, in inherently confused situations. In many other cases involving multiple defendants, again quite apart from race, jurors found themselves confronted with hard moral choices. A jury composed of twelve adult males, for example, found it impossible to fix a murder conviction on any of the five young white boys who in the summer of 1866 kept on throwing stones into a scow until one of them happened to brain old Samuel Shaw. The elimination of this one case from the statistics on interracial trials, together with the cases from the riots, would show more clearly that Philadelphia juries were not normally harder on black defendants than on white.[19]

The relative impartiality of homicide verdicts was paralleled in patterns of sentencing. Until the very end of the period, whatever the color of the victims, black defendants were far less likely than whites to be hanged for murder. Hanging was not a common fate for anyone in the late nineteenth century, and it drew much more attention than the numbers warranted locally. The Commonwealth of Pennsylvania, like most eastern states, had outlawed public executions well before the Civil War, and the gallows in Philadelphia's own Moyamensing Prison was left in storage more years than not, leaving the newspapers to search all over the state and even the world to fill their appetite for stories of last rites and rituals. Whatever their tastes as readers, citizens in the jury box were reluctant to convict for murder at all, and were especially reluctant to convict for murder in the first degree. Virtually all killings were prosecuted, in form, as potentially capital offenses, but jurors, if they brought in guilty verdicts at all, typically knocked them down to manslaughter. And if jurors did not flinch, judges did, and back of the judges was the governor or the pardons board, neither of them eager in an increasingly humanitarian age to assume responsibility for taking life. The result was that from 1860 to 1901, when there were 927 first-degree murder indictments, 831 trials, and 414 convictions, just 31 men and one woman were hanged for murder.[20]

The route by which a killer reached the gallows was almost as capricious as the rest of the sentencing process, but it had a moral basis. The law said that two kinds of homicides should be treated as murder in the first degree. One of them was a killing committed in the course of another major felony, such as rape or robbery. The other was murder "with malice aforethought," cooly premeditated, as in revenge, the elimination of a rival, or the pursuit of an inheritance. In practice, the ultimate sanction was applied only if the criminal as well as the crime was shocking or frightening enough to outrage all of the people, from jurors to the board of pardons, who had some share in the decision.

Prior to 1900 only two blacks and two whites were convicted of first-degree offenses in interracial cases. Of the whites, William Killer was sentenced in 1888 for clubbing his black roommate, David Lewis, presumably for a small amount of missing money. Ten years later Harold Bloomberg, disappointed in love, shot Emma Otis, or Deery, a black woman once apparently adopted into a white family. Both sentences were commuted. Of the blacks, Jeremiah Dixie, also known as Sol Holland, was clearly a menacing character with a bad local reputation, but the act of knifing Peter Martin on a summer night in 1862 was not enough to hang a man, and the Governor so ruled. The margin was a little tighter for William Turner, or "Face" Epps, who with Sam Dodson planned to rob Mary Ann Lawlor's coal and grocery shop on a January night in 1898. While Dodson stood watch, Turner slapped or pushed the woman into a fatal fall. But he appeared contrite at the trial, and during the long wait between sentence and execution he so impressed his jailers with an innocence of soul that the sheriff himself led the movement for his commutation.[21]

These near-exceptions only prove the rule that the majority of interracial killings were too ordinary, too humanly impulsive, to qualify as murder in the first degree. So were virtually all of the killings involving blacks alone. No one in these cases was accused of mass murder, or insurance fraud, or poisoning a wife or mother for her money. Until the 1890s only one black defendant, in fact, other than Dixie was condemned to die, and there was never any chance that Annie Cutler would be hanged.

Cutler had waited in ambush for nearly an hour before shooting William Henry Knight in the face on a crowded sidewalk, Arch Street above Eleventh, on the afternoon of April 22, 1885. She had been practicing with the pistol earlier that week and, as clinching evidence of premeditation, had written notes to her mother a month before predicting that she would shortly jeopardize her soul in a matter involving "love and revenge." But Annie was a woman wronged. Two years earlier, at eighteen, she had followed Knight from their native Newport to Philadelphia, where she took a live-in servant's job. Sometime thereafter he told her he had married another woman. While Cutler's letters forced a verdict of murder in the first degree, they also eased the work of the interracial committee formed as "Friends of Annie Cutler." After begging God's forgiveness, Cutler had urged her mother to "give my love to all my friends, and tell them for me never to get in love with a man so they cannot leave him." Instructing that there should be no graveside ceremony and nothing more than a plain pine box, she made a final request: "please bury Henry's picture with me." The Board of Pardons—gentlemen, Victorians, and politicians—could do no less than deny her wish.[22]

The first black hanged in Philadelphia since the prewar era was thus William Moore, a thirty-two-year-old stevedore, who in September 1892 shot down another black man, Charlie Matten, in a pool room near the corner of Sixth and Lombard. The issue, as with Cutler, was love and jealousy, in this case a rivalry for the attentions of Adeline Johnson. Like Cutler, Moore also announced his intentions in advance—not to his mother but to a policeman, Officer Mickens, who was unable to talk him out of it. Without the element of gallantry to interfere, the law took its course in 1893.[23]

But none of these cases was a precedent or preparation for the sudden events at century's end, when seven black men were hanged for four crimes in three years between 1899 and 1901. Three of them—Charles Perry, Henry Ivory, and Amos Sterling—were convicted in the robbery-murder in 1900 of Roy Wilson White, a socially prominent white lawyer. The White case was one of the most publicized of the century. Robbery-murder was a rare event, and so was any crime involving blacks and upper-class whites. It does seem that whites were growing more fearful about black violence toward the end of the century, and the fact that a number of unusually distinguished white lawyers stepped forward to defend the accused trio was backhanded recognition of the fact that the case had stirred racial prejudice in the city and that leaders of the bar were determined to avoid all appearance of a legal lynching. But the case turned on hard physical evidence and an undisputed confession; the death sentence was mandated for felony-murder. And the element of racial revenge was irrelevant in all the other capital cases involving blacks. At the time of the White case, Robert Brown had already been convicted of stabbing his wife, George Weeks and George St. Clair of shooting a black prostitute. Eugene Clements, a Republican party worker, was involved the next year in what seemed otherwise the routine shooting of his wife's lover.[24]

Despite the late-century flurry of black hangings, then, Philadelphia's court system was not normally harder on Afro-American defendants than on white. For ordinary cases of theft and violence, the criminal process was indeed shaped by the popular pressures of black and white complainants who brought their own cases to the courts. But party politics had little to do with this. The justice records reflect the fact that stealing and killing, unlike vice, found little political protection, and that prosecution was not much biased racially.

· 4 ·
THE WAGES OF SIN

BLACK CRIME in nineteenth century Philadelphia was paradoxically both serious and easy to ignore. The city's white elite could overlook theft as no more than an occasional annoyance, and vice as a problem for other people, with other habits, in other neighborhoods. But with legitimate opportunities so often blocked from the city's black population, criminal activity was very important to it, helping to define and shape much of its culture and its relations with the wider world. Afro-American crime was distinctive in significant ways. And, sometimes, it paid.

For black Philadelphians, theft and vice were, among other things, forms of economic behavior, some of which were purely internal and some of which involved the outside white world. Stealing or dealing within the black population itself added nothing to its collective wealth and sometimes subtracted from it. But to steal successfully from whites or to sell illicit goods and services in the wider market was potentially to add to the slender resources available to the city's Afro-Americans, considered as a group, and, from a purely economic point of view, to compensate them for their exclusion from more legitimate activity. Although no hard dollar figures are available, contemporary sources provide a kind of accounting that, apart from the wider social impact of criminality, gives some idea of its economic importance. Each form of illicit behavior differed in terms of the net gains and losses involved for the race as a whole. Most of the varieties of theft were typically unprofitable. So were gambling and the illegal sale of alcohol, despite their importance for the individuals engaged in them. Thus, only the business of prostitution, along with the complex of activities that surrounded it, consistently transferred money from the hands of white customers to those of black entrepreneurs.

THEFT

The image of black men stealing into chicken coops and melon patches was one of the staples of nineteenth century folklore, a legacy of slavery and the early minstrel shows that easily survived the postwar transition into tenantry, sharecropping, and vaudeville. Slaveholders like Thomas Jefferson understood that a people defined themselves as private property could hardly be expected to have much respect for the rules which told them what was theirs and what was "massa's." Others had more complex reasons for tolerating and even encouraging the kind of petty theft endemic to the plantation. Since the whole system of race relations rested on their own sense of moral superiority, every item taken reinforced that system by confirming, in their eyes, the "childlike" and "irresponsible" character of their black dependents.[1]

This was a widespread as well as a useful sentiment for those whites who held it, and it had some echoes in postwar Philadelphia, but neither blacks nor whites were normally so tolerant. The majority shopkeepers, householders, and working classes of a busy commerical and manufacturing city managed to feel the superiority without granting the indulgence. The black population, which under slavery had distinguished between "taking," as from the master or whites in general, and "stealing," as from each other, had little economic margin for absorbing theft within the group. Citizens of both races, then, went often to the authorities when they suffered losses, however small.[2]

Thievery in Philadelphia was far more important in black lives than in white. In the whole period between 1860 and 1900, blacks were seven or eight times more likely than whites to be convicted of property crimes (see table). In the years around 1870, the only ones for which there are figures for arrests resulting in overnight jailings as distinct from convictions, about 3.5 percent of all black males over fifteen were annually committed for stealing. This figure means that, if there were no repeaters, the so-called "average" man had, by the age of forty-five, been jailed at least once on a charge of theft.[3]

The situation was even worse for Afro-Americans as a group because most types of property crime in which they engaged were not typically profitable. The world of the late nineteenth century was a heyday—perhaps the heyday—of professional criminals in America, including pickpockets, burglars, and confidence men. These people made a living, occasionally a handsome one, entirely out of theft, but at a price. Full-time professionals could expect to spend between a third and a half of their adult lives behind bars, a figure remarkably similar to that for our own generation. A number of black Philadelphians paid that price, but

IMPRISONMENT FOR ALL CRIMES OF THEFT, BY RACE AND SEX, AND
BLACK:WHITE RATIO OF RATES OF IMPRISONMENT PER 100,000 POPU-
LATION, 1859–1901.

Years	No. in prison		No. in jail		Totals by race	B:W ratio[b]
1859–1861	8 BM	1 BF	180 BM	58 BF	247 B	
	115 WM	5 WF	670 WM	118 WF	908 W	7.1:1
1869–1871	22 BM	0 BF	197 BM	48 BF	267 B	
	195 WM	1 WF	754 WM	112 WF	1062 W	8.1:1
1879–1881	89 BM	9 BF	316 BM	57 BF	471 B	
	490 WF	10 WF	1763 WM	83 WF	2346 W	5.5:1
1889–1891[a]	176 BM	9 BF	331 BM	53 BF	569 B	
	973 WM	12 WF	1220 WM	62 WF	2267 W	6.5:1
1899–1901	89 BM	3 BF	630 BM	92 BF	814 B	
	295 WM	2 WF	1300 WM	98 WF	1695 W	9.5:1

a. No published prison report for 1891; prison figures from 1892. Reformatory added
to prison totals, 1889– . Holmesburg Jail added to Moyamensing totals, 1899–1901.
  b. See note 3.

it bought them little, because color prejudice was as effective in keeping
them at the bottom of the criminal ladder as of the straight.[4]

The handicaps that plagued black criminals were not quite the same
as those that faced their fellows in the wider economy, but they had
much the same effect. In the period following the Civil War, the world
of urban professional crime was highly specialized and roughly graded
in several tiers. Forgers and counterfeiters rated at or near the top, as
did bank thieves. The better pickpockets, working in mobs or at least
pairs, could bring in large amounts of cash when working the right
territory. Hotel thieves or sneaks were not the same as second-story
men. Among burglars, safeblowers outranked safebursters in the recognized hierarchy, and safebursters in turn outranked safebreakers. Afro-
Americans, however, were confined largely to the simplest, most direct,
and least rewarding of crimes by the very nature of the business. The
most successful crooks, whatever their individual talents or specialties,
were all in some sense confidence men, skillful actors, in a way that no
black could be.[5]

Urban bank robbers like Max Shinburn typically did not operate like
such crudely rural characters as Jesse James. The art of robbing banks,
as they practiced it, was not intrinsically violent; banks were instead

taken at night, quietly, when safes could be blown at leisure. Those who were good at this could commonly steal tens and even hundreds of thousands of dollars at a time. The critical planning stage involved days and even weeks of posing as bankers or businessmen themselves, making friends and palming keys, plotting deals and taking measurements. The final phase sometimes involved returning some of the stolen and non-negotiable paper, in return for a promise not to prosecute. To an outsider, the resulting conference between banker, lawyer, perhaps detective, and thief could look much like four confederates plotting to capture a railroad.[6]

What was true at the very top—Shinburn was an international traveler, a "count," when it suited him, and sometimes a millionaire—was in lesser degree true all down the line. To follow Willie Sutton's apocryphal dictum and go "where the money is," a criminal had to look comfortable with those who had it. Hotel and jewel thieves posed as legitimate guests, pickpockets followed the crowds and the seasons, and business was always better at Ascot or Saratoga than on the horsecars of Philadelphia.

Inspector Thomas Byrnes's treatise *Professional Criminals of America,* first published in 1886, contained not a single black face in its portrait gallery of 204 typical burglars, confidence men, shoplifters, and fences. A similar compendium put out in 1895 by Boston's chief detective had just one black representative, the Cuban burglar Edward Smith, who was included for his daring and athletic breakout from an urban courtroom full of police. At a time when their proportion of any northern city's population was no more than 4 percent, Afro-Americans not in livery stood out too boldly in those shops and public places where the money was.[7]

For Afro-Americans, then, the problem of breaking into the more profitable crimes of guile and even education, such as fraud, embezzlement, forgery, or taking money by false pretenses, was a direct analogue of the problem of breaking into white-collar employment more generally. These white-collar offenses were always rarer in the courts than the blue-collar ones, although they grew more common over time with the increasing sophistication of the economy and of the population. In 1859–1861, for example, white-collar offenses amounted to only a little over 5 percent of the property crimes for which men and women were sentenced to hard labor in the county jail; by the turn of the century the average had reached nearly 16 percent. Blacks did proportionately fewer of these crimes, or less than 1 percent in the earlier period, which was a single case of "taking money by false pretenses," and a little more than 4 percent around 1900. More important, in terms of the way that crime did or did not pay for the group, the problem was that although in fact people were born every minute who were willing to buy the Girard Avenue Bridge, few of them were willing to buy it from a black man. Thus, when blacks committed fraud, they did so usually at the expense of other blacks.

Of thirty-one newspaper accounts of black men and one of a black woman involved in some sort of fraud, the color of the victim or mark is not clear in some cases, as when a man was caught begging money to bury his still living mother or a woman solicited money to build a church. But a clear majority of complainants or prosecutors were black people. Sometimes the confidence man's own color or background was part of his "edge," as when John Anderson, a black man, collected small sums from several householders in 1880 to "conjure" the location of buried treasure in their cellars. Other frauds sold bogus tickets to fraternal outings or played street games like three-card monte. The most common scam, however, was color-blind; white as well as black "agents" from phony employment companies took money from young women, newcomers to the city, on the promise that these "fees" would bring them jobs as servants either in Philadelphia or on the Jersey shore.[8]

Only eight frauds by blacks were clearly directed against white victims. In two of these cases the black man was a subordinate partner to a white principal: one was a stablehand in a barn where farmers were fleeced of their loads, the other was a night porter who allowed an embezzling bookkeeper to do his work after hours. The other six cases involved rubber checks or forged orders for amounts under $10 or the "embezzlement" by a waiter of the price of several meals not turned in to the cashier. The outstanding exception was the case of John Brooks from Albany, who in late 1899 and early 1900 forged deeds and documents in the names of prominent local blacks as part of a scheme to bilk a white broker out of mortgage money. Inasmuch as truly professional forgery was rated at the very top of the criminal ladder, Brooks's audacity earned him a savage sentence of fifteen years in separate and solitary confinement. This was apparently the second longest sentence given any black man for any offense short of murder in the first degree, a fact that underlines the exceptional nature of any attempt at entry into the white world of the criminal elite.[9]

For the great majority of black thieves, who were confined to the miscellaneous unskilled and marginally profitable offenses, the economics of black thievery was much like that of the lesser kinds of urban thievery in general. The Philadelphia Police Department provided figures on the economics by keeping a record of all stolen property recovered and returned to the owner. The itemized list includes the price of every lot or article, the name of the person from whom it was taken, and the name of the thief. Only the detectives at central headquarters did not ordinarily itemize in this kind of detail; much as nineteenth century detectives loved publicity, they could not stand scrutiny and required a certain haziness to work in. Some of their activities involved arranging deals between thieves and owners in which stolen profits were split up without further question, or even simpler deals in which thieves and detectives did the splitting without involving the owners at all. In 1880, a typical year, the nine plainclothesmen at headquarters recorded only unitemized totals amounting to some $26,000 in cash and goods, not counting an indeterminant but smaller amount "located by the officers at different pawn offices, where it is obtained by the owners, and no receipts are obtained by the department." The dollar figure presumably covered the bigger individual cases aborted or solved by the department. The rest of the recovered stolen property, amounting to something over $48,000 or almost two-thirds of the total value, was accounted for by the "special officers" attached to the districts or by those well-placed patrolmen who were able to catch a thief in the act.[10]

The average worth of all 759 lots or items on this list, including horses and handkerchiefs, chickens, stickpins, and lawnmowers, came to about $62. This average, however, is in several ways a misleading figure. The horses, for example, most of them with wagons, were the most expensive items, on average, at nearly $200 apiece. But few thieves were trying seriously to steal and sell a horse. Young men simply climbed in and drove off with them, as nowadays with commercial vans, and abandoned them after emptying the wagons; only an inept and unlucky minority were actually captured sitting in the driver's seat. In several other categories, too, the average worth was distorted by the occasional big score, such as a "trunk and contents" valued at $600 or a professional burglary of "908 pairs of fine shoes" at $1500. As illustration of the profits of more typical thieves, the more meaningful figure is the median or typical theft, valued at $19.

Except for cash and other items meant to be used directly, all stolen items had to be pawned, fenced, or sold at second hand, a process which cut the take severely. At best, for professionals who had carefully destroyed all clues to the original ownership, a fence gave no more than a quarter of the face or replacement value of stolen goods. The profit from the typical recorded theft thus came to about three to five dollars. This was not a negligible sum at a time when $10 a week was good wages, but the price level also helped account for the persistence of prosecutors, to whom the lost shirt, rake, or baby carriage was worth much more than it was to the thief.[11]

The pattern of thefts committed by blacks was in no way unusual. In 1880, for example, the average value of the goods taken by identifiable blacks was somewhat higher than the general average, or about $78 if

David Anderson, Jr.'s, $712.50 in cash and jewelry taken from his father is included. Without that intramural lot, the average was somewhat less, or $58.

The real difference between black and white theft was not so much the nature of the crimes as of the criminals, for blacks were far more likely than whites to be repeat offenders rather than first-time amateurs. The official statistics on this matter are highly suspect, since any experienced thief knew that "old offenders" drew longer sentences. In an era when there were no social security cards or registered fingerprints and only late in the period a carelessly administered collection of photographs at police headquarters, a man's name or identity was whatever he cared to tell the authorities. If no one recognized him immediately, he had every reason to claim that he was young, illiterate, orphaned, desperate—and above all caught up in the law for the first time in his life. The list of "prior convictions" after a person's name in jail was based on little more than an honor system, especially if he had been sentenced in some other state or county. Every study has shown that the majority of white men brought in for stealing in nineteenth century towns and cities were typically young and amateur criminals, for whom one or more of these small adventures had been followed by the inevitable arrest, and for whom a few weeks or months in jail was a once-in-a-lifetime experience. In Philadelphia the official figures indicate that about two-thirds of white convicts fit this description. A better if more conservative guess would be about one-half. Among black men brought in for stealing, given their far higher rate of conviction, probably two-thirds or so had established, under a variety of names, the sequence of theft and arrest as a recurrent pattern, a way of life.[12]

Although most of these repeaters stole the same things as the amateurs, they were in fact professional or at least semiprofessional thieves. Of those arrested in 1880, Ed Smith from Boston, who stopped in town long enough to rifle a cash drawer, was the only black man so recognized in the published guidebooks to the underworld. But Philadelphia's own Jefferson Brown, for example, had all of the requisite skills. A pickpocket with a smooth line and an eye for the right mark, Brown was found by a detective on April 9 with $200 in cash stolen from a white stranger whom he had been taking on a tour of the city's downtown resorts. The incident was only one in a long series; Brown was arrested at least nine times over a quarter of a century, always for the same kind of offense. After the penultimate conviction, in 1899, he had broken out of Eastern State Penitentiary by characteristically conning the administration into transferring him to Norristown State Asylum, a place from which it was easier to escape. Other names on the 1880 police list of stolen property were almost equally familiar. Twelve of the 89 blacks reported by the *Public Ledger* as arrested for theft in that year—and the paper listed only a fraction of the total—were reported twice, despite in several cases the intervention of a short jail term.[13]

If jail was truly a "nursery of crime," a large number of those people—three, six, or eight-timers—had earned an extensive if elementary education, graduating as professional or at least experienced thieves. The black population was small enough so that its criminals typically knew each other by sight or reputation. They often worked together, stashed their stolen property with wives or women friends, and made sure that someone else did the pawning or fencing for them. But while these simple precautions were the hallmarks of experience, experience alone was not enough to get them into the big time. Although a number of blacks were skilled pickpockets, limited only by their lack of access to the richer marks, most other criminal specialties were beyond their grasp. Only John Brooks qualified as a forger. The newspapers reported no black counterfeiters, no safeblowers, bursters, or breakers, no bank sneaks or hotel thieves in the ordinary sense. Each year several black men were convicted for burglary, which involved breaking into a locked placc, whether a store, an employer's bedroom, or a fellow boarder's trunk, but there were about ten times as many convicted of the lesser crime of simple larceny. Only Charles Elliot Purnell and his group behaved like first-class professionals, and their fate tells much about the limits imposed on black criminality.

Purnell worked with three other men, the brothers "Doc" and Jimmy Sawyer and Tom Johnson. All of them lived in Philadelphia, but they had previously worked out of New York and Baltimore, and none of them had local police records. The group usually confined their depredations to smaller towns and cities outside of the metropolis; it was only when they abandoned this precaution that they got caught. On April 10, 1892, a Sunday night, Purnell was caught rifling the second-story bedroom of Louisa de Bonneville, on South Sixteenth Street, and on his way out he took a shot at her. The detectives immediately rounded up the "usual suspects," and de Bonneville identified one John Moss, who had earlier done some work around her house. The District Attorney then cleared the tracks for a railroading, and Moss was prepared for trial on Wednesday. Purnell in the meantime had been arrested in possession of an overcoat stolen with a lot of other goods from the suburban estate of Frank Thompson, vice president of the Pennsylvania Railroad. Some of de Bonneville's personal articles were also found in Purnell's stash, together with items from at least ten other burglaries. After the jury voted to acquit Moss, who had an alibi, the police secured a confession from Purnell, together with the identities and whereabouts of his accomplices. On April 21 Purnell was remanded to the authorities in Delaware County, one of the three jurisdictions in which he was wanted, to begin the process that eventually earned him a forty-year prison sentence, the longest on record for any crime by black or white.[14]

The unusual circumstances of this episode explain the severity of its outcome. Both the prosecution and the victim were embarrassed by the trial of John Moss: de Bonneville had sworn that she would "never forget his face." More important, the shock of surprising an intruder in the home always evoked a special kind of fear, and the Purnell gang, as the story unfolded, had twice been discovered by suburban house-holders and had once been the target of some shots. But Purnell's fate, when added to the John Brooks sentence and the triple hanging follow-ing the murder of Roy White, suggests the limits to judicial impartiality. Blacks were no more liable than whites to be judged guilty when accused of a given offense, but equality of sentences hid another form of prej-udice. Far more blacks than whites, when brought to the dock, were repeaters, a status that would normally have earned them longer terms in jail. This situation was ordinarily balanced by the fact that black criminality was so often practiced on other blacks, or was so petty in character, that it posed no threat to the class to which the judges be-longed. But when an Afro-American broke out of character and behaved in a more directly threatening way, the judges overreacted out of surprise or fear.

The surprise may have resulted from one important difference be-tween the patterns of criminality then and today. Even successful crim-inals like Max Shinburn were capable, when cornered, of shooting it out with policemen, and burglars occasionally tied up or threatened householders in the course of a job. But burglary was normally a non-violent crime and, if successful, was not even known to its victim until some time after the fact. The sudden trauma of finding a Purnell in the bedroom was a nightmare in part because it was so rarely a reality. Sober, respectable Philadelphians ordinarily had little cause to fear crim-inals in the starkly physical senses, simply because armed robbery was for unclear reasons virtually unknown then in the urban East.

Robberies sometimes occurred when men, but never women, were attacked or mugged in slum areas, overpowered, and stripped of clothes or cash. But this was not a common crime, or perhaps not a commonly reported one because of its connection with prostitution. In any event, the newspapers never carried more than a dozen or so stories in any single year. And despite the fact that weapons were widely available and commonly used in ordinary fights—knives always, guns increas-ingly—these muggings never seem to have involved even the threat of cutting or shooting. In the 1890s the press was much concerned about choral hydrate, also known as knockout drops or Mickey Finns, in the hands of robbers, a successor to earlier fears about chloroform. But when a saloon in the North Bronx was held up by a gunman in November 1895, the news rated a front page in Philadelphia, and although no one was shot or hurt, the story lingered on for days. The New York police concluded sagely that the robber must have been someone from the Wild West Show currently playing the town.[15]

There seemed to be a code that distinguished what would today be called muggings or simple beatings from armed robbery. A man, especially a well-dressed stranger to the neighborhood, was perhaps fair game, someone probably up to no good, looking for a game or maybe a woman. Or after a fair fight it was perhaps all right to lift a wallet as one of the spoils of victory. In any case, to threaten a victim with a deadly weapon was not done by black or white. Most cases of robbery in Philadelphia usually grew out of rolling drunks or snatching purses, the latter offense an especially common one among young blacks.[16]

There was thus a large number of black thieves in the city, but most of them did no great harm, as they simply grabbed at whatever opportunities lay about. And it was not hard for the authorities to keep this class under control. A few black men and women were charged each year with receiving stolen goods, but almost no one of any color was prosecuted for receiving in the usual sense, that is, as pawnbrokers or second-hand dealers who traded with criminals. These people in fact usually had working relations with the police, which gave detectives the power to solve most of the local thefts, by local people, that they really felt thay had to crack. The only risk to dealers was the loss they might suffer when made to surrender stolen items to the owners, a risk that gave them another incentive to pay as little as possible for anything suspect. The people actually charged with receiving stolen goods were typically the confederates of thieves, often women given goods to store or sell. They in turn were rarely convicted, because they too had a role to play in the detective system. After pleading ignorance of the source of whatever shoes or sealing wax had been entrusted to them and fingering whoever actually did the job, the women were let go. The conviction rate suggests that as of the mid-1890s, 400–500 black men practiced professional or semiprofessional thievery. Another 1500 or so were liable, in the course of a lifetime, to serve a single sentence for some crime against property. But as a group, these men posed no more threat to private property than they did to private persons, at least as part of their work.[17]

In particular, black male thieves could have added little to the total transfer of wealth from whites to blacks, even without subtracting for their wages lost while in jail, on the grounds that they could have earned little more than subsistence in any case. About a quarter of all black male thefts reported in the papers involved items taken from other blacks, as in the case of young David Anderson. The real figure was undoubtedly much higher. The *Public Ledger* as of 1900, for example, reported only a fraction, about one-eighth, of those cases that resulted in convictions. Although the bulk of these petty thefts and burglaries were not intrinsically interesting, the editors presumably thought that interracial crimes, such as purse-snatchings and shopliftings, were more newsworthy than the everyday pilferage of shirts and wallets from cousins and neighbors. A majority of the Afro-Americans arrested for theft were probably accused by their fellows, blacks being noted for their willingness to go to court when wronged. And since the set of blankets that meant at best a dollar or two to the thief was worth six or eight dollars to the landlady, the effect of this sort of crime on the Afro-American population as a whole probably subtracted rather than added to its resources.

The economic impact of black women thieves was different, however, and more important in terms of both their relative activity and their earnings. Although men of both races were more likely to be caught stealing than women, Afro-American women were much more heavily involved in the business than white women, both absolutely and relatively. And in the two largest occupations available to them, domestic service and prostitution, they typically accounted for larger thefts and enjoyed greater immunity from prosecution than their black male counterparts.

The greater involvement of black women than of white showed up in the different proportions of men and women convicted of various crimes against property. In the years 1859–1861, white men were imprisoned at six times the rate that white women were, black men at only three times the rate for black women. This disparity between the sexes continued to grow, for both races, over the next forty years, but more steeply among whites than blacks. As a result, around 1900 white males were imprisoned at sixteen times the rate for white women, and black men at twelve times the rate for black women. Given the much higher proportion of black thieves, these figures show that twelve times as many black women as white ones were jailed in the earlier period, relative to their numbers in the city's population, and fully nineteen times as many in the later period.

More important than their numbers alone was the fact that these Afro-American women were able to steal impressive amounts, especially in cash and valuables, from white marks, and were often able to get away with it. In 1870, for example, the two biggest thefts, $400 and $200, reported by black men were from other blacks, but the largest amount reported stolen from a white man was $125, taken by Jane Martin. In

1880 the record take was Barbara Minor's $1000 in government bonds, whereas the biggest theft by a black man was the $712.50 which David Anderson, Sr., lost to his errant son. In 1895 Hester Pitt stole $3500 in cash and $500 in jewels from her employer; two confederates were caught with part of this loot, but she was able to get out of town ahead of the detectives. The largest male theft reported in that year was only $380, taken by William Bagby from Joseph Pinket, the nearly blind black president of the Twenty-ninth Ward Republican Association; the money was Pinket's profit from a card game at the club. And in 1900 two operations tied for the largest score of the year. Mary Stroller stole $3000 in jewels from a private home, and a woman known only as "Ella" took $3000, which included $2000 in bank notes, from another. Ella retained her anonymity because she was able to make her escape. The biggest black male score that year was "several hundred dollars in jewelry, etc." stolen by a janitor from tenants at the West Philadelphia apartment-hotel where he worked.[18]

Domestic servants, as some of these examples show, lived close to where the money was, and since more women than men had this kind of access to rich white households, whatever they could get away with was at least a short-term gain for the black group as a whole. Some pilferage of food and household goods was traditionally accepted as a kind of perquisite. The taking of small or perishable items may have led to some firings, but the people who hired servants, unlike neighbors and shopkeepers, did not generally prosecute in these cases. Silverware, however, was taken seriously, in both senses, and a number of domestics were jailed each year for household theft.

These small items could be stolen directly only at risk. Often it was immediately obvious that, if not the butler, the maid had done it, especially if she were new or had fled the household. The detective process could then operate on two fronts, searching for the woman or for the spoons. Larger and more expensive items, however, might be worth the risk to a servant. And if she could stay calm under questioning, she might also serve as guide or pilot to a burglarous friend or gang on the outside. The arrest in 1900 of Fannie Smilie led eventually to four different men, burglars and "receivers," all of them white. White criminals rarely associated with black men, perhaps because they were too well-known or vulnerable to be trusted, but working with black women might be a winning proposition.[19]

The special advantage enjoyed by prostitutes over either domestics or any other class of thieves was the odds on beating prosecution. In this case, uniquely, there was an added edge in being black. While servants made the most dramatic scores, the robbery of customers, who were usually but not always white men, was per episode by far the most profitable kind of black theft in nineteenth century Philadelphia.

There were several varieties of this ancient game. "Panel thievery" was the name given to the version in which a man, perhaps hidden behind a panel, crept in to rifle pockets in pantaloons not currently occupied by their owners. The "badger game" involved the sudden appearance of a large male confederate, the woman's alleged husband, in the middle of a tryst. The victim might then be blackmailed or simply forced to flee without his valuables. In Philadelphia it was called "badger thieving" when a woman or group simply stripped, rolled, or picked clean a man who, as the *Ledger* put it nicely, "placed himself under their care and fell asleep in their presence." Most of these incidents involved black women and no men at all, other than the victim. In at least one case two black women managed to eliminate the middle act in the usual drama as well: Malvina Braxton and Jessie Augustus were arrested in May 1900 for "enticing" a young man into an alley and braining him with a blackjack.[20]

The usual badger operation, however, began with the turning of weakness into strength. The best brothels, with the most attractive "inmates," worked hard to give their visitors a sense of comfort and security, allowing them to indulge their fantasies about welcome and even romance in an effort to bring them back repeatedly. Badger theft in Philadelphia was instead practiced by people in places that encouraged no illusions of this kind. Black women worked all over town, but they usually worked as badgers only in the lower end of the Seventh Ward, into the Fifth or the Fourth, on St Mary's, Alaska, or Hurst Streets, in Middle Alley, and at other hardcore slum addresses. Most had less to lose than the men did, and they could count on that advantage in the effort to fend off prosecution.

None of them robbed all of their customers. Common sense suggested that they pick on the least aggressive or the least awake, especially those who were strangers to the community. Many immigrants were simply afraid to go to the law. The color bar was helpful in embarrassing married men into shutting up and slinking home. Sailors were less concerned about their reputations, but like some of the immigrants, they were only passing through town and found it hard after a long night to retrace their steps and identify the right woman at the right address. It took time, too, to put in a complaint and follow it through two hearings and a trial.

A tough audience awaited complainants if or when they finally made it to a courtroom. In June 1860 Georgiana Coleman, accused of taking $10 from Bill Fine, announced at her arraignment that "she would rob any white man who went with her; they might send her to prison for it, but after she came out she would continue to play the game." She was sent home free. While the law represented the official moral sense of the state, the unofficial function of the jury, or sometimes of the judge, was to register the moral sense of the community. The key to the actual administration of justice was often the complainant, and complainants in badger cases were not seen as wholly innocent victims, especially those who had been consorting with black women. In 1881 Judge Allinson, while dismissing Mick Albright's case against three prostitutes, turned the tables entirely by declaring that, "if there was anything which would justify the reestablishment of the pillory or whipping post it would be that such a man might be publicly and properly punished."[21]

An attitude like Allinson's had a discouraging effect on prosecution. The police did crack down sometimes, and in 1880 a repeat offender, Emma Burk, who had killed a man seventeen years earlier, drew two years for badgering. But experienced prostitutes—and there were few innocents on Hurst Street—knew that the odds were strongly with them, and the risk of punishment was low.[22]

The temptations were even more attractive than the odds. Philadelphia was a port of embarkation and debarkation, and sailors, immigrants, and emigrants sometimes carried big rolls of money on their persons. In November 1880 Bernard Mullen, a pedlar, was robbed of his life savings, $1275 in cash, on the eve of his departure for his native Germany. Mullen remembered celebrating in "Doc" Edwards's oyster house, where the proprietor, a black man, had performed a playful marriage ceremony uniting him with one of the two white women who hovered around his booth. But he was much too hazy to make identifications, and the money was never recovered.[23]

An archetypical story was that of Barbara Minor, a black woman who contrived in May 1880 to badger $1000 in United States bonds out of a visitor from out of town. Lizzie Archer, who had been arrested for a domestic theft in April, then went and told the police. Minor managed to break Archer's arm on the way to headquarters, but that was the only damage suffered by either woman. It is unclear how many of the bonds were returned, or to whom, after the detectives had done with the pair, but no one went to jail.[24]

Badger theft, then, was often a successful business, but like theft by domestics, it was an exception to the rule that stealing was not in general a profitable activity for Philadelphia's Afro-Americans. Perhaps in fact it is not properly classified as theft at all, but as vice, part of a considerably larger and more significant pattern of illicit behavior.

VICE

Commercial vice in black Philadelphia was economically far more important than simple theft, and socially it was more complicated because it was both more distinctive and more fully integrated into the wider white world. The patterns of illegal black drinking, gambling, and prostitution were different from the white, and so was the level of involvement in each. At the same time, viewed simply as businesses, these occupations, like their legitimate counterparts, required networks of wholesalers, moneylenders, contracts, and customers in which Afro-Americans did not operate independently but were often intimately involved with whites. And all of the people involved in vice, regardless of color, had constantly to deal with the legal authorities who alternatively harassed and protected them.

This ambivalent relationship with Philadelphia's police and politicians was another reflection of the complex interrelations between the criminal and the straight worlds, whether black or white. Illegal vice in the United States has generally been hard to distinguish, if not from virtue, then from legal enterprise. The line between licit and illicit has been drawn differently in different times and places, but the sale of alcohol and other drugs, along with the businesses of gambling and professional sports, of entertainment and prostitution, have always been entangled with each other. In Philadelphia during the 1890s, as in Chicago under Prohibition or in Las Vegas today, all of these enterprises were shaped by politics also, making the distinction between the permissible and the impermissible much more complex than the law alone would have it.

In some nineteenth century cities, though by no means the majority, the gap between differing moralities was bridged in part by the establishment of official or quasi-official "red-light districts." Nothing was that neat in Philadelphia. The city's police and magistrates had to tolerate, even to protect, illegal enterprise in some degree, determining in a rough way who might carry it on, how, and where. But while brothels and other places of nighttime entertainment were concentrated downtown, there were few large sections of the city wholly free of commercial vice, and no locality where it was safe from prosecution. Selling liquor to minors on Sunday or without a retail license was unlawful. Gambling of any kind was equally illegal; so was streetwalking. It was a crime to maintain a disorderly or bawdy house or, after 1885, an opium den. But the agents of law were often products of the factional politics as well as of the broadly decentralized and responsive system of justice. Prosecution for vice offenses was episodic, as a result, and its outcome uncertain, but complaints were heard, pressures were felt, and at least a few violators were arrested every week.[25]

One result of the tangled and complex relationship between illegal enterprise and public authority was that the criminal records were untrustworthy guides to the extent of vice in general and of black involvement in particular. But a number of contemporaries outside the justice system were also concerned with illicit activity and its effects. Many of them testified to the size and nature of the black underworld and to the way in which illegal liquor sales, gambling, and prostitution worked for both races, sometimes separately, more often together.

Both the consumption and the illegal sale of drugs of any kind were less important in the late nineteenth-century black economy than other forms of vice. Morphine was typically a middle-class addiction; opium was used exclusively by Chinese and whites; cocaine, by century's end, was not yet common in the streets. Alcohol was the only drug ordinarily used and sold by Philadelphia's Afro-Americans, and drunkenness was not a major social issue, at least relative to others. Illicit alcohol dealing, however, was a problem of sorts, largely because of some unintended effects of the contemporary Temperance Crusade.[26]

The oldest and strongest moral reform in the nineteenth century was the crusade against strong drink. Gambling and prostitution were only secondary targets, because they were thought to be typically secondary effects, the result of passions already inflamed, judgment destroyed, or ruin brought on by indulgence. Reformers in several states succeeded before the Civil War in passing prohibition laws to curb the evil. One lasting result of these experiments was to arouse the liquor industry and its lawyers to challenge them, as well as to strengthen precedents concerning the laws of search and seizure, probable cause, and permissible evidence. Virtually all prohibitory laws were repealed by the 1870s. Although prohibitionist sentiment never died, practical reformers between the Civil War and the end of the century turned to more moderate tactics.[27]

The work was helped, in ways that few reformers understood, by the economic transformation that continued through these years. The demand for order and rationality was not compatible with the heavy indulgence that had been common in the early republic. Drunken behavior grew less acceptable among the middle and upper classes. The medical establishment attacked the popular notion that drink was a source of physical strength as well as courage. And the per capita consumption of alcohol declined markedly as the century progressed.[28]

The police and local authorities in big cities all over the country cooperated with these developments by arresting drunks in staggering numbers. The battle against public intoxication was related to the wider campaign for control of the streets, and everywhere by the 1870s the police were winning, as drunk arrests, which had peaked in the mid-century decades, were declining. In Philadelphia, typically, arrests on drunk or disorderly charges averaged 15,601 a year between 1859 and 1861, representing some 51 percent of all arrests, or 28 arrests per every 1000 residents. These arrests climbed further in the three-year period 1869–1871, averaging 22,168 annually, 56 percent of the total, or 32 per 1000, and they stayed high in 1879–1881, averaging 26,259 a year, 61 percent of the total, or 31 per 1000. The curve fell toward the end of the century, down to 23,181 in 1889–1891, 48 percent of the total, 22 per 1000, and down to 24,834 in 1899–1901, 39 percent of the total, or 19 per 1000.[29]

Although the police and politicians went willingly to work at clearing the streets, they were not so eager to move against illegal sellers. Up to 1887 it was easy enough for a citizen with fifty dollars and references to get a liquor license in Philadelphia. Beer and spirits were sold in virtually every hotel and eating place in the city, hundreds of cigar stores, and thousands of places which dealt in nothing else. The requirement that no alcohol should be sold on Sundays or to minors was widely and openly violated. Sunday was the only day off for a workingman, and most young people went to work years before reaching their majority. There was little basis in the political culture shared by the police and magistrates to support these Protestant restrictions, and even less in the ethnic cultures of the city's large German and Irish populations.[30]

Party politics was one reason for the handful of arrests and the even smaller number of convictions for illegal selling that occurred in every year from the 1860s through the 1880s. In a typical raid in 1879 under the Stokley regime, the owners of twenty-nine "rum holes" on Alaska Street were charged with Sunday sales; twenty-three of the names were Irish, and bail money was supplied in eleven cases by "Squire" William McMullin, Democratic leader of the Fourth Ward. The grand jury ignored every single indictment, with the result that Stokley got credit for the action, McMullin for the rescue, and nobody got hurt at all. But politics in the narrow sense was not the only consideration. Some owners were taken in following thefts or fights on their premises; neighbors or landlords complained about disorder; anxious wives and mothers complained about debt and credit extended to drunken menfolk. And every year a dozen or so dealers out of the thousands in operation were sent to Moyamensing for terms of a few months.[31]

The city's black population, meanwhile, had comparatively little trouble with either drunk arrests or liquor violations. The only police records that distinguish arrests for simple drunkenness from other offenses by race are those from the county jail during the years 1869–1871. On average, 193 blacks were jailed for intoxication, out of a total of 3737 such jailings. Thus, the black 3 percent of the population accounted for

5 percent of the commitments for drunkenness. This ratio is surprisingly low, given black poverty and misery. It also illustrates the relative fairness of the justice system, showing that Afro-Americans were not systematically singled out: blacks were far more likely to be arrested for property offenses or violent ones, crimes with real and often strident victims, than they were for the largely discretionary offense of drunkenness, one of the few offenses for which policemen routinely made arrests on their own initiative, without responding to citizens' complaints.[32]

All other evidence reinforces the conclusion that blacks were not especially subject to arrests having to do with liquor. The police records give only arrest totals by race or ethnic group, without breaking them into categories. But the fact that intoxication, the biggest single component of these arrest totals, ordinarily led to no criminal prosecutions makes it possible crudely to measure the comparative liability of various groups. The result of dividing each group's total arrests by its total convictions, mainly for crimes against persons or property, gives a ratio which suggests the relative importance of the less serious charge of drunkenness. By this measure, blacks during 1860–1900 had consistently the lowest ratio of drunk arrests for any major ethnic category. The Irish-born had by far the highest, with non-Irish immigrants giving way to native whites in the 1880s, when the relatively heavy-drinking Germans were replaced with Italians and Jews and the second-generation Irish joined the "native" group. Moreover, the proportion of black commitments to the House of Correction, a reformatory reserved mostly for vagrants and habitual alcoholics, was consistently about the same as the proportion of black drunk arrests, or from one and one-half to two times their proportion in the population as a whole, which was far less than their representation in any other charitable or correctional institution.[33]

The justice system was not the only agency to confirm the low incidence of black alcohol abuse. The city's health records are no more trustworthy in specifying causes of death than was nineteenth century medicine itself, and "alcoholism," as a scientific label, is only somewhat more precise than "intemperance." Death certificates for the poor were signed by often marginal physicians, attendants in charity wards, or doctors assigned to the office of coroner. But in part because their judgments often mixed popular stereotypes with physical diagnoses, their finding that at century's end blacks were less than half as likely as whites to die from either "alcoholism" or "cirrhosis of the liver" is especially significant. In 1899–1901, for example, there were three black deaths and 264 white deaths from alcoholism, 11 black deaths and 538 white deaths from cirrhosis.[34]

Only by the elevated moral standards of a W. E. B. Du Bois or the evangelical *Christian Recorder* did the abuse of alcohol rank high among the host of social problems afflicting the city's blacks. Drinking among the poor is always more visible than among the rich. The streets in the lower wards at night were full of passing figures carrying pails of beer, or "rushing the growler." The founders of the Octavia Hill Association were easily shocked by the sight of men and women drinking on stoops and sidewalks. But the drinking habit among blacks was shaped by class, neighborhood, and personal choice rather than by ethnic culture. Most, under slavery, had only limited and episodic acquaintance with alcohol. Further back, there was no African tradition of regular or heavy consumption. Most black Americans belonged to churches historically hostile to strong drink, and many fit their actions to their beliefs. The Prohibitionist parties of Pennsylvania and elsewhere treated blacks with respect, as candidates for office and potential allies rather than special targets. If many in Philadelphia used liquor to kill pain or to spice good times, by contemporary standards they handled it well.[35]

It was not the abuse but rather the sale of alcohol which posed special economic problems for the group. Because prohibition seemed politically impossible in the post–Civil War years, and because prosecution was obviously ineffective under existing law, the antiliquor forces developed another weapon. They persuaded a number of states, including Pennsylvania in 1887, to adopt new laws changing the ways in which liquor licenses were administered and, above all, charging steeply higher fees, or several hundred dollars for the right to sell in amounts less than one quart. This essentially modern approach to retail sales had several purposes. Tightened requirements would drive out disreputable sellers and cut down the number of those who remained. While prosecutions would continue as before, the real threat to a licensed seller who sold after hours or to minors would be surrender of his investment and forfeit of his bond. Forfeit was determined by purely administrative procedures. The county's quarter sessions judges were impaneled to act as a special license court to hold hearings, every spring, to decide who should get and who should lose the privilege of dealing.[36]

These hearings, lasting over two months or so, were the subject of intense local interest, especially in the early years. Individual complainants had a chance at every name brought up, and most important agents of the Law and Order League had a hit list of their own, drawn up after months of prowling the city in search of rowdiness, immorality, and other violations of the terms of license. The League, organized by the same reformers who had lobbied for the new law, played in fact a quasi-official role not only in these hearings but year round, demanding police action, organizing raids, and bringing evidence to court.[37]

The system in practice worked much as was hoped. The judges of the license court were generally recognized as honest and apolitical, unlike the city's magistrates and police. The new law was administered strictly and fairly from their end. But like any major change in the code governing drugs or liquor, it had unexpected consequences, some of which had a devastating effect on black business.[38]

Small restaurants and barrooms were traditionally the kinds of enterprise begun by new migrants to the city and people with little capital. Black men and women ran perhaps several dozen of these businesses from the 1860s into the 1880s. Many more sold liquor when catering private parties or dances, and catering was the most characteristic of small black enterprises. But beginning in 1888, the law required a $2000 bond and a $500 license fee, at a time when $500 was a good year's wage for a workingman. The owners of many small establishments did not bother to apply. Most who did apply were turned down as unsuitable. The license court, after its first set of hearings, granted only 1257 applications out of 3457, cutting the total number of legal outlets to less than a quarter of the 5773 allowed in 1887.[39]

A related problem emerged that first year when Alfred G. Baker, president of the Academy of Music, proposed that Andrew F. Stevens, society's favorite caterer, be given a license to sell wine and spirits at the balls and special functions occasionally held on the premises. Despite the efforts of two of the city's leading lawyers, the judge ruled that no such "floating" or partial grant could be issued. This ruling could be evaded, with some difficulty, if a caterer maintained an open bar with free liquor. But it could not be flouted; two years later the Academy was busted when it tried.[40]

More ominous was the reception given the few black saloonkeepers able to get up the fee and apply to the court, a procedure that revealed a serious cultural gap. Elite Philadelphians drank at home or in all-male clubs. Many of the city's working-class Irish or native whites also thought of the saloon as a basically masculine refuge. The respectable newspapers looked askance at any place that welcomed women, drink, and music all together, and a number of raids in the 1880s were directed at "concert dives" in the city's entertainment section. The formal charge was generally selling alcohol to minors, but underlying it was the moral outrage that men and women were meeting to drink beer and dance, or even to sit and listen to tunes from *La Traviata*.[41]

This attitude was not shared widely in the Seventh Ward. Just five black men applied for liquor licenses the first time around, and each of their saloons provided some kind of music. Alfred Bettencourt, who had run a saloon at 1132 Lombard Street for fourteen years, was questioned about disorderly or disreputable characters, a recent killing just outside his door, and piano playing on the premises. Sounds carried a long way on hot nights in an era before air conditioning made it possible to keep the windows closed. Residents who lived near a hotel owned by John Brown at 336 South Eleventh Street complained of the "perpetual thumping of an unknown musical instrument"; he too confessed to maintaining a piano. Preston Price at 1234 Pine Street and Amos Scott at Eleventh and Pine were subjected to similar complaints.[42]

Gil Ball, whose second floor at 720 Lombard Street was undeniably a dance hall, spoke for all black saloonkeepers when he was asked directly, "Would you be willing to abandon [it] if the court granted your license?" The veteran saloonkeeper was not easily cowed: "If it is against the law I would abandon it. But I would like to know if it is against the law." The judge, after what seemed to be a startled pause, could only reply that "there were a great many things contrary to public policy which were not actually prohibited by law." Ball's application was then held up, a rare procedure, until he promised to give up the dancing, although not the piano. Magistrate Izzy Durham and Councilman Chris Perry testified for Bettencourt; Brown, Scott, and Price also made the cut.[43]

But not for long. Brown and Scott lost their licenses in 1889, Ball in 1890, Bettencourt in 1893, and Alfred Govens, his successor at the same address, in 1895. The testimony or accusations were in every case the same. The law forbade all licensees from allowing "disorderly conduct" or "disreputable persons" on their premises. If these were code words in effect demanding sexual segregation, or at least discretion, no black saloon could fulfill them. Black women, with rare exceptions, went where the men went. Or if "disorderly behavior" meant music and dancing, and if "disreputable persons" were people who enjoyed both, or had criminal records, or who mixed and coupled across the color line, the result was inevitable. Ball, when asked about "immoral women" at his place, pleaded vainly that "it is the custom of the neighborhood, your honor." All the places that lost their permits were accused of such "violations." And it was hard to find new applicants, as the fee rose to $800 and again to $1100 by century's end. There were times during the 1890s when Preston Price was the only Afro-American in Philadelphia who sold liquor legally. As late as 1910 there were no more than two.[44]

This situation did not drive people out of business but only into illegality. Two years after the new law went into effect, at a time when there were roughly 1200 licensed places, a church group put the number of illegal saloons at 6000. Secretary Clarence Gibboney of the Law and Order Society thought it closer to 3000. A few years later, Robert Patterson, president of the Retail Liquor Dealers Association, suggested it was 3500 to 7000. That seems a good guess, given the fact that as of

1890 919 wholesalers were licensed to supply the 1173 businesses that legally sold alcohol by the pail or glass.[45]

That the estimates of Gibboney and Patterson were so close was no accident. While the League and the Association were at odds each spring at the license hearings, they were functionally allies through most of the year, because the legal dealers were almost as eager as the reformers to shut down their illegal competitors. That goal was beyond reach. But the strange bedfellows, working with the police, generated several hundred arrests each year and enough heat, if not to close the speakeasies, at least to keep them unrespectable. Most of them remained hole-and-corner enterprises, furnished with barrels and planks, a dozen cases of beer, and a few gallons of spirits. The black bars were typical, except perhaps for the greater number of female customers. A few dozen enjoyed a shadow of legality, those that doubled as political clubs and theoretically served only "members," who gave donations rather than paid by the drink. These were uniquely all-male enclaves, since only men had the vote, and they often doubled as places to gamble. Some of the rest were open only on weekends, their proprietors part-time entrepreneurs who held other jobs or who sold alcohol in addition to groceries and cigars. The newspapers suggest that blacks were arrested for liquor violations at no more than their numbers would warrant, although the jail records indicate a considerably higher rate of conviction. In 1889–1890, 10 of 126 people sentenced for illegal liquor selling were black; in 1899–1900, 27 of 104 people sentenced for this crime were black. During the mid-1890s, in fact, perhaps 4–5 percent of Philadelphia's speakeasies were black-owned and operated, or by this conservative estimate, around 120 or 150 places.[46]

The net profits to the Afro-American population from the sale of alcohol, not counting allied enterprises such as gambling or prostitution, could not then have been high. Many blacks patronized white saloons and speakeasies in addition to their own. Given the fact that blacks had no wholesalers, on the one hand, and that as a group they did not drink heavily, on the other, alcohol probably cost blacks less than it did some other nineteenth-century ethnic groups and also provided some of them with significant entrepreneurial experience. Neither of these economic benefits was as important as the social fact that virtually all of this experience was forced into illegal channels.

Gambling in the nineteenth century was for blacks a more important source of gains and losses than was drinking. A few men made a living as professionals in the money sports. Many more played with cards or dice for cash and recreation. Above all, playing policy was as important in black neighborhoods then as playing the numbers is now—a source of hope and jobs, an almost daily tax on income.

Most team sports, through the 1890s, were reserved for schoolboys, collegians, and amateur clubmen; only baseball was a workingman's game and a popular spectacle. Philadelphia's Phillies joined the National League in 1883, and the Athletics were only one of several other professional or semiprofessional teams that flourished for varying periods. But while black New Yorkers, thinly disguised as "Cuban" Giants, came down sometimes to play in or near the city, they had no counterparts in Philadelphia. Only the older individual sports, boxing and horse-racing, had room for black professionals.[47]

The post–Civil War years were the heyday of black involvement in thoroughbred flat racing. The best American horses were bred on plantations in western Kentucky and other areas of the once-slave South. Much of the work around tracks and stables was traditionally done by black men, and Isaac Murphy, the best jockey of his day, won a record three Derbies in the 1880s. He was rewarded with a piece of each purse and reputedly left some $125,000 at his death in 1895. The New York *Age* sounded a modern note with its concern over the fact that sixteen of the city's black jockeys in 1890 averaged somewhere between $2500 and $8000 a year, far more than most professionals could hope for.[48]

This kind of moral danger was less acute in Philadelphia, if only because the city and indeed the state had no flat track to race on. Point Breeze and Belmont were reserved for gentlemen and trotters; the modest course at Gloucester, New Jersey, offered the only opportunities nearby. But Gloucester boasted perils of its own in that era, as a favorite resort for Philadelphians of both races. A continuous ferry service linked the larger city to "the poor man's Cape May," down the river, and as many as 15,000 excursionists made the trip on summer Sundays. Attractions included bathing, boating, and a boardwalk; sandwiches, frankfurters, pig's feet, hot corn, and fish cakes. But above all else, the place was an escape from the Sabbatarian restrictions which, beginning in the 1880s, were increasingly enforced in Philadelphia and across the country. On Sunday the Athletics played ball in Gloucester, the boardwalk was lined with carnival games and roulette wheels, and the town itself boasted open gambling casinos. The city limits were a barrier to much state law, and everywhere on Sunday a thirsty customer could buy a glass or even a bucket of something labeled "nectar" or "ambrosia," which smelled like more familiar brews. The *Inquirer,* as part of its periodic campaigns against "Sin City of the Delaware," stressed the lurid atmosphere in the black-and-tan pavilions by the beach: "The white man had weaned the mulatto girl from her negro companion, and there was murder in his eye . . ." This was for the Sunday supplement; the sports page continued to relay the daily racing card and odds.[49]

But the sporting empire run by Billy Thompson, "the Duke of

Gloucester," was often under siege. In the fall of 1893 a local prizefight between two black Philadelphians helped the reformers' cause by creating a scandal, as J. B. Johnson killed "Skewbald" Charlie Burke. Gambling was the issue in the county elections two weeks later, and Thompson's men were badly defeated when the county sheriff's deputies beat the local police at the polls. The state assembly then closed down the racetrack, a move that coincided with the national campaign to bar Afro-Americans from riding thoroughbreds at major meets across the country. Murphy's successor, George Simms, left for England early in 1895; the less distinguished Philadelphians either scattered or lost work.[50]

It was little consolation to these men that, as racing closed down, the ring remained open. Professional boxing, though a growing business, was not only brutally dangerous but illegal almost everywhere, including Pennsylvania. The prohibition was more strictly enforced in the City of Brotherly Love than in most others. Mayor King in the early 1880s broke up a scheduled fight between Irish Mike Cleary and John L. Sullivan, and often fighters were forced to pose as amateurs to beat the law. The ruse fooled no one. When Joe Garragan killed nineteen-year-old Ed Sanford right before Christmas in 1900, it turned out that both men had been fighting under assumed names and that Sanford, as "Frank Barr," had been knocked unconscious only the week before. The taint of illegality, in any case, did little to hurt the sport or its heroes. In 1860, just four days after a local bout had been broken up, a crowd of youngsters mobbed a man who merely looked like the champion John C. Heenan. "Gentleman Jim" Corbett and Bob Fitzsimmons were subject to the same sort of adulation when they stopped in town some thirty-five years later.[51]

There was big money at the top, and in the early 1900s blacks like Jack Benjamin and Joe Butler would make Philadelphia one of the centers of the sport. But no one in their class, of any color, had developed through the 1890s. Butler had begun his career, but the black most often mentioned was Walter Edgerton, "de Kentucky Rosebud," a man of middling weight and ability, whose career probably reached its height with a loss in 1895 to Baltimore's great Joe Gans. The fact of mediocrity combined with illegality to keep Edgerton and most other Afro-Americans out of the money and generally out of the city.[52]

The threat of legal action limited advertising and thus the size of crowds. Many matches were fought in barns on the outskirts of places like Clearview or West Chester, for purses in the fifty-dollar range. In 1888 the police raided a barroom at Sixteenth and Passyunk to find two boxers, two seconds, four reporters, and just seven other onlookers. One of the principals was Fred Stewart, "Colored Middleweight Champion of Pennsylvania," who was fighting for whatever the spectators would donate.[53]

It was legally possible to break out of this format only by giving "free" exhibitions, sometimes in connection with the amateurs sponsored by the city's several athletic clubs. Nothing better underlined the hypocrisy of the law and the real economics of the business. The Colored Amateur Championship of Philadelphia, held at the Southwark Athletic Club in 1891, was fought before a crowd of roughly a thousand, "made up without respect of color, age, or previous condition of servitude." The *Inquirer* noted the presence of "sports from Gloucester with glossy silk hats and a profusion of jewelry, sports of the lower element with a handkerchief tied round their neck instead of a collar, colored sports from Lombard and Locust Streets, and sports of all sizes and descriptions." The amateurs flailed away for four rounds each, followed by come-on three-rounders by the professionals. Edgerton was on the card with several others, including Black Barney Boykin, "a bad man from Gloucester," who was evidently setting up the bettors. After showing "a marked unwillingness to fight" and generally disgracing himself, Boykin roared a challenge to anyone who would meet him the next week, across the river in Gloucester. "De Rosebud" jumped at the chance and into the ring—matchmaking was simpler in those days—and the bet is that Boykin had saved much more for the home folks than he had shown on the road.[54]

There were no census lines for illicit occupations, so it is hard to tell just how many black men earned a living with their fists. The papers blurred the line between amateurs and professionals, perhaps deliberately. The title "colored pugilist" was awarded as often in the news or crime column as in the sports page, and there is no knowing whether it was won in the ring, on the streets, or at the polls. At any given time during the 1890s two dozen or so may have fought at least occasionally for prizes.

All of them were in some sense gamblers, the allies or employees of gamblers both white and black. A number of the black sports at ringside effectively advertised their vocations with top hats, silver-headed canes, bright neckties, and patent leather shoes. Some worked out of political clubs or with other criminal types. Amos Scott, who fought on the same card with Edgerton and Boykin, was a minor politician, quondam saloonkeeper, embezzler, and later convicted burglar. Joe Butler himself, drafted into the Republican army, was in 1900 arrested three separate times for larceny, vote fraud, and illegal liquor sales. Like the better professional thieves, these men sometimes traveled between cities in search of new marks, and Gil Ball hosted "Four Kings" West and other New Yorkers at a Philadelphia Club dance.[55]

Few black men, however, set up regular books on horses, as part of a larger operation. They usually bet man-to-man, at ringside or the races, with others white and black. There was no color bar at some of the city's seldom-raided gambling houses or casinos. But professionals had no edge on each other, and truly wealthy white marks probably did not play with black men for big money. Poker was a popular game in black neighborhoods, and so was craps, but in the absence of outside money, the sums put up were often modest. In the summer of 1900 "Bright Eyes" Lucas, a professional from Washington, D.C., killed Forest Braxton outside Delmonico's in an argument over fifty cents.[56]

From an economic viewpoint, neither the sporting events nor the weekend crap games were nearly as important as the daily round of playing policy, what the *Christian Recorder* called "the favorite form of gambling among our people here." The game was organized much like its modern counterpart, the numbers. Dealers, generally small businessmen, employed agents or runners, working on commission, who canvassed specific beats and encouraged people to place small bets on the identity of a four-digit number or complex of numbers to be drawn at the end of the day. The runners recorded each bet on a slip, which was then relayed to the dealer, who paid off at odds far smaller than the actual 1000:1 that most bettors faced. The whole operation was ultimately backed by "bankers," men of capital, who took much of the profit in exchange for insuring the dealers against undue losses and, sometimes, against official harassment.[57]

Playing this game, in some form, was a business that stretched back well before the Civil War. For years the police paid little attention to a game played openly "on almost every street" downtown. Beginning in the late 1880s the new concern with immorality pushed the police into making several dozen arrests each year. But neither the rate of conviction nor the punishments meted out were enough to discourage the trade. Reformers by the end of the century were worried about the connection between gambling and politics, a concern sharpened by the fact that many public employees were allegedly in debt to the full-time runners who worked in City Hall. But the older, deeper complaint, one that made policy a more important target than, say, bookmaking, was the fact that the bets were so small that it was always the game of the urban poor, who could least afford the losses.[58]

Although policy was played all over the city, mostly by the whites who made up the majority of the population, it was always associated with blacks. The attractions were obvious. A daily bet—and by the 1890s the minimum was a single penny—meant that the player "always had something going." The appeal was emotional, the game an anodyne, as the mind could turn from dull routine and empty future to the always living chance that the day could bring a "hit." Everyone who played did win now and then. And the excitement of the windfall helped to hide the odds, the toll exacted by the tiny losses that dripped out every day.

Then, as now, the game was rich in the folklore of gigs and dream-books, guides to luck and fate. One major difference between the modern numbers and the policy played in the 1890s is that it was easier then for the backers to cheat. The crucial numbers were not published by a neutral source, as part of the daily treasury balance or some other recurring set of figures. The winning numbers, whether single or in complex combinations, were drawn by the spin of a wheel, and many backers drew their own. Given time between the day's last bets and the hour of the drawing, backers could avoid the numbers that had been heavily played and add to their already handsome odds. But while cheating brought profits, it could also bring trouble.[59]

Police protection was essential but fragile, good only if the game was running smoothly. Much like the enforcement of the liquor laws, it was part of a complex political process. Bankers and dealers were vulnerable to pressure from reformers or to factional shifts in power, and even Bob Hamilton, reputed policy king of the city, was jailed for eight months in 1894. Black men and women often testified against white runners. At times these witnesses were people who were in chronic trouble with the law and thus open to whatever the police asked them to do. At other times they were simply wives distressed when husbands stole to play the game or lost the money for the groceries. But for Ellen Johnson and many others, such testimony was an expression of anger, a way of fighting back. Johnson hit for $370 in June 1900, on a bet of just $1.07, and the dealer welshed. The criminal complaint in her case had much the effect of a civil suit: the target had either to settle up or to take his chances in court. William Smith, a black who entered the same kind of complaint, made clear that he would drop his prosecution in exchange for a "stake" from the man he had fingered. The effect of reform efforts that threatened the security of the game was to increase these hassles by frightening bankers into changing the rules, or the odds. In July 1900 there was a riot on Ninth Street when several black men protested the payoffs given out by "Four Dollar Charlie" Beach, who owed his ironic nickname to the size of his favored payoff.[60]

There are no accounts of black bankers in the city, only dealers and runners. Stories of cheating or welshing are then doubly significant. The practice meant that bettors lost money at a rate even greater than the odds would have it. And at least some black men and women did business directly with white runners rather than black ones.

The *Public Ledger* in 1900 put the number of policy shops in the city at more than 800. Each of these places employed a minimum of three people on average, including a tally clerk, back at the cigar store or barber shop, and at least two runners. In the 1870s maybe as many as 3000 Philadelphians made a living out of gambling of all sorts. This total mounted to about 4000 by the 1890s. Blacks were heavily overrepresented among those convicted for gambling, as for the illegal sale of liquor, accounting for seven of the 32 jailed during 1889–1891 and five of the 26 jailed during 1899–1901. At a conservative estimate, they furnished the same proportion of professional gamblers as they did of the whole city's population. Their number included several dozen boxers and jockeys, and in comparison with their white colleagues, relatively few of them worked as bookies and casino employees and relatively more worked as policy runners. The total was perhaps 200 to 250.[61]

These men, and a few women, could make up to several times a workingman's daily wages, not counting whatever some of them brought in through the sale of liquor or other trades. The business of gambling thus had the effect of building up the class of illegal entrepreneurs. But whatever their numbers, most of their profits were taken from the policy money that leaked steadily out of black neighborhoods. So long as black professionals worked for white bankers, the most important economic effect of gambling was to transfer money, every day, from black hands into white.

This was not true of the business of prostitution, however, which was economically more important in black neighborhoods than either illicit liquor sales or gambling. The significance of prostitution is shown by the fact that the very location of the city's brothels and streetwalkers was determined in part by the somewhat uncertain boundaries of Afro-American settlement. Uncertain boundaries ruled the business in other respects. The actual number of women involved, especially the number of Afro-American women, was obscured by the blurred lines between legitimate and illegitimate activity, and between black and white. Yet the oldest profession was one of the most profitable in all of black Philadelphia.

Its importance in the downtown wards was due to geography, the fact that in Philadelphia, as in many cities, the red-light district was partially located in the area of densest black settlement. One reason was political, in that while police and magistrates were not usually thought capable of eliminating vice, they could at least set bounds to it. And "Little Africa" was ideally suited in all respects. Many black Republican activists, or troop leaders, had an interest in the business, and the legitimate black elite was not strong or independent enough to protest effectively, to keep it out of their neighborhoods. Those neighborhoods were also ideal from the standpoint of urban ecology, with the port, the railroad terminals, and the major thoroughfares all near enough to make them convenient to transients. Most important, other places of amusement of all sorts were located in or close to black areas.[62]

Nighttime entertainment in the city often began at the theater, whose association with illicit sex was not entirely the product of overheated

Protestant imaginations. Quite apart from the private lives of actresses, or suggestive sights and dialogue on the stage itself, some of Philadelphia's theaters had been built with a special "third row" where professional prostitutes might parade their attractions. The major houses were also found downtown, a few blocks on either side of Market Street running from Broad Street to the east. After an early evening's amusement, a visitor strolling either north or south would shortly find himself in one of the two city neighborhoods most heavily settled with brothels, one largely white, the other black, but neither exclusively so.[63]

During the 1890s, before the advent of the movies, a great city offered a remarkably rich and varied nightlife, ranging from the serious to the salacious. During a single week in 1895, the Academy of Music offered three different Wagnerian productions and the Chestnut Street Opera House offered Beerbohm Tree in *An Enemy of the People* and five other plays. None of the attractions at Philadelphia's sixteen major theaters was scheduled to run for more than seven nights. Only three, in fact, were not changed daily, notably a special performance of *Uncle Tom's Cabin,* at the Strand, which featured a $3000 version of Eva's Golden Chariot and an appearance by the Hyer Sisters jointly playing Topsy while rendering "the duets which have made them famous." Most of these shows were comedies or melodramas; four were vaudeville or variety bills in which the dog acts were overshadowed by trapeze artists in tights or by a "chorus of pretty and shapely girls." At the Dime Museum at Ninth and Arch, visitors could catch the Hula Hula Girls, including Madji, the Beautiful Sandwich Island Queen, in her Hula Kau Kaulilua "Muscle Dance!"[64]

Afro-Americans were engaged in this kind of show business in many ways. Sometimes, instead of impersonating tropical dancers, they were themselves impersonated. Blackface minstrelsy was already past its peak, but the Cairncross Opera House still featured a resident troupe which put on new shows every night. Several of the variety acts, too, featured dialect humor and songs, and an imaginative version of the Old South was a popular setting for melodrama, occasionally providing employment for black actors rather than white ones in burnt cork. Nat Salsbury's enormous production of *Black America* also came to town in August for an unusual three-week run. The show provided some three hundred jobs for its all-black cast and traveled in nine railroad cars. It opened with a grand parade downtown, to the accompaniment of Ascher's Military Band and a detachment of the Ninth Cavalry.[65]

Philadelphia's black men and women went to these shows—Ball was once arrested in a fracas outside of *The Planter's Wife* at the Haverly— but there were not enough of them to support a genuinely black theater on a regular basis. Church groups in the 1880s sponsored a number of one-night Star Concerts at the Academy of Music, featuring touring artists of all kinds. The Afro-American Amusement Company was a mixed affair, which included some of the same performers as the Star Concerts together with others who belonged in the minstrel tradition: the singer Bessie Lee and R. Henri Strange, "The Black Booth," had to share the stage with "The Whistling Coons," and the ticketholders were later invited to join in a pie-eating contest and cakewalk.[66]

The audience participation was fully appropriate, for cakewalking, as done by the more graceful black performers, was in part a spectator sport, and the city's several dancing academies advertised contests and balls in the same amusement pages which advertised the theater. The entertainment district, too, boasted many halls which rented out for dances, black and white. On March 20 the "George W. Roop Association" gave its so-called "Annual Ball" at the Musical Fund Hall on Eleventh and Locust, near the heart of the Seventh Ward. George Roop and his brother Harry were both bailbondsmen and "fixers"; Harry also ran a well-known saloon farther north, and later that year George was involved in an elaborate shakedown and bribery scheme involving a madam on Schell Street. The ball was accordingly a raffish affair. The *Inquirer* was there, in a patronizing mood, to cover the customs of the Tenderloin. Neither the men nor in some cases the women were willing to surrender their cigars while waltzing, and small groups sometimes lifted their skirts and broke into the houla-houla and the can-can. The event was normally policed by six police in uniform, but this time the superintendent pulled back the protection, a move that allegedly cost six men their watches and the barkeep some $30 in change.[67]

Roop's guests, like those at many downtown dances, were racially mixed, or drawn from "all strata of the lower shade." Throughout the period whites went to basically black affairs at least as onlookers. Events such as the Coachman's Ball had once been exclusive, by invitation only, but standards began to slip in the late 1880s. Many black groups organized dances simply to raise funds, with tickets available to all, and large numbers gathered to see who would "take the cake" in the contest finale. The Colored Janitors Ball, held the week after George Roop's, was such an occasion, with music provided by F. J. R. Jones and his band. The *Inquirer* was at pains to note that there was little drunkenness and no fighting and that the attendants went home by two in the morning. The crowd was not so quiet the same night at Heyser's Hall, where "two rival colored organizations clashed" and sent several to the hospital.[68]

Whatever the character of the group inside, there were in these neighborhoods always streetwalkers on the outside, and brothels no more than a few blocks away. The bigger of the city's two centers of prostitution began along Arch Street, north of Market, encompassed the gambling and opium dens of Chinatown on Race Street, and stretched as far up as Spring Garden, especially along Ninth, Tenth, and to a lesser extent Eleventh Streets. The parlor houses, massage parlors, dance halls, and hotels of this district were largely white. South of the business center, generally closer to the river, was another and poorer class of places, especially along Front Street, Bainbridge east of Fourth, and in the densely tangled black and immigrant slums which wound in and out of Bay, Barclay, and Hurst Streets and Soap-Fat, Currant, and Middle Alleys. Both districts were racially mixed, although in different proportions.[69]

The profession of prostitution probably reached its peak numerically between 1850 and 1900. The figure given for New York City in 1900 was 30,000 women out of a population of some 1,800,000. If reduced by the appropriate ratio, this number would suggest more than 18,000 professionals for Philadelphia, which had over a million inhabitants by the middle of the decade. But such an estimate seems high, even considering the sexual imbalance among several immigrant groups and the continual traffic of sailors, salesmen, and other transient males who greatly multiplied the number of potential customers in any seaboard city.[70]

A closer estimate of the city's brothels emerged from a series of hearings into municipal corruption in 1895–1896. The investigation stemmed from State Senator Boies Penrose's withdrawal of his name for the Republican nomination for mayor of the city, apparently under threat of publication of a photograph showing him leaving a famous bawdy house at dawn. His replacement was City Solicitor Charlie Warwick, an opponent of the Penrose-Durham-Quay alliance which, with black support, had been the dominant faction in the party. Soon afterward Penrose, as leader of the Senate, ordered the hearings into Warwick's management of the city. This was only a year after New York's Lexow Committee had given the nation a close look at life in Manhattan's West Side Tenderloin, and after a short time spent on paving contracts, the Pennsylvanians rediscovered the elemental fact that illicit sex and politics sell papers.[71]

Counsel Silas Petit brought a line of ex-policemen, madams, doorkeepers, and streetwalkers before the committee to underline the link between police and prostitution. The outlines of their testimony were familiar enough. Streetwalkers were held up irregularly for $1 to $1.50, sometimes for tickets to police excursions. Modest parlor houses paid $25 a week. Several women complained that the police would not stay bought, that after paying for protection they did not get it. The safest places were presumably those in which policemen themselves had an interest. Two of the city's black officers, for example, owned a piece of one bawdy house on Lemon Street.[72]

Detective Eugene Lyons gave information on the number of houses in thirteen police districts, or half of the city. By far the largest number, some 280 places, were located in the Eighth Police District, which ran east from Broad to Sixth Street and north of Vine to Poplar. The Sixth District just to the south, which covered the business and entertainment center from Vine south to Chestnut, housed 150 more bawdy houses. From there the numbers fell off sharply, though the houses were well scattered through the city: 40 each for the Second, Third, and Seventh Districts; 25 in the Tenth; 20 in the Ninth; 15 in the Twelfth and Twenty-eighth; 12 in the Eleventh; 10 in the Fourth; 8 in the First; and 6 in the Eighteenth, for a total of 626 brothels in the districts singled out by Lyons. But the political complexion of the investigation was revealed in the fact that it omitted the other half of the city's police districts, roughly that half whose leaders were loyal to Senator Penrose. Most of the Seventh Ward was left off entirely. When an estimate for the fifteen missing districts, many in the roughest parts of town, is added to Lyons's count, the total comes to about 1000 houses. And 1000 was the number independently compiled in the same year by the Reverend Frank Good-child, a social reformer who had studied prostitution in the city for some time. The minister was careful both to count houses block-to-block in some districts and to discount higher estimates.[73]

Various numbers of "inmates" lived and worked in each of these houses. In the bigger places, those that attracted police raids, eight to twelve or more women usually worked, but Goodchild put the average at five. This meant that 5000 women worked in houses. But a large number of other women worked in other settings, ranging from kept mistresses at one end of the social scale to streetwalkers at the other, many of whom rented their bodies only part-time as a supplement to other or occasional employment. On the usual assumption that those outside brothels represented roughly half of the prostitutes in the city, the total number for Philadelphia in the mid-1890s was close to 10,000.[74]

The role of black women in this traffic has been obscured for two related reasons. The popular mythology of prostitution in this era was shaped in part by the *Police Gazette,* with its prurient images of demi-mondaines in striped tights. That mythology owes still more to those earnest late Victorians who sought to draw a straight and terrible line between female innocence and ruin. Both visions played on real emotions in the people they addressed. But they worked on the imaginations of white audiences only when the principals were also white.

The prostitute as victim required a seducer; as temptress, a target. Thus, the business provided four roles that either men or women could view with some mixture of fear and anger, empathy and jealousy. All of these feelings depended, for maximum effect, on sexual attractiveness. Given the conventional prejudice against blackness, the woman must be, if not white and middle-class, then as close to white and middle-class as possible. It is no accident that the adjective *octaroon* was almost never applied to men, or indeed to women in any context but the sexual. *Uncle Tom's Cabin* was still a favorite on the bookshelves as well as on the boards, and Harriet Beecher Stowe knew precisely how to manipulate the emotions of her readers. The awful peril awaiting Emmeline at the slave auction was clearly heightened by reference to her "fairer complexion" and her "white, delicate hands."[75]

The notion of virginity at peril rested on a concept of innocence that whites were unlikely to grant black women. In the real world women were in fact sometimes "procured," by deceit or even force, to work in brothels. Many of these were recruited to the city by the offer of servants' jobs in private establishments, only to find, on the scene, that the "house" was not a home as promised. Rural blacks were especially vulnerable to this kind of betrayal, but they did not figure heavily in the literature of "white slavery."

Mythology aside, then, Afro-American women were heavily involved in prostitution. The effort to find out how many is helped by the fact that illicit sex of all kinds left tracks on the record, no matter how indirect.

The justice system is an obvious source but not a good one. The men who ran it were too worldly to be outraged at the mere existence of prostitution, and left alone, they might even have legalized it. The police in particular often came from the same classes as these working women and had little trouble with them. Policemen did harass prostitutes sometimes, usually over money; Stephen Crane's *Maggie* is drawn from life. But the police were also patrons, even partners, and nothing annoyed reformers more than the sight of uniformed men on hot afternoons leaning sociably into the windows of parlor houses or chatting with streetwalkers on the steps of the station house. To the extent that their efforts were directed from above, by higher government or political authority, they aimed not to eliminate "the social evil" but to contain it in certain localities. The Fifth and Seventh Wards were clearly among these. Carl Bolivar complained about the way in which the authorities had worked to clean up the southern and eastern borders of the silk-stocking Eighth Ward by sweeping its madams and gamblers back into his own, the largely black Seventh. By century's end the dominant Republican faction not only condoned but actively worked to protect at least some of this activity in black neighborhoods. Brothels were precisely the kinds of places, with many bedrooms, from which it was possible to register improbable numbers of party voters. And during the reform campaign of 1900 J. R. K. Scott, the most notorious of machine lawyers, served as counsel not only in vote fraud cases but, rather unusually, in cases of prostitution.[76]

The decentralized nature of the justice system did not allow Scott or anyone else to protect a large number of streetwalkers from successful prosecution. Prostitution was a summary offense handled by the police magistrates. No records were kept, and most of the accused had no counsel of any kind. They submitted to small fines and perhaps six weeks in the House of Correction as episodic costs of doing business. Legal action, as with liquor violations, was often initiated by people outside of the formal agencies of law enforcement. Organized reformers pushed for periodic raids, and sometimes neighborhood complaints were too loud to resist. The Society for the Protection of Children from Cruelty often acted to rescue runaways from brothels, and policemen in these cases sometimes shared their indignation. But the fact that nine of the 15 people jailed for maintaining bawdy houses during 1889–1901 were black, and 21 of the 36 jailed during 1899–1901, is no better guide to the racial composition of these brothels than to their number. The criminal records do provide clues to the number of Afro-American prostitutes, but they are indirect, measures not so much of the business itself as its byproducts, or the situations that typically led to it.[77]

As other means of birth control were at best uncertain during the nineteenth century, the abortion rate was by later standards high. Through the middle of the century it was neither illegal nor unrespectable to end a pregnancy before "quickening," or about six months along. But physicians, inspired by a better understanding of the process of conception, demanded changes in state law. Their campaign was successful, and by 1860 abortion at any stage was made illegal almost everywhere. As the better doctors stopped performing operations and fewer married women asked, the numbers dropped off markedly. At the same time, in Philadelphia the number of criminal prosecutions rose, to reach a peak in the 1880s.[78]

Because information about these cases is scarce, it is hard to tell how many blacks were involved. The court summaries normally gave no information at all about the aborted women themselves, except for occasions when death or near-death resulted. Of the twenty deaths between 1860 and 1900, eight of the victims were black.[79]

For many black women, especially those without friends or connections, abortion was financially out of the question. Reliable operations could cost from $100 on up. Many desperate women had no choice but to bring unwanted pregnancies to term. A few chose then to take the final step of killing their infants at birth or shortly after. Infanticide was always a crime, and some of those who committed it were brought to trial. But while these cases gave the state an opportunity to reaffirm, through ritual, its interest in the sanctity of life, they were an embarrassment in practice.[80]

The problems emerged clearly in the case of Lizzie Aarons, locally something of a cause célèbre when tried in May 1881. Aarons had been arrested in the attic room of a lodging house in January of that year, shortly after having come to town, alone and pregnant. Much thrashing and moaning were heard from the room on the night she took it, including the unmistakable cry of a new-born infant. Lizzie, next morning, was still alone, but a tiny body was discovered in the courtyard below. Some months later she was put on trial.[81]

Aarons's canny court-appointed defense lawyer did no more than describe the several days proceding the fatal night. Lizzie Fleck, herself a modest widow with two children, had found the pregnant woman walking ragged, nearly barefoot, without stockings in the snow. Three times she had taken her into the kitchen and, lacking room to put her up, had given her enough for lodging through the night. Ida McMun, the last two days, had taken Aarons on a tour of the city's social agencies. Toland's Home Mission wanted $1 for a ticket back to New York. The almshouse directed her to a magistrate for a warrant. The Lying-In Hospital on Cherry Street wanted a marriage certificate and $5 in advance. The secretaries at the Y.W.C.A. sent them from branch to branch before one young Christian woman told Aarons that she could not be helped "on account of her condition." The district attorney at that point abandoned the case and "spoke feelingly about the way the defendant had been treated." The judge was equally moved. The jury acquitted Aarons without leaving the box, and the spectators took up a collection.

The case inspired charitable citizens to organize a special home for foundlings, but no one in that era had any solution for the problems of unwed mothers. The justice system had the grace to let them be when possible. Coroner's juries found ways to excuse or mislabel infanticide when they found it; juries rarely convicted; judges often suspended sentence. The shame and guilt that enveloped these cases were compounded by the fact that only the most luckless or distracted women were ever brought in, the ones whose babies, battered, strangled, or drowned in the communal privy, had been killed without any attempt at concealment. Of the 41 cases that reached the trial stage in this period, at least 12 of the accused were black.[82]

One reason that the men who ran the system were so reluctant to punish infanticide is that they knew the official cases were only a small fraction of the number which really occurred. Thousands of babies died in Philadelphia every year, many of mysterious or ill-defined causes, such as "inanition" or "suffocation," perhaps "overlaid," allegedly, by exhausted or drunken mothers who had slept with them in bed. One indication of the extent of the guilty deaths is the number of "unknown" infants found dead each year in the city's streets, lots, and cesspools. They were counted not through the justice system but by the health department, under terms of the registration act passed in 1861. There was no legal or even medical reason to note the race and sex of these small bodies, even when it was possible, and in later years these matters were recorded only erratically, if at all. But during the last four years of the 1860s, when the registration act was still new and the number of dead infants reached its height proportionally, some 140 black bodies were counted and 343 white ones.[83]

Many of these small unknowns were dumped out, the police believed, by women who ran baby farms. These places were the private answer to the problem faced by a mother with a child she could not raise herself. Philadelphia had few institutions equipped to bring up foundlings; no one had yet developed an adequate substitute for human milk, and without wet-nursing, virtually all abandoned newborns died in infancy. The almshouse demanded stringent tests, and for those under one year old its death rate was close to 100 percent. Baby farms were thus places where a mother could buy some minimal care, a diet of bacterial cow's milk and sugar water, for the weeks or months a child would normally survive. The usual fee, or "guilt money," was $2 to $3 each week, which was well beyond the means of most poor or even working-class women, except for prostitutes. Of seven accounts of baby farms, all were racially segregated: three black ones, four white.[84]

Perhaps even more than pregnancy, many women endured disease as a kind of occupational risk. There was even less information about treatment for venereal disease than there was about birth control, and syphilis was an important killer still. Its incidence provided another indirect measure of the relative extent of prostitution among the races. In the 1890s some 82 blacks and 325 whites, most of them infants, were recorded dead from syphilitic infection in the city.[85]

The only direct count that gives the ratio of black to white prostitutes was taken by the Philadelphia Vice Commission during 1912–1913. The Vice Commission, one of dozens set up during the Progressive era, sampled the race and nativity of 861 professional prostitutes, 214 of whom, or just under a quarter, were black. The relatively greater number of black women in the city in 1912–1913 than in, say, 1895—close to 6 percent of the total as compared to less than 5 percent—tended to cancel out the canvassing of the better houses of the northern white districts than of the shabbier black neighborhoods by agents of the Vice Commission. On the whole, therefore, the proportion of blacks to whites was roughly the same for both periods. Black prostitutes represented a fifth to a quarter of all those in the city, based on a conservative estimate that blacks, averaging 4 percent of the city's population, accounted over a considerable period for 40 percent of its known deaths from abortion, 29 percent of its prosecutions for infanticide, 25 percent of its unknown infants found dead, 20 percent of its official deaths from syphilis, and 43 percent of its known baby farms. A fifth to a quarter of the prostitute population represented about 2000 or 2500 women, a figure with important implications both socially and economically.[86]

These women were not necessarily hopeless or pitiable figures. Only a small fraction of them were physically forced into the life. The rest were there by choice, and even if it proved unhappy or even tragic, it was at least a choice, an effort to assert control. In a world in which women's bodies and their labor were exploited in many other ways the decision to rent themselves to strangers seemed at least economically a rational one.[87]

This perspective fit black women better than most. Domestic service was the only real alternative, a life notoriously subject to the whim of others, to sexual harassment and the loss of dignity. Blacks more than others strained against the restrictions imposed, insisting on nights off, for example, and the right to live their private lives as they saw fit. If prostitution was not fully freedom, it offered more than day work, and at several times the income.[88]

The price for many was social stigma, the loss of family and of contact with the wider or straight world. But Philadelphia's Afro-American prostitutes were part of a large subgroup, a population that included a number who held different jobs in the same neighborhoods or houses. It was traditional in much of the country to hire blacks exclusively to work as maids and other employees in parlor houses, and the better ones generated loads of laundry. Philadelphia's fancier houses, such as Lottie Stanton's place, made work for piano players and doorkeepers or bouncers, as well as cooks and maids. All of the scattered references to these employees, in murder trials or other investigations, were to black men or women.[89]

Unlike middle-class whites, farm girls, or immigrants' daughters far from home, these people worked in familiar neighborhoods. Many worked only part-time, as streetwalkers, when the need arose. Some, like Mary Dorsey, were parents, or married, and in most respects lived lives much like others in the straight economy.

Many of them either hired, worked for, or worked with white women, also. Blacks and imigrants lived next to each other throughout the Fourth, Fifth, and Seventh Wards, and many brothels housed inmates of both races, people whose common trade and problems must have pulled them close together. One of the rare accounts that hints at this life followed the death of Mary Ray, or Wray, in January 1895. Ray was a middle-aged white who had once had a place of her own. She was brought to the hospital on a Saturday night, suffering from a knife wound to the stomach. When she died next morning, the police, in default of other suspects, arrested everyone found living at 627 Middle Alley, her last address. An investigation found that she had been stabbed elsewhere and stumbled home, where four blacks, Theodore and Rachel Scott, Kate Johnson, and Katie Green, had worked to save her life and then carried her to the hospital.[90]

From an economic point of view, black prostitutes regarded white colleagues as less important than white patrons. Men of all races visited prostitutes, but the number of adult black males—well under 20,000 in 1895—was not big enough to provide more than a fraction of the custom. Philadelphia's black population was also unusual in that adult women outnumbered men, a balance which suggests that the need for commercial sex was felt less strongly among them than among Italians, Jews, and the other southern and eastern European groups in which the ratio ran heavily in the other direction. Most male transients, such as sailors, salesmen, and other proverbially heavy customers, were also typically white.

Racial etiquette demanded, in theory, that whatever the color of its inmates, a given house should cater to either black men or white but not to both. But streetwalkers were not, or could not, be covered by this rule, and no sailor could have been naive enough to imagine that he was getting racially exclusive services in the houses lining Soap Fat Alley. Even some of the better places found ways to beat the system. Complaints from the neighbors in trial testimony indicate that "Better Days" Stewart, who ran a house on Lemon Street off North Tenth, entertained black callers during long and sociable afternoons, then whites, alone, at night.[91]

The income from these visits was by contemporary standards enormous. The estimated price of a single "trick" in that era began at fifty cents and ran up to several dollars. As the Philadelphia Vice Commission later put it, the common use of "unnatural means," or oral sex, "accounts in some degree for the extraordinary number of men received by one woman in a given time." With domestic service at just $2 to $4 a week, there was no mystery to the attractions of prostitution. The cheapest of streetwalkers could earn several times that sum, or much more than a workingman steadily employed. At a place like Stewart's, after giving up half her income to the madam, a black woman could easily clear more than $25 a week, or perhaps $1000 a year, a sum that placed her in the highest of black income brackets.[92]

The money from prostitution was enormously important to the black population. Unlike petty free-lance theft, it was part of a genuine business which had some status in the eyes, if not of the law, then of certain agents of the law. While gambling and illegal liquor sales enjoyed some of the same protection and were important for the entrepreneurs involved, neither—in the absence of prostitution—was a significant way of transferring money from whites to blacks. The business of keeping a brothel, or even streetwalking, was central to a number of other activities as well. A full accounting of its economics must include not only direct payment for sexual services but the wages given musicians, maids, and bouncers, the business brought into neighborhood speakeasies, and the cash obtained from robbing marks. The gain was at least enough to cut sharply into the overall losses from drinking and especially gambling. Probably in fact it was enough to overbalance these completely, so that the black population made a net profit out of illegal activity of all kinds. But whatever the year-end accounting in cash, the long-term costs are best measured on other scales entirely.

· 5 ·
THE PRICE OF CRIME

PHILADELPHIA'S Afro-American murder rate was far higher than its over-all murder rate in the late nineteenth century. The black rate, as meas-ured by the number of men and women actually tried for homicide, climbed unevenly from 6.4 per 100,000 residents annually during the 1860s to 11.4 during the 1890s. Many of these killings resulted directly from involvement in criminal activity, such as theft and vice, and some resulted from an increasing resort to handguns to settle disputes. All three phenomena—crime, gun use, and homicide itself—were in turn related not only to each other but to the systematic exclusion of the black population from the opportunities opened up by the urban in-dustrial revolution.[1]

The effect of this exclusion was twofold. It contributed to high levels of criminal activity among the ambitious and the desperate both. And it deprived Afro-Americans of the security and the sociopsychological changes that were working to reduce the incidence of violence in the dominant population. Although the urban experience had a generally settling effect on European immigrants, it had a corrosive and unsettling effect on blacks. The full significance of the Afro-American murder rate was not simply that it was high, and rising, but that it was rising just as the white rate was falling. The citywide murder rate, having peaked at 3.6 per 100,000 just before the Civil War, fell to just 2.1 in the 1890s.[2]

PATTERNS OF VIOLENCE

The murder rate is the only trustworthy measure of the comparative incidence of violence. Differences among the official statistics on rape, for example, may record not a different incidence of the crime itself but a changing level of faith in the justice system. Assault, which shares with rape the need for a cooperative complainant, best measures not behavior but the social sensitivity to behavior, as a Saturday night's brawl may be a form of popular entertainment in one neighborhood and a matter for prosecution in another. Homicide, in contrast, was a crime taken seriously by the authorities all across Philadelphia. And murder or manslaughter was an index to other forms of aggression, the visible tip of a much larger pyramid of assaultive behavior, the result of the one quarrel out of thousands that got fatally out of hand. Its accuracy as an index can be measured by comparing black and white murder rates with the record of hospital admissions for fighting. Between April and September 1880, for example, 36 of the 210 people reportedly brought in as victims of interpersonal violence were black, precisely five times the figure expected on the basis of population and very close to the black-white disparity in homicides. That disparity is hard to measure precisely, since blacks can be identified only in the 90 percent of murder indictments that actually came to trial. But however calculated, the murder rates of both groups revealed significant racial differences in behavior, specifically in the roles played by women, by male gangs, and by deadly weapons.[3]

Except for the special and hard-to-measure crime of infanticide, women in the nineteenth century were, as always, less likely to kill people than men were. But the gap was much smaller among blacks than whites, as a result of the generally more active role of black women. Fewer blacks than whites stayed home, away from the paid work force, as housewives and mothers; far more, proportionally, were out in the streets, at work, or doing criminally dangerous things. The relative lack of sexual segregation in black social life meant that women were more likely to be there, and active, when men got to fighting. Victorian white women were overwhelmingly victims rather than killers, murdered by stronger or better-armed males by a ratio of more than two to one, while black women, in contrast, were nearly as likely to kill as to be killed.[4]

Street brawls among men accounted for many of the homicides, especially at mid-century. Young white men roamed the streets in small gangs, or packs, stopping often to drink and sometimes to attack other groups or even lone outsiders. Black men did not carouse so often in this way, partly because bar-hopping was less a part of their culture, and partly because there was no substantial area that they could call home turf, and a group of traveling roisterers might prove dangerously provocative. The difference in the resulting murders was considerable. Over one-quarter of all killings by white males between 1860 and 1901 involved multiple defendants, with two, four, and sometimes eight men accused of stomping or otherwise killing a single victim in a sidestreet or saloon. Black men, like women of both races, were typically indicted as individuals, and less than 10 percent of murders by blacks involved more than one attacker.

But the most important difference, in terms of its effect on murder rates and its impact on the culture, was the greater proportion of black men who killed with weapons. Over the postwar period 58 percent of blacks indicted for murder had used a weapon, as compared to 43 percent of whites. The pattern was explicable in terms of two phenomena: racial fears and, increasingly, criminal activity.

Racial fears contributed to a felt need for protection from white attack. Black men were often targets of gang aggression in strange neighborhoods, and through the election riots of 1871 there was some danger of being hunted down in their own. Uncertainty always ruled. In Philadelphia or any other city an encounter might suddenly turn ugly, and it was thought best to go forearmed.

The need for protection never fully disappeared, and as late as the 1890s George Queen, Frank Monroe, and Scott Irwin were all tried, and acquitted, for killing members of small white gangs who had assaulted them. All of these gangs were composed of men with Italian names, just as earlier in the century most of those who attacked black men were Irish. But the important difference was one of scale; the assaults of the 1890s remained isolated incidents, not comparable to those forty or fifty years earlier, in the heyday of race rioting, when Robert Purvis had had to stay awake all night, in his own home, with a rifle across his knees. In terms of purely racial fears, Afro-Americans late in the century had less reason to carry weapons than they had earlier. And yet, even as the wider city grew steadily less violent, the use of handguns, especially, continued to increase within the black population. During 1860–1880 only 24 percent of black males tried were accused of killing with guns, a proportion that increased by half, to 37 percent, during 1881–1901.[5]

Some of this increase was a byproduct of widespread illegal activity. The word *byproduct* is important, as most black theft was essentially nonviolent, and armed robbery was an extraordinary event. But theft and, more important, commercial vice were activities often conducted in an atmosphere charged with the possibility of assault and even sudden death.

Some of the association between illegal enterprise and violent behavior was a result simply of the fact of illegality itself. Secrecy and corruption made any tensions tighter than they needed to be. The fact that business disputes could not be taken to civil court meant often that they were settled by force, directly. But no matter what the law, much of the increase resulted from the very nature of the activities themselves.

The word *vicious,* after all, is simply the adjective form of the noun *vice.*

Drinking in our society has always been associated with impulsively reckless behavior, the release of those inhibitions that protect us from thoughtless aggression. It is possible to gamble in relatively dispassionate ways, by playing games such as policy or the numbers where the players are not pitted directly against each other but against an impersonal luck, or fate—barring the shenanigans of a "Four-Dollar Charlie" Beach. But most games are not so impersonal. And the classic ones, like poker, craps, or faro, cannot be played at all without betting for stakes, without hopes suddenly raised and then blasted by a flesh-and-blood opponent just a reach or slash away. The sale of sex, too, even between consenting adults, is not always a victimless crime. The business is often risky, quite apart from the threat of robbery or of arguments over prices quoted beforehand and satisfactions received afterward. Men go to prostitutes to fill needs more than physical, and the actual experience may lead to jealousy, deflation, or sudden shame. Any streetwise woman, accustomed to meeting alone with sometimes big or boisterous strangers, had best be well prepared to deal with trouble. Consider, as example, four episodes in the career of Hattie Stewart, or Harris, later known as "Better Days."[6]

The first episode occurred in July 1895, when Stewart was arrested for shooting four times at Mary Jackson, a housemate at No. 2 Smith's Court. Jackson never showed up at the hearing, and there was talk that she had been spirited away. It seems that Stewart had friends on the police force, for when Viola Jackson was jailed for running a brothel at 1024 Lemon Street, the way was cleared for Stewart to take over the premises. The next truly memorable date in her short life was the following October 14, when William Green stopped by the new place about noontime. Green was a black chiropodist and, incidentally, an agent for the State Liquor League, but his visit was not professional. He had once been a "special friend" of the mistress of the house but had lately fallen out of favor, and he had come to make clear that he was not going to take the demotion lightly. Over a period of some hours and several drinks, he took at least two shots at her before she and the other women were able to calm him down. By the time that Joe Robinson and Ivan Brooks arrived later in the afternoon, Green was able to sit down sociably enough, even to take a little teasing about being a stool pigeon for the Liquor League. But he would not stand for a direct challenge. Brooks crossed the line when he told Green, "You've been shooting at these women all day—you've got a pistol but you can't bluff me!" In the ensuing gunfire Brooks was killed instantly, and Robinson was winged.

In 1898, after a brief stay in the House of Correction, Stewart emerged angry enough to put another former lover, Charles Harris, into Jefferson Hospital with five slash wounds to the head and face. Two years later, at thirty-one and now known as "Better Days," she was murdered herself in the small hours of Friday, March 2, when Eva Dillon hit her in the head with a lighted lamp, setting her afire. Dillon later claimed that she had acted out of self-defense, in an argument sparked by Stewart's insistence on hiding her clothes and holding her in something like slavery. Stewart's own dying declaration was that she had stopped Dillon from rolling a white customer, an act that would have compromised the reputation of the house.

An even more compelling example of the atmosphere surrounding illegal enterprise, which this time included prostitution, bootlegging, and gambling, occurred on four consecutive nights in the lives of George St. Clair and his friend George Weeks. St. Clair was the quintessential late-century badman, a native of Washington who had moved to Ballinger's Court in Philadelphia's Tenth Ward. Convicted once of felonious assault in 1892, he still carried scars inflicted by "Too-Much" Johnson, souvenirs of what was reportedly his only losing fight. His business was gambling, and he went about it habitually with a two-gun holster strapped beneath his coat. On weekends and holidays he laid in some liquor, too, to sell to the marks in the crap games he held in his home. In December 1898 his running feud with the two prostitutes next door took a turn for the worse when they discovered that he was afraid of ghosts.[7] As Alice White and Lucy Johnson pressed their advantage by making his nights miserable with rattles, tincans, and catcalls down the chimney, St. Clair called in his friend George Weeks to sleep with him for company. One night, as Christmas approached, the two returned from a game to find that someone had stolen their beer. They suspected the women next door, and decided to settle scores simply by killing them.

St. Clair, at his trial for murder, described a scene in which he and Weeks had gone over to Mrs. White and Mrs. Johnson's place, knocked, complained, and been set upon by several men, white and black, who were visiting there. He and Weeks had fired blindly, only in self-defense, before retreating. St. Clair was wounded, and to the best of his knowledge Charlie Moore, one of Mrs. White's guests, was the only other person hit by a bullet. Several witnesses agreed that something roughly like that had happened—but on Christmas Eve, the night before the fatal shooting, which had occurred on the holiday itself. Since Mrs. Johnson was not killed and Mrs. White survived long enough to make a deposition, both were able to testify that St. Clair and Weeks had shot down their door on Christmas night, shot them in the head, and fled the apartment through a window in the back.

On the night following the murder, St. Clair, apparently unconcerned, was picked up at a ball at Seventh and Lombard, as he went about his usual rounds wearing his usual weapons. George Weeks stayed equally cool. He went on courting Nancy Lincoln, asking her out for a walk along Emeline Street, where as the *Inquirer* put it, "he made a proposition in which she did not concur." He showed his annoyance by taking a shot at her. Lincoln, equally annoyed, called a policeman who made the arrest. They discovered at the station house he was wanted on a graver charge.

Casual killers such as Weeks and St. Clair were not typical, but they did belong to a much wider criminal subculture whose need for weapons had an effect that reached far beyond its own membership. The fact that the city's blacks and its vice were concentrated in the same neighborhoods posed dangerous problems for everyone who lived in those areas, as excited, nervous, or angry young men of both races roamed their streets and alleys, often unable to tell respectable residents from others. As the handguns introduced in the 1850s grew steadily more available and cheaper—by the 1880s the price of a revolver had dropped to about two dollars, or two days' pay—it was inevitable that many blacks would manage somehow to get hold of them, with equally inevitable consequences for the murder rate.[8]

Other things being equal, the presence of knives or razors reduces the odds that a given quarrel will turn fatal, and a revolver reduces them further still, making murder a matter of an instant's flash of anger, a few pounds of pull on the trigger. It is true that the two-dollar pistol of the 1880s was by no means a routinely deadly weapon, and an astonishing number of people were up and around shortly after being shot. The underpowered bullets of that day were deflected by ribs, brow, and even cheekbones. In the St. Clair–Weeks affair, for example, the two women were both shot between the eyes, at close range. Mrs. Johnson's bullet was deflected into her palate and surgically removed without trouble, while Mrs. White lived on for nearly two more weeks. But however weak by modern standards, these nineteenth century handguns were more dangerous than knives, and as more men carried them, the effect was to increase the number of truly reckless and thoughtless killings. When a roistering black man, for example, spotted an old acquaintance during a celebration and yelled, "There's Brown—I'll shoot off the crown of his hat!" his boast proved fatally inaccurate by inches.[9]

The climbing rate of homicide was thus explained not simply by the spread of the gun culture but even more simply by the spread of the guns themselves. Both contributed to the problem. Yet neither the subcultural nor the purely material or technological reasons account in full for the fact that black and white murder rates were moving in opposite directions at the same time.

THE EFFECT OF EXCLUSION

Although cheaper handguns were available to all, white Philadelphians were increasingly less inclined to use them. This fact suggests that guns were not, by themselves, a sufficient explanation for the rising murder rates among blacks. Moreover, criminal violence was declining generally, not only among most Philadelphians but among the citizens of Massachusetts, London, Stockholm, Sidney, and virtually every other place where the phenomenon has been studied. The widespread nature of this drop in criminally aggressive behavior suggests the enormous power of the social and economic changes that had made it happen. Conversely, it suggests the enormous impact of exclusion from these changes, of the fact that the American black population in the late nineteenth century was uniquely cut off from the experience of the urban industrial revolution. The new economic order brought not only a new level of social order and economic prosperity to the city but also changes in behavior among those who participated directly in it. Thus, the exclusion of blacks meant not only that they failed to become full beneficiaries of the public order and rising real wages which marked the post–Civil War years but also that they did not share in the process which imposed a new social psychology, and thus lower crime rates, on other groups, such as Irish immigrants.

In terms of social problems in general and crime rates in particular, the Irish were the archetypical white ethnic group of the nineteenth century. No immigrants had a more difficult time than those who fled the famines of the "hungry 'forties." No city, until the full onset of industrialism, had jobs enough to absorb the waves of peasants who invaded them over the next several decades. All of the institutions of charity, sanitation, and education were strained by the effort to cope with Irish misery and desperation. So especially were the police. The problem of law and order, as seen by local authorities in many northeastern cities, was specifically an Irish problem throughout these decades, with the newcomers earning a reputation for hard-drinking, aggressive, riotous behavior wherever they settled.

One basis for that reputation was the murder rate for Philadelphia. Although the worst murder record had been compiled in the 1840s and 1850s, during 1860–1873 men and women with Irish Catholic names were indicted for murder at an annual average of 4.7 per 100,000 of population, a rate far higher than the citywide average of 2.9.[10]

Once fairly settled in, however, the "wild Irish" settled down. The new economic order following the Civil War offered them the opportunity to move up, especially in Philadelphia with its strong industrial base. After 1850 the proportion of "common laborers" among them, once about a third of the total, moved steadily down with every census. Rapid occupational diversification into skilled, factory, and entrepreneurial work assured that by 1870 less than a quarter of male immigrants and only 8 percent of those born in this country were still listed as "laborers." Many of those raised in Philadelphia were able to take advantage of an ambitious system of parochial schools, and the lessons of personal discipline and self-control were reinforced by a network of temperance societies which, like the schools, reached their highest development in the City of Brotherly Love. Even more rapidly than their fellows in Boston, New York, and elsewhere, the Irish in Philadelphia learned the kind of patience needed to stand in line, keep out of trouble, and climb up the predictable white-collar ladder best symbolized by jobs in civil service. The result was reflected in the record of violence. By 1874–1887 the rate of murder indictments among the Irish had dropped to 3.1 per 100,000 of population, and by 1888–1901 to 1.8, or well below the citywide average for all groups of 2.1.[11]

The black experience was strikingly different in virtually all respects. There are problems in measuring murder rates among the Irish, just as among blacks, because of the overlap between the names of Irish Catholics and those of other ethnic groups. It is nevertheless clear that the murder rate for blacks was several times higher than that for their Irish neighbors and rivals. Between 1860 and 1880, the annual rate of black murder trials was 8.7 per 100,000 of population. This rate was unique not only in its size but in its climb, reaching an average of 9.5 between 1881 and 1901.

These figures indicate as clearly as the occupational statistics that those blacks who lived in the city were shut out of the urban-industrial revolution at a time and in a place where others were signing on in growing numbers. A fortunate few, men and women, were able to break into the professions, but skilled workingmen lost ground, and most blacks, unlike the Irish, stayed mired in unskilled, dead-end, service jobs. As doors to the new factories and offices stayed shut, there was little incentive for children to remain for long in school. The Institute for Colored Youth, unlike the vast pariochial network, was restricted to a handful of elite youngsters, while no more than a dozen black Philadelphians had graduated from the public high schools as of the late 1890s. The lesson of discrimination, as Du Bois put it, was that "it is useless to work . . . education will get you nothing but disappointment and humiliation."[12]

The impact of all this on urban black behavior was to leave it in an essentially preindustrial state. What was missed even more than opportunity was the training, or the regimentation, provided and demanded by the new economic order, the kind of training that redirected the aggressive impulses of so much of the white population. Without this redirection, blacks typically remained where the majority had been before the Civil War. The new technology brought them only handguns, to add to the uncertainty of their lives. The new prosperity only multiplied the sense of deprivation, as immigrant neighbors no more qualified than they moved up and past them. Psychologically, when blacks felt frustration or aggression, they continued to direct their feelings outward rather than inward. Not only was their murder rate higher than that for any other group, but their suicide rate was lower. No more than 20 black suicides were counted for the period as a whole, as compared to 3092 white suicides.[13]

The false promises of politics under freedom only added to the sense of frustration. Before the Civil War blacks had been locked into a caste position, clearly citizens of a second class, without the vote and without the right to attend white schools, sit on juries, or practice law. After emancipation the bars were lifted in theory but often not in practice. Philadelphians won the right to ride on streetcars but not to drive on them, the right to vote but not the power to make a difference. And while the figures are too small to be significant statistically, it is at least suggestive that the murder rate reflected the political and economic situation even over relatively short periods of time.[14]

Black murder rates in Philadelphia remained at relatively low levels during the Civil War years and after, the period that witnessed the Thirteenth, Fourteenth, and Fifteenth Amendments, the early hopeful years of Reconstruction in the South, and in the city itself the shared excitement of military service, the streetcar fight, and the Equal Rights League. In the years between 1860 and 1869, the generally prosperous period bounded by Lincoln's election and the final push toward the Fifteenth Amendment, the rate was 6.4 per 100,000 annually. The next decade began with the evident failure of Reconstruction and the assassination of Octavius Catto, and continued through a major depression and the frustrating inability to win political office in the city. The rate leapt up dramatically to 10.8. Then came the expansive 1880s, the period when Philadelphia's Afro-Americans made their first modest political gains and the last possible decade during which a hopeful young man such as the columnist Charles A. Minnie could imagine that hard work and good credentials would earn him a chance at the American Dream. The murder rate dropped down sharply to 7.2. But the 1890s were a different era. The decade began symbolically with the nearly simultaneous deaths of Gil Ball and the Force Bill and continued through an increase in lynchings and a systematic denial of the vote in the South, another national depression, and a painful loss of political dignity and office in Philadelphia. The rate of black homicide accordingly jumped again to 11.4. It was by then five and a half times higher than the trial rate for white Philadelphians, during the same period.[15]

Black men and women in Philadelphia by the end of the nineteenth century were being tried for homicide at a rate higher than the official F.B.I. rate of 9.8 for the whole United States in 1980, as measured not by trials but by the far higher number of "crimes known to the police." This homicide record was a significant index to the amount of physical aggression in general which plagued the residents of the city's black neighborhoods. Economic discrimination had helped to create the poverty and insecurity which led to underworld activities that were always rich in the potential for violence. The heritage of racial fear, inspired by a long history of white persecution, contributed to the growing popularity of handguns. Most important, exclusion from the urban industrial revolution meant that blacks were far more likely than whites, even Irish immigrants, to retain an older or preindustrial social psychology, in which aggression was primarily directed outward, at others.[16]

All of these sources of violent behavior were related to each other in terms of not only their common roots in white prejudice but also their effects. Each reinforced the other in an upward spiral that contrasted sharply with the downward spiral in criminal behavior experienced by most other Philadelphians. And that upward spiral had an impact which reached well beyond the official statistics or the events recorded in the daily press, to affect the attitudes and behavior of virtually all of the city's Afro-Americans, whatever their habits, class, or occupations.

· 6 ·
CRIME AND CULTURE

CRIMINAL BEHAVIOR worked deep into the culture of black Philadelphia, as vice and violence reached well beyond those directly engaged in them to affect the lives of thousands who were not. Two groups of Afro-Americans encountered special problems as a result of the illicit activities of others. One group included the middle-class leaders who were struggling to achieve respectability; the other group included all those who sought to raise families in the city.

The conditions of black life in Philadelphia, or indeed anywhere in the late nineteenth century, meant that "respectability" was always a precarious quality. The Afro-American elite of educators, professionals, civil servants, and legitimate entrepreneurs shared the same fundamental values as their white counterparts. These values, tirelessly encouraged by the black press, included in addition to simple material success those standards summarized in the motto of the Citizens' Republican Club: "We Believe in Education, Morality, and Equality under the Law." None of these virtues was easy to achieve or sustain. A special problem was symbolized by the emblazoning of the motto itself on a parade banner intended for display before primarily white crowds. Respectability was a matter not only of achievement but of recognition. And recognition by the dominant white group was critically important for those blacks who sought to win respectability both for themselves and their families and, through their own success, for the whole of their race.

In this situation the growth of an active criminal subculture, led by a large and powerful class of illegal entrepreneurs, posed multiple problems for the legitimate black elite. Leaders had to struggle not only to achieve middle-class status but also to defend it and, finally, to transmit it through their children. Their efforts were threatened on two fronts. One threat came from within the black group itself, where the middle-class standards of some people were subverted by the behavior of others. The other threat came from the white group, whose hostility and contempt seized upon any evidence of black unrespectability, especially of vice or violence, to reinforce stereotypes about the whole of the race. Black leaders tried to mount intellectual and social defenses in order simultaneously to bolster their own morale, protect their own values, and uphold the reputation of Afro-Americans as a group.

Their efforts had generally failed by the end of the nineteenth century. The intellectual defense against racism relied upon another, scarcely more supportable set of stereotypes, which blamed problem behavior on backward southern blacks, who were allegedly less evolved, or civilized, than long-term urban residents. This model served the psychological function of suggesting that the Afro-American condition was improving over time, with the move from South to North, country to city. But all such optimism was denied by the realities of Philadelphia. Ultimately there was no defense against the deteriorating conditions of family and street life which, however unevenly, affected all the city's blacks together.

THE SEARCH FOR RESPECTABILITY

The black bourgeoisie, or urban elite, was noted over the years for its exaggerated insistence on respectability, even puritanism, and its refusal to identify with the great mass of the black population. W. E. B. Du Bois first pointed to a tendency among the educated in Philadelphia to refuse leadership, to set themselves apart in manner and action. At the same time, these men and women justifiably resented being lumped together by whites with others they thought less deserving. The social rituals of Philadelphia's black elite are best seen as part of a struggle not to reject the working class but to distinguish themselves from the criminal class.[1]

Virtually all leading black Philadelphians were engaged at some level in the politics of race, and their activity extended well beyond their obvious self-interest. Lawyers such as John Durham and elder statesmen such as Robert Purvis retained a genuine concern for the economic problems of black workers. The editor H. Price Williams noted forcefully that party politics was a means of opening blue-collar opportunities to new voters. So did the redoubtable Bishop B. F. Tanner, who declared on the ninth anniversary of the Fifteenth Amendment that he was opposed to "too much gush" about it and wanted to see more "practical Christianity" in the form of jobs on the streetcars. But all members of the urban elite were presumably hostile to the "Better Days" Stewarts and George St. Clairs among them, men and women whose attitudes

and activities worked in several ways to undermine the economic progress and social respectability they were trying to win for themselves and
for the whole of the race.[2]

While the black press and the "Negro columns" of the white press
were filled with elite achievement, racial politics, and church and lodge
activities, ordinary white readers were exposed more often not only to
comic stereotypes but to the crime news and to hints and echoes of the
songs, myths, and folkways that made up an entirely different side to
black culture. Hints and echoes were all they normally got because white
reporters were not students of black culture, and when a murderer sang
a song to himself, they gave some of the words but not the music, just
as they reported that Robert Craig played piano at Tillie Maguire's
fancy house but not what he played on it. It is never certain, moreover,
whether reporters were making up the dialogue as well as the spelling,
as when they reported after a big vice raid that the captives broke into
a popular song, "I Guess I'll Hab to Telegraph Mah Baby," while the
bystanders replied with "I Don't Care If You'se Never Come Back."
But sometimes there was no mistaking the truth of an account. When
Thomas Grobes shouted "Hear my bulldog bark!" as he fired a pistol
at his best friend, the line was straight from the legend of Stagolee, the
most celebrated of mythical late-century badmen.[3]

Afro-American culture was marked by an aggressively competitive
strain compounded of bold display, semiritualistic insult, and an ad-
miration of violence in verbal form at least. "Playing the dozens," a
contest involving the exchange of often sexual insults directed not only
at the participants but at their families, especially their mothers, was
one example of this strain, perhaps illustrated by the exchange between
William Brooks and Ivan Green in Hattie Stewart's parlor. Another
example was "toasting," an oral art that stressed skill in the telling of
rhymed or alliterative stories of violent struggles for domination among
either mythical animals or men. Both forms of exchange required an
urban rather than a rural or closed setting in which to flourish, since
they depended for inspiration on new audiences and fresh players and
ideas. And both, although they combined earlier American and even
African elements, came to full maturity well after the Civil War. The
stress on violence in particular dated from late in the nineteenth century,
when "black lore was filled with tales, toasts, and songs of hard merciless
toughs and killers confronting and generally vanquishing their adver-
saries without hesitation and without remorse."[4]

The timing of this violence is significant. The era of slavery and, later,
of severe repression in the rural South typically produced a folklore that
centered on the trickster, the master of masks and of indirection who

dealt with a hostile, or white, world much as Br'er Rabbit dealt with the fox, by turning apparent weakness into strength. But the later decades of the nineteenth century witnessed the beginnings of that long trek to the city which would transform Afro-Americans from an overwhelmingly rural to a disproportionately urban people. Life in the city at least freed blacks from the kind of direct surveillance which had fostered themes of disguise and deception. But at the same time it had a harshness of its own, which encouraged other themes suited to a life lived in or near the fringes of a growing illegal underworld. Toasts involving powerful characters such as Stagolee recognized and even celebrated the overwhelming importance of aggression in human relations. These men, unlike most legendary white bandits, "preyed upon the weak as well as the strong, women as well as men." Wholly without social purpose or redeeming qualities, they were "pure force, pure vengeance, explosians of fury and futility." Some of them were loosely based on the real lives of contemporary killers, and Philadelphia provided a number of potential models in men like George St. Clair.[5]

Although these violent tales and rituals are now recognized as elements of a genuine culture, the contemporary black elite was understandably less enthusiastic about them than modern collectors of folklore. Its own "high culture," as represented in the black press, was an amalgam of black and white models, of spirituals and opera, of Afro-American poetry and Shakespeare. There was no toasting at the church-sponsored Star Concerts held at the Academy of Music. And the leaders, who could regard the romanticizing of the criminal class as a matter only for regret, viewed the behavior that lay behind it as a much more serious threat.

One line of defense against this threat was to develop a rationale for explaining black social problems that would serve simultaneously to maintain morale within the group and to protect its reputation in the face of external criticism. Booker T. Washington, who by the 1890s emerged as a leading apologist, implied the formula for achieving both ends in the title of his later autobiography, *Up from Slavery*. To locate the blame for contemporary problems on the long heritage of bondage allowed blacks to feel an automatic sense of progress as that heritage receded in time. It had the further advantage, in the face of continual discouragement, of shifting attention away from conditions in places like Philadelphia back to the rural South. Setbacks and discouragements could then be laid to the continual stream of migrants, ignorant, as yet uncivilized newcomers who persisted in infecting the city with problems imported from points both geographically and socially distant. This kind of scapegoating was especially useful because of its appeal to white audiences as well. Durham's charge that rising crime rates in 1900 were the result of southern migration was echoed by both the *Public Ledger* and Police Superintendent Francis Linden.[6]

Although these sentiments were voiced by several Philadelphians, such as Durham and Mrs. Nathan Mossell, they were elaborated most fully by a visitor to the city, the young Du Bois, who spent several months in 1896–1897 living and taking notes in the Seventh Ward. The resulting study, *The Philadelphia Negro,* is arguably the best piece of sociology written by an American in the nineteenth century. It portrays conditions bleak enough to indict the white attitudes that had helped create them, but not so bleak as to discourage work and hope. Its central message, on which this book is based, is that racial prejudice had destroyed the promise of the city, that economic discrimination was growing worse, and that blacks were not only losing jobs but being shut out of the newer ones. He might then have concluded that social problems, which he linked to economic conditions, were growing worse as well. But in treating crime and criminality—which he ranked at the top of the list of internal problems that the black population had to overcome—he shrank from the dismal implications of his own findings, with the result that his frequent references to crime, drink, gambling, and prostitution are collectively the weakest parts of the book.[7]

Part of the explanation for this may be that nothing in Du Bois's background at Harvard, Heidelberg, or the A.M.E.'s Wilberforce College had fully prepared him for life in the Seventh Ward, where he must have seemed to long-term residents as alien as his German gloves and cane, his accent and pince-nez. A great deal of what he saw and heard affronted the new bridegroom's late Victorian personal, political, and sexual morality, which may explain why he was able to count only fifty-three prostitutes in the whole ward. The police, just months ahead of his arrival, had flushed out forty-eight one morning, in an area just two blocks long and two blocks away from his settlement-house apartment. Almost every Sunday, the *Inquirer* reported, there were raids like that in "Little Africa, which netted a courtroom full of women of all shades, from inky black to old gold, all young, all tough, and all much given to swagger and vile oaths."[8]

More important even than Du Bois's personal morality in blinkering him to the full impact of crime in the city was the intellectual framework imposed on him by contemporary social science theory. After the Civil War the doctrine of Social Darwinism at its starkest had suggested that the freedmen, once removed from the protection of their masters, would die out as a result of being thrown into "the struggle for life" in competition with superior white labor. Although the census returns of 1880 had laid that notion to rest—Isaiah Wears of the Equal Rights League noted proudly that "the race had not died out, as had been prophesied. They were rather kind of 'dyed in' "—two other related ideas were harder to kill off. One was that blacks were indeed moving upward, but only along the lower rungs of a metaphorical evolutionary ladder. The other was that, like all social problems, the difficulties encountered in the city were simply matters of adaption, or adjustment to new conditions, which would automatically smooth out in time.[9]

When faced with the need to explain criminality in particular, Du Bois found it hard to resist these arguments. If moral behavior was disappointing, "stealing and fighting are ever the besetting sins of half-developed races." If theft was rampant, "naturally, then, if men are suddenly transported from one environment to another, the result is . . . lack of harmony with social surroundings leading to crime." What most embarrassed Du Bois's analysis was that his evidence, though flawed, showed on its face that black criminal behavior was actually on the rise. Both absolutely and relatively to the white population, he noted, the proportion of black men sent to prison had increased substantially over the previous decade, accounting for 14.9 percent of all new convicts during 1885–1889 and 22.43 percent during 1890–1895. In every other instance, however, partly out of a sociologist's naive faith in unexamined statistics, Du Bois systematically, if unconsciously, minimized the relative extent of black crime in the city.[10]

The ominous suggestion that criminal behavior was actually on the rise was perhaps too bleak for Philadelphia's black leaders to face, certainly to admit or discuss openly. The situation was especially acute in the fearful 1890s. William Dorsey's interest in filling hundreds of pages in his private scrapbooks with newspaper clippings about southern lynchings on the one hand and Afro-American crime on the other amounted to an obsession. The fact that black crime through the early 1890s was not yet a major issue for Philadelphia's white elite was only because it had yet to reach them in any significant way. The stereotype of the black man as one whose uniquely violent impulses required violent control was already in place in the South. Below the Mason-Dixon Line, the stereotype in its most virulent form was an excuse that cost hundreds of lives each year, and much hard-won political power. In the last decade of the century the lynching phenomenon reached its peak with over a thousand black victims, and at the same time, not coincidentally, the process of segregation and denial culminated in a successful drive virtually to deny the franchise to blacks in most of the former Confederate states. The *Christian Recorder,* which circulated in the rural South as well as the urban North, went so far as to plead with its readers to inform on any rapists they might be harboring.[11]

Closer to home, the lynching phenomenon had a definite effect on the racial atmosphere of the city. The editorial pages of the leading papers were opposed to the practice, but violence sold. The front-page stories of lynchings, apparently written by southern correspondents or stringers, assumed that all victims were guilty of whatever heinous murder or other crime was charged to them. Given an average of over 100 of these episodes a year, literate Philadelphians, black or white, began most days with headlines about a "Savage Killer," "Negro Fiend," or "Black Brute." Despite these circumstances, the city was relatively immune to the myth of the black rapist, simply because it was a myth. Although intraracially the crime itself was common enough, alleged black rapes of white women were rare in this period and, when they did occur, were never sensationalized. The jury hung in an 1870 case involving an unnamed "colored lad" and a white child. A reported attack was made in 1890 on a "young white woman" in "a secluded part of the city"; the incident then dropped out of the papers. One black man was caught by his wife in 1879 while attempting to rape the daughter of a white friend and neighbor; he got five years in prison, quickly and quietly. But at the same time that this most explosive of issues was normally dormant, crime both real and imagined had a heavy impact on everyone who lived in the city's black neighborhoods.[12]

The fact that both men and women commonly worked out of the house meant that the premises were left unguarded all day long. The board of health in 1860 noted that black homes, many of them mere cellars, were typically patrolled by vicious dogs let out to roam only at night. The *Christian Recorder* railed against the criminal tendencies of young Afro-Americans, a complaint sharpened by the fact that "Mother" Bethel Church itself was repeatedly burglarized. Elite Philadelphians were embarrassed in 1878 when Judge Jasper Wright, once head of the Pennsylvania Equal Rights League and later appointed to the federal bench in South Carolina, was robbed by two fellow black men on a return visit to the city.[13]

The criminal stereotype was economically most harmful toward the bottom of the ladder, where it threatened the jobs of thousands of men and especially women. Many domestics lost jobs to white immigrants. Some of this loss was due to the endless discussions of the "servant girl problem," which in 1890 led to the establishment of the Association of Housekeepers, later renamed the Fidelity Servants' Reform Association. By the next year the group had become a fixture in Philadelphia and was planning a charity fundraising ball. Mrs. M. H. Roberts, wife of Pennsylvania's commissioner to the Paris Exposition, urged in 1890 that the best domestics were European or English orphans, given special training in "proper principles." At the same time, reform councilman C. Oscar Beasley, president of the Association, announced that he was keeping a file of some 600 acceptable names—and a blacklist of 2000, compiled after a "careful investigation of their morals and habits." Later that year Beasley complained bitterly that black votes he had counted on had somehow deserted his cause.[14]

For black leaders, however, and respectable members of the middle class, the problem of crime was not so much economic as social. Some of the issues they faced and did not face were illustrated by the little group of long-term residents who advised Du Bois on his study of the city, including the historian Carl Bolivar, the school principal Jacob White, Jr., and the civil servant, artist, and bibliophile William Dorsey. These elders supplemented the younger man's observations with their own memories. Among the blacks they recalled was the imperious caterer Thomas Dorsey, William's father, a man of "real weight in the community" who eventually got more notice in *The Philadelphia Negro* than any other leader who survived the Civil War. Dorsey had not only served, and in some cases refused to serve, the great and famous, but had entertained a long list of antislavery crusaders of both races at his prestigious Locust Street establishment. Although the elders told Du Bois about the old abolitionist, who had died twenty years earlier, it is not clear whether they mentioned that his daughter Mary, the one who adopted a white girl, had operated a whorehouse just down the street, that Sam St. Clair was arrested for running a dog fight at the same address, and that Aaron Dorsey was even then managing a speakeasy at the old place. Like many others, Du Bois believed, because he wanted to believe, that crime was mostly the business of the poor and desperate, of ignorant migrants slow in learning how to adjust to the urban environment. The city's native black leaders, however appealing they found this explanation, must surely have known better.[15]

They and their counterparts in New York and Boston sought to claim that the natives of northern cities were socially and even morally superior to southern migrants, but the claim did not ring true. Those born in northern cities were in fact not less but more likely to be plagued with those social problems that the census measures, such as single-parent families headed by women or low occupational status and prospects. In Philadelphia itself, earlier leaders such as Octavius Catto, Robert Purvis, and William Still were all southern born; so were the majority of business, political, and professional leaders listed in a directory published in 1910. Even if criminality had in general been the result of the ignorance and desperation of southerners, that would not have explained the situation most directly confronting the city's legitimate elite, for whom the problem was often not the poor and shiftless but the rich and powerful.[16]

Most forms of criminality did not benefit the city's Afro-American population as a whole, but for illegal entrepreneurs, as individuals, the plain fact was that criminal activity was not the result of a failure to adjust to the city. On the contrary, it was an often highly profitable means of adjustment, offering the only opportunity for many people to achieve material prosperity and success. Much legal enterprise had been driven underground by moral legislation, exclusion, and denial. By the end of the 1890s there were, by various estimates, 350, 200, or just 45 legitimate black businesses in the city. Whatever the actual number, there were far more illegal black entrepreneurs than legal ones. And many of the legal ones surely operated at least partially outside the law. The story of Andrew Stevens's troubles in getting a license to sell alcohol at the Academy of Music shows how thin was the line between catering and bootlegging. The barber shop was proverbially the place for a man to lay a bet; second-hand stores often dealt in stolen merchandise. Collectively, then, the proprietors of speakeasies, policy shops, and brothels, together with the people who worked out of them, comprised much of the economic middle and even upper class among blacks.

One problem with this big, relatively rich, highly visible group of criminal entrepreneurs was that they were able to enjoy middle-class incomes and privileges without the discipline imposed by middle-class lifestyles. Gamblers, prostitutes, and other illegal actors lived lives marked by insecurities and tensions. These entrepreneurs in many cases simply expressed, in flamboyant fashion, the older psychology shared by the great majority of people, black and white, who were denied the repressive experience of factory, bureaucracy, or schooling. They often had literally to fight their way to success and were therefore driven to enjoy it while it lasted, before the cards, the police, or the election returns toppled them suddenly, or the inroads of age and hungry competitors pushed them off more slowly.

Their behavior was a direct threat not only to the elite struggle for recognition but to its integrity as a group. The characteristic work habits and values of professionals and legitimate merchants combined with the tight formalities observed within the highest circles to insulate them as far as possible from meaningful contact with the "criminal element." But residential segregation forced more closeness on the respectable middle-class than it wanted. And sometimes there was simply no defense against exposure to other lifestyles. Parents in particular faced hard choices. Any broad or public occasion, a ball or an outing, necessarily exposed the younger generation to the top hats, stickpins, silk clothes, and cakewalking high style of the illegal entrepreneurs. Some of them reacted with a strict puritanism; others were themselves tempted into extravagant dress and other forms of conspicuous consumption, perhaps in self-defense. The first strategy may have accounted for the cautious self-segregation often noted; the second strategy effectively blunted, for many blacks, the ability to follow the classic white middle-class route to prosperity through self-denial.[17]

This last problem may have contributed to the growing estrangement between the city's Afro-American leaders and their historic allies among the Society of Friends. Some disputes centered around specific issues in the Society's schools for black children, ranging from salary levels and the locus of power to the teaching of music. There were wider cultural differences as well. The Quakers were firm exemplars of a middle-class ethic that many blacks found hard to achieve or appreciate. Problems arose, Bolivar noted, when blacks failed to understand that what the "Quakers exact from themselves they demand from others," that "an appointment for a certain hour means just that," and that "they have always paid promptly and bidden others do likewise."[18]

The problem of achieving or maintaining middle-class respectability was complicated for many lawyers, who found that exposure to criminality was not merely a residential hazard but an occupational necessity. No group was growing faster, beginning with a single practicing attorney as late as 1891. Attorneys Theophilus Minton and John Stephen Durham regularly worked for the federal government, but most other lawyers had to scrabble for criminal work. One feature of illegal enterprise was that it did its legal business in criminal court rather than through civil suits. The Republican party retained experienced counsel for many blacks accused of murder, prostitution, liquor offenses, and vote fraud, but there was still a deal of legal work to go around. The judges in quarter sessions, or oyer and terminer, appointed a number of black attorneys to cover killings by black suspects. The custom was normally for black lawyers to refuse, or be refused, those cases in which the victims were white. Several black lawyers turned down the opportunity in 1899 to defend Sam Dodson and "Face" Epps in the robbery-murder of Mary Ann Lawlor, and in 1900 a distinguished battery of white lawyers defended Charles Perry, Amos Sterling, and Henry Ivory in the Roy Wilson White killing. But beginning in 1896 blacks became active in such cases. M. L. Nicholas joined Henry Bass in defending Robert Brown; A. F. Murray and T. H. Wheeler represented Marion Stuyvesant; and Aaron Mossell, first black graduate of the University of Pennsylvania Law School, served as counsel to several accused murderers, including Mary Bradshaw and Dora Whittaker, both of whom were indicted on charges of infanticide. The procedures and atmosphere of the criminal courts constituted a kind of occupational hazard for these men, as they did for their often sleazy white associates. Murray, for example, was arrested for fighting in the corridors, and Mossell for stealing a client's bail money.[19]

Mossell's brother Nathan, too, was one of several blacks involved in one of the medical byproducts of prostitution when in 1890 Ella Brown accused him of having performed an abortion on her. The case was unusually sensitive, for Nathan Mossell, first black graduate of the University of Pennsylvania Medical School and founder of the Douglass Clinic, was emerging as the leading black physician in the city. The *Inquirer* smothered the story for a time, and several white colleagues at the Pennsylvania Hospital closed ranks to help quash the indictment. Mossell pleaded that he had treated Brown only for a fibrous tumor, which the other doctors testified was commonly mistaken for pregnancy. The district attorney then chose to ignore the woman's testimony as to what she had asked for.[20]

Deeper problems of professional status and reputation remained for all black doctors in the city. The legal or licensed practitioners had typically graduated from the best universities. The University of Pennsylvania Medical School had accepted Mossell in large part because Harvard Medical School had showed the way in the case of Afro-American medical students. But even a prestigious degree was no guarantee of success. On the one hand, there were some 1700 white physicians in the city, and no one after Dr. David Rossell was apparently able to win a significant number of white patients. On the other hand, black physicians still had to deal with a number of conjure women and spirit healers, who had kept the field almost entirely to themselves through the Civil War. In fact, the great majority of black "doctors" and "physicians" listed in the 1880 census were unlicensed practitioners. Many of these people practiced useful or consoling arts, but by the late nineteenth century there was already a substantial difference between folk healers and university-trained physicians. Although the enumerators and the ill-educated could not tell the difference, members of the black elite were at pains to establish it. The Afro-American papers were proud of the city's black doctors, such as Robert J. Abele who had set a state record on the licensing examination. But others were graduates of such institutions as the Eclectic School of Medicine, a fradulent diploma mill where one black man got a degree by attendng four lectures and paying $20. These unlicensed practitioners made the news only when they were cited for signing death certificates illegally, poisoning patients, or above all killing young women who had come to them for abortions. At least two blacks performed or assisted in fatal abortions on white women.[21]

The abortion issue was sensitive for everyone involved. Older doctors remembered a time when the operation was routinely pereformed on the most respectable of women, and many others felt at best ambivalent about the law. To deny a requested abortion was often to drive a woman to an unskilled quack, perhaps one of the "graduates" of the notorious

Ecletic School of Medicine. People like Mary Bradshaw and Dora Whittaker would never have needed the legal help of Aaron Mossell if they had previously received proper medical advice from his brother Nathan. No one, at that stage in the history of medicine, had any cure for the children of diseased mothers, the "misconceived and misbegotten," who were condemned to blindness if not death.[22]

The problem faced by Dr. Mossell and other trained Afro-American doctors was in some ways unique, in that "status" in their case was partly a matter of law, and medical licenses were essential both to their own careers and to any wider effort to help the black population as a whole. But in most respects their experience was similar to that of other professionals and businessmen who had to struggle to maintain their reputations and values in difficult circumstances. All of them were affected by the problem of criminal activity—sometimes in the form of clients or competitors, always as part of neighborhood and family life in the city.

FAMILY LIFE

Men and women of both races in the late nineteenth century were much concerned with the character of family life among Afro-Americans. The principal issue from their perspective was sexual morality, with a special emphasis on the chastity of women. Even sympathetic white observers, given their typically religious backgrounds, were at best baffled by the sexual mores of places like the Seventh Ward. Helen Parrish, a founder of the settlement in which Du Bois later lived, was involved in continual argument over the casual living and loose marital arrangements of the people with whom she worked. Black leaders shared her late Victorian premises about virginity, monogamy, and fidelity. Mrs. Nathan Mossell, who wrote a family column for the New York *Freeman,* agreed with Booker T. Washington that female morality left much to be desired, but she blamed the situation on the heritage of slavery. The issue was especially important to Du Bois, who, in urging racial self-help, ranked the need to improve family life ahead of the need to reform work habits and only just behind the need to control criminality.[23]

Yet a workable sexual morality and family life had in fact flourished in the slave South. Although the model did not fully fit the contemporary or Victorian ideal, it was in some ways better, having less rigidity about premarital behavior and allowing for more equality between the sexes. The bond between husbands and wives or between parents and children was often necessarily weakened because southern law did not recognize the legality of relations among slaves, but much of the pain was eased with the help of extended families of cousins and uncles.[24]

Social science has recently concerned itself less with sexual behavior than with the "female-headedness" of families. According to the census records, single black women were left to raise children by themselves much less often in the late nineteenth century than today. These findings are probably fair enough, despite questions about the accuracy of the census. And the number of parents in the household is a better test of the strength of the family than the chastity of females, and easier to put on the computer. But neither is a really good measure. The real measure is how well parents are able to raise children, to maintain good relations within the network of kin, and to transmit useful cultural values across the generations. On this point, all of the evidence from nineteenth century Philadelphia points in one direction. The conditions of urban living were deeply subversive of black family life.[25]

One measure of that subversion is the extent of intrafamily violence, as measured by the murder rate. In general, the murder rate was several times higher among blacks than whites, and the difference in family killings was proportionally even greater. The officially recorded percentage of family homicides was about the same for both racial groups, accounting for about one-fifth of all trials for murder between 1860 and 1901. Among whites, there were 134 family episodes, or 22 percent of the 633 white cases in which this relationship could be determined, while there were 26 such episodes among blacks, or 21 percent of the 126 black cases that specified family relationships or their absence.

But these raw figures do not allow for other facts that indicate an even greater racial disparity in the real world. Afro-Americans were somewhat less likely to marry than white Philadelphians, and were notably more likely to have smaller families, so that there were proportionally fewer legal kin to serve as potential victims of homicidal anger. As of the 1880 census, for example, only 18 percent of the black population was composed of children under ten years old, compared with 23 percent of native whites, and fully 31 percent and 34 percent of first-generation Irish and Germans, respectively. Moreover, the often sketchy newspaper accounts that provided these figures did not always note common law or collateral kinship relationships. Expansion of the category of family to include lovers, rivals, and other people who shared the same address would add 36 black episodes, or 29 percent of the black total, and 61 white episodes, or 10 percent of the white total. By this expanded definition, then, family killings accounted for less than a third of white homicides but nearly half of black homicides. Case after case testifies to the tensions of claustrophobic living conditions in black households, compounded by a cultural pattern in which weapons were easily available in bedrooms and in kitchens. John Fitzgerald in November 1870 killed an old family friend who tried to intercede when

Fitzgerald broke up a Sunday prayer session by accusing his father of sleeping with his wife. Twenty-four years later, in January 1894, young Henry Hill murdered his mother in an argument over a stolen dime.[26]

Even more fundamental than violence was the unique economic situation which demanded that a high proportion of women, higher than in any other group, went daily out to work. Unlike those in rural communities, urban black women worked outside of the home, usually for wages in money. In the absence of day care—and in the 1880s the kindergarten movement was just beginning to draw support from black leaders—this meant that children were left alone and untended. Mrs. Mossell warned against the apparently common practice of drugging infants to keep them quiet during long hours of absence, or of locking them in single rooms or even closets. Frequently children were burned to death in poor neighborhoods, as all heat and light came directly from fire, and in the city this increasingly meant volatile liquid fuels instead of the wood and candles of tradition. Newborns occasionally were killed by rats. Most older children left school after the three primary grades. Du Bois noted that the small amount of child labor was a problem not a blessing: "There is very little that Negro children may do." Factory work was closed to them, as to their parents, and they could find few legal ways of adding to the family income. "Their chief employment," he reported wishfully, "is found in helping about the house while the mother is at work." Approximately 38 percent of the families of the Seventh Ward kept lodgers to help ends meet. These were single men mostly, sometimes out of work themselves, who often had alternative suggestions as to ways in which adolescent girls might spend their time. And there was always the street.[27]

The attraction of the street was measured by the unhappy statistics from the House of Refuge. The House was established in 1829 as the city's juvenile reformatory for children up to age sixteen. Although the figures from jails or prison were occasionally higher, no institution in the city had a consistently higher proportion of black commitment. In 1859–1861, of those admitted from Philadelphia, 791 were white and 228 were black, or 21 percent of the total; in 1869–1871, 422 were white and 122 black, or 20 percent; in 1879–1881, 475 were white and 134 black, or 22 percent; and in 1889–1891, 606 were white and 160 black, or 21 percent. These black children were not typically victims of discriminatory justice or of any attempt to impose white morality on them or their families; 56 percent of them were committed at the request of parents, relatives, guardians, or friends, who found them incorrigible, rather than on a magistrate's own initiative. And as final refutation of the idea that criminality was imported from the South, these children were overwhelmingly native Philadelphians. Most southern migrants were childless young adults. Only 16 percent of blacks committed to the House were listed as southern-born.[28]

The proportion of commitments was especially striking because there were proportionally fewer black children in the city, as compared with adults, than in any other major ethnic group. The census indicated that black women across the United States had high fertility rates in the late nineteenth century, far higher than those for whites. The ratio in 1890 was 1.542 black children aged four or younger for every white child; in other words, black women had more than 50 percent more small children than whites. This high ratio was achieved only because of the extraordinary fertility of rural Afro-Americans, the very opposite of those who lived in urban areas. In Philadelphia in 1890 the black-white ratio was .815 to 1.000, meaning that black women had nearly 20 percent fewer children than whites, a figure that in 1900 dropped to .716 to 1.000, or nearly 30 percent fewer. Despite the high proportion of young adults in Philadelphia's black population, then, the fertility rate consistently fell not only below the white average but below the rate needed to maintain the size of the group, or less than zero population growth.[29]

This phenomenon is hard to explain, since even the middle classes were not widely acquainted with reliable methods of birth control, other than abstinence, and the mass of blacks were presumably less well informed. Prostitution may well have had a unique importance in this regard. Given that infertility was usually the most serious effect of gonorrhea among females and that, whatever their effectiveness, contemporary strategies of birth control, including abortion, were most likely to be available among those whose living depended on them, the impact of commercial vice must have been considerable.

Probably only around this time, when prostitution was at its peak, and only in places where the black population was still small, was it possible to have so large a proportion of black women in the business. In Philadelphia in the mid-1890s a total of 2000 to 2500 black prostitutes represented somewhere between one-seventh and one-eighth of all black females between the ages of fifteen and forty-five. Many of these were relatively casual or occasional streetwalkers, but those who counted on the income were, if not effectively infertile, at least powerfully inclined to avoid or postpone child-rearing. Contemporary observers suggested that the average working life of prostitutes of all races was something between five and six years. This figure was misleading as applied to blacks, because these sources tended to emphasize the experience of relatively middle-class white women, who had other options, and of women who were confined in houses rather than on the street. Reformers also wanted to believe that death, disease, or reformation cut short most careers. Black prostitutes actually worked many years longer than this average. Du Bois noted a couple over fifty years old, and Emma Burk, who in 1863 was acquitted of killing a customer who had slashed her, was jailed seventeen years later as a "notorious badger thief." Moreover, since the average figure included all those prostitutes who were working at a given time, the effect of any turnover at all would be to increase the proportion of those who, by middle age, had at one time walked the streets or worked the brothels of the city. All told, perhaps a quarter of Philadelphia's black women who reached the end of their childbearing years had at some time had exposure to the diseases and habits associated with prostitution. This figure would account almost precisely for the difference between black and white fertility in the city.[30]

Contemporary black leaders saw this situation as part of a larger pattern which threatened the preservation of their own values. And the Christian ministry, at least, never stopped fighting it. Successive editors of the *Christian Recorder* complained continually about vice in black areas and about the indifference of the police—"Watchman, what of the night?" At the Senate hearings of 1895, the Reverend H. C. Gibbons complained that many black parents refused to send their children to the Binney School, in the Fifth Section, on account of daily insults to their daughters. H. L. Phillips, pastor of the Episcopal Church of the Crucifixion at Eighth and Bainbridge, also expressed concern to the senators about the special problems that aggressive streetwalkers created for parents in his parish and, more generally, about the universal cynicism felt toward the law and the police. "The children seem to grow up in an atmosphere in which they lose all sense of the distinction between right and wrong . . . it is impossible to counteract it."[31]

The minister was speaking to an audience of politicians; Judge Peter Gordon two years earlier instead addressed his concerns about criminality to "the philanthropic colored people of the community," whom he hoped might "see what is radically wrong . . . and correct it." Both appeals were equally misdirected. Phillips should have understood that it was politicians, much like those who had rather cynically called on him to testify, who had in effect "zoned" his neighborhood as a center of vice. And Gordon should have understood that few black leaders were in any position to object. The illegitimate among them profited directly from the situation, while the legitimate were often fearful, compromised, and ultimately dependent. Back in the 1860s, Carl Bolivar remembered, Jacob White, Sr., had led a vigorous if vain attempt to rid the Seventh Ward of its gamblers and madams. In the 1890s, no such campaign was mounted even in the face of apparent attempts by the white authorities to "clean up" portions of the Fifth and Eighth Wards by driving their "undesirables" further into the heart of black Philadelphia. The same arrangements that raised the Gil Balls in the population to something close to respectability simultaneously demeaned the Andrew Stevenses, the Christopher Perrys, the E. C. Howards and William Warricks, who were pushed into acquiescence. All hope of breaking out of this situation was defeated by the events of the 1890s, which marked the final surrender of the politics of race to the politics of Philadelphia.[32]

It was impossible, then, to mount any collective resistance to a system that trapped all blacks together. Individuals could find partial routes to escape: Constantin Hubert, who refused to obey the machine; Robert Purvis, who lived, isolated, on the far fringes of the city; and some of the women who refused to bear or raise children in the atmosphere of black Philadelphia. But none of them could break fully free of the conditions that made all of them subject, if not to the direct effects of criminality, at least to the prejudices and stereotypes it encouraged.

By the end of the century apparent changes in the targets as well as the level of violence combined to add a final element to the situation and to realize the deepest fears of the black elite. In 1893 Judge Gordon noted, after sentencing ten black men to many years in jail during a single April's term of court, "There is nothing in history that indicates that the colored race has a propensity to acts of violent crime. On the contrary, their tendencies are most gentle, and they submit with grace to subordination." Most black leaders would have objected to his version of their history under slavery, if only because of their own wish to claim that criminality was a heritage of the past and not a product of ongoing conditions in the city itself. But the judge's patronizing stereotype about subordination was at least less harmful than the fears and hatreds that would follow later in the decade."[33]

Gordon spoke out in the same month that witnessed the first execution of a black man since the Civil War, namely William Moore, also known as Scott Jennings, who was hanged for killing another black. The escalating pace of executions later in the decade was confined largely to other men who had also committed intraracial murders: Robert Brown, George St. Clair, George Weeks, and Eugene Clements. It is not clear how elite blacks viewed this parade to the gallows or the rising rate of homicide in general. But they must have grown apprehensive when blacks began to be accused of murdering middle-class whites.[34]

The first such incident occurred when Marion Stuyvesant was indicted, although not tried, for killing the bibliophile Henry Wilson in 1897. The next year "Face" Epps barely managed to escape the ultimate penalty after confessing to a fatal assault on the shopkeeper Mary Ann Lawlor. But the felony-murder of Roy Wilson White by three black men at the end of the century symbolically opened a new era in local race relations when it broke the earlier taboo against armed robbery. Its impact was felt the next year when Mary Wright was put on trial for the ax murder of her white employer, Sarah Higgonbotham, on evidence no stronger than the fact that Wright was the only one who could be placed in the old woman's house on the fatal day. The city's blacks had always had to live in an atmosphere created by white discrimination; now, as even elite white Philadelphians tinged their earlier paternalism with nervousness, blacks would have to live with the consequence of white fear as well.[35]

This element of fear completed the vicious cycle that constricted black Philadelphians by the turn of the century. As the number of Afro-Americans grew larger and more concentrated over the years, white reluctance to visit the barbers, upholsterers, and caterers among them increased accordingly, further stifling the development of a legitimate middle class. Despite individual success stories, the middle class remained disproportionately composed of professionals and civil servants. Its members, increasingly on the defensive, were unable to help others break out of the cycle. The members of the black elite found themselves instead surrounded by criminals and victimized in several ways. Sometimes robbed or beaten, at other times demoralized, they were never fully able to dissociate themselves from their unwanted neighbors. Vice and violence, originally reactions to exclusion and poverty, worked to reinforce the exclusion and to perpetuate the poverty by subverting efforts at escape. As criminal behavior weakened the structure of the family and compromised the potential leadership, it worked ultimately, in white eyes, to justify the prejudice on which the whole cycle had been founded.

EPILOGUE

THE CRIMINAL subculture established in late nineteenth century Philadelphia may be traced not only through the later history of the city but
across the whole of urban America. Black and white rates of homicide
for the city through the first three decades of the twentieth century fit
closely with the national figures available from that time on. The gap
between black and white has fluctuated throughout the twentieth century, usually widening or, more rarely, narrowing in response to changes
in the same kinds of social and economic conditions that originally
created the disparity between them. Most other patterns of black criminality in the 1980s may also be traced back to those of the late 1800s.
In many respects, then, the present is simply the past writ large, the
result of those successive waves of migration through which millions of
Afro-Americans left the rural South to come to live in cities. Each group
of migrants and their descendants have faced similar problems and have
adapted ways of coping much like those pioneered by their predecessors,
ways that have long since hardened into cultural or subcultural patterns
of behavior.

Despite the similarities, the present situation also has differences. The
first third of the twentieth century brought little change in the condition
of urban Afro-Americans, the second third was a period of real hope,
and the most recent third has witnessed a series of contradictory and in
many ways unprecedented developments. The result is that, while the
forms of criminality remain much the same, their relative emphasis and
impact differ, and so do the social, political, and eonomic contexts in
which they operate.

PHILADELPHIA, 1900–1930

The Philadelphia story through the early decades of the twentieth century was similar to the later decades of the nineteenth. The Afro-American

population grew considerably, especially during the great migration of World War I, when southern blacks left for northern cities in huge numbers. But the black condition remained much as before, with similar causes breeding similar results as measured by the continuing disparity between black and white rates of conviction for murder.

The contrasting role played by Irish immigrants in the nineteenth century was filled even more dramatically by Italians in the twentieth. Mostly peasants without urban skills, who were far less literate than Afro-Americans and almost wholly lacking in the English language, the Italians came to Philadelphia from a country that had the highest murder rate in Europe. Other factors aggravated this violent tradition among those who migrated here. Unlike the Irish, the Italians arrived at a time when the urban gun culture was fully established. They often came as single young men, always the most aggressive element in the population, for whom the usual tensions and insecurities of a new life were heightened by the special problems of sexual imbalance and the lack of family life and responsibilities. Their rate of homicide, as measured not by trials or indictments but by imprisonments for murder and voluntary manslaughter, was very high in the early years of the twentieth century—for a time even higher than that of the blacks. Of the 909 people convicted for killings in Philadelphia during 1901–1928, 388 were members of the city's Afro-American population and 181 were members of the considerably smaller group of those born in Italy. The total among all other Philadelphians in the same years was only 340. Thus, blacks and Italians, together comprising only a little more than 10 percent of the city's population, acounted for a whopping 63 percent of its homicide convictions.[1]

In Philadelphia, as in other American cities, the escalating influx of Italians and Afro-Americans in the first three decades of the twentieth century helped to mask the continuing effect of the urban industrial revolution as shown by the declining rate of violence. Outside the United States the decline was still clearly evident, as murder rates began to reach the bottom of the long U-curve that they started to describe in the mid-nineteenth century. The official statistics of murder were uniquely distorted in the United States, however, by the impact of in-migrating peoples who were not yet full participants in the urban industrial revolution that was responsible for giving the U-curve its shape. This distorting effect was more evident in places other than Philadelphia. The Quaker City received relatively few Italian immigrants, and since it had a relatively large number of blacks to begin with, the impact on it of Afro-American migration during the early twentieth century was not as marked as on, for example, New York or Chicago. But even in Philadelphia the effect of high murder rates among these two groups was apparent. The conviction rate for the whole city was 2.3 per 100,000 residents during 1901–1907, dropping to 1.6 in 1908–1914, then rising again to 2.0 in 1915–1921 and to 1.9 in 1922–1928. The white rate alone, discounting people of Italian birth, was markedly lower and somewhat differently curved: in the same for periods it was 1.3, 0.6, 0.7, and 0.6, respectively.[2]

Among the Italians, however, truly high murder rates began to moderate, as they and their descendants settled down in a remarkably short period of time. Those born in the old country were imprisoned for homicide at the record rate of 26.5 per 100,000 annually in 1901–1907, which dropped to 11.4 in 1908–1915. A sharp jump in the World War I years created an upward blip to 17.1 in 1915–1921, followed by an even sharper drop to 5.2 in 1922–1928. The later arrivals were clearly moving into a more secure and predictable neighborhood culture. The patterns already established by white working-class Philadelphians in the previous century proved especially attractive to these latest newcomers, as they too found factory jobs, joined savings and loan associations, settled into row houses, and raised big families. As testimony to the strength of this newly emerging family culture, of the 909 people jailed for killings over the first twenty-eight years in the twentieth century, only 10 were second-generation immigrants with Italian surnames, and none of these were born in Philadelphia.[3]

The problem of Afro-American criminality, meanwhile, grew with the population, which itself rose from 63,000 in 1900 to 85,000 by 1910, swelled during wartime to 135,000, and reached nearly 200,000 by 1928. This growth rate, coupled with the failure of the city's native black population to reproduce itself, ensured that a large proportion of blacks living in Philadelphia were always immigrants from the South. So, accordingly, were those convicted of murder. But neither the new arrivals nor the murderers were typically rural people who had come directly from the farm. Five-eighths of migrant householders surveyed in 1924 had come from urban areas. Almost half of the southerners sentenced to the Eastern State Penitentiary during 1922–1928 had been born in cities, principally Baltimore, Washington, and other nearby places such as Norfolk and Lynchburg, but a number also came from Macon through Mobile down to New Orleans. Many of the rest had left their rural origins to migrate through a series of progressively bigger places before ultimately arriving in Philadelphia, "sharpened and prepared for crime," as Du Bois had put it earlier, "by the slums of many cities through which they had passed."[4]

The destructive elements of the culture of black Philadelphia were by no means unique to that city. Most of the conditions which had created a subculture of vice, theft, and violence could be found in almost any urban setting. In the South the problem was often heightened by a justified mistrust and even fear of the police and the court system, another legacy of the failure of Reconstruction. The lack of institutional support and protection drove even respectable blacks to settle their problems directly, through confrontation and aggression.[5]

Whatever their background, migrants to Philadelphia found the same pattern of exclusion and disrimination that had faced their predecessors. Individual success stories continued to multiply, as they always had. The philosopher Alain Locke, a graduate of Central High, was the first black man to win a Rhodes Scholarship, in 1910. Arthur Huff Fauset, a pioneer student of Afro-American folklore, established a literary magazine in 1927. And Sadie Alexander, a member of the remarkable Mossell family, became an assistant city solicitor in 1928. But factory and white-collar work stayed closed to most blacks, and so did the city's labor unions. From the turn of the century through the 1930s, improvements in the occupational distribution of black workers were marginal at best. New arrivals, if lucky, joined the older hands as railway laborers, street and sewer cleaners, and trash collectors for the city. Many of the rest continued to do domestic and personal service. Still others, ranging from the desperate to the ambitious, presumably continued to flow into the established channels of the hustling subculture, gambling, pimping, whoring, and now selling illegal drugs as well as alcohol. The drug culture, often associated with prostitution, grew especially after the turn of the century. Female users all over the urban Northeast had long found that morphine, or later heroin, was an anodyne, and males believed that cocaine was an aphrodisiac.[6]

Politics continued the downward slide of the 1890s. The columnist Carl Bolivar, just two years before his death in 1914, announced that presidency of the Citizens' Republican Club, once the bastion of elite believers in "Education, Morality, and Equality Before the Law," had passed to Amos Scott. Scott was the ex-boxer convicted of multiple burglaries in the fall of 1900; he continued to sell illegal liquor into the 1920s and did well enough to win a position as president of the Frederick Douglass Memorial Hospital by its twenty-fifth anniversary in 1920. He failed, however, in a bid to become the city's first black magistrate. Real power remained in other hands: Henry Bass won election to the Pennsylvania House of Representatives in 1910, but beyond that the group was unable to win any office higher than common council, or— in contrast to 1890–1891—in any district other than the Seventh Ward. That was the only ward, too, which boasted a black ward leader through the 1920s.[7]

As was appropriate for these decades of stasis, the Afro-American murder rate simply started high and stayed there. It began at 12.9 convictions per 100,000 population during 1901–1907, dropped marginally to 11.6 during 1908–1914, and during the next two seven-year periods held at 10.7 and 13.3, respectively. The great majority of killings that accounted for these statistics were, as always, committed within rather than across racial lines. But as the absolute numbers rose with the continuing influx of newcomers, the authorities came to view Afro-American violence as a problem and responded with repression. From the late 1890s, in strong contrast to earlier decades, blacks were not less but more likely than whites to pay the supreme penalty for homicide. For example, they accounted for 14 of the 21 convicted killers hanged in the city between 1901 and the installation of the electric chair in 1913. The gap between black and white rates of conviction for homicide meanwhile continued to widen. The rate of conviction among all whites dropped to just .8 in 1922–1926, or about one-sixteenth of what it was among blacks.[8]

PHILADELPHIA AND THE UNITED STATES, 1930–1960

The middle years of the twentieth century witnessed the most important changes in the position and prospects of Afro-American citizens since the era of the Civil War. Two of the most important developments were that the urban-industrial revolution begun in the previous century reached its height toward the end of the 1950s and that black Americans were able for the first time to begin to participate fully. This new turn had an impact on the murder rate of black and white not only in the city but across the nation.

The economic and political developments that combined to scramble many of the familiar patterns of Afro-American life began with the Great Depression and continued through World War II. During the 1930s the appeal of Franklin Roosevelt's New Deal began to move black voters in a massive voting shift out of the "party of Lincoln" and into the Democratic column. Philadelphians shared in this movement, although the pace of change was slowed for two decades by continued Republican control of the city. But during the third Roosevelt administration the city's blacks were able to take advantage of what was potentially the most important change of all, the nationwide wartime demand for their labor. From their perspective, on the homefront the most important result of American involvement was that it opened the gates to factories and other previously closed employment all over the country. There was some resistance, and in Philadelphia, symbolically, federal troops were called in 1944 to break one last white strike against the hiring of black men as streetcar conductors. But this time, unlike World War I, the gains were real and lasted beyond the few years of active fighting. The new opportunities overbalanced losses in some traditional areas, notably a declining demand for domestic service, and contributed to a measurable betterment in urban living conditions. Improvements in public health, for example, and in institutional support, combined with a decreasing involvement in prostitution, raised the rate of black fertility in cities across the country. Millions of men and women accordingly left the rural South in search of these new advantages.[9]

In the war and postwar years, then, as black groups gathered strength, the demand for civil rights was added to the national political agenda. A series of dramatic breakthroughs led in 1954 to *Brown* v. *Board of Education,* the critical Supreme Court decision which declared that segregation in the public schools was contrary to the Constitution of the United States, a ruling that was increasingly extended to other areas of national life.

The most thorough investigation ever into the patterns of criminal homicide was conducted in Philadelphia during this hopeful period, from 1948 through 1952. This was in retrospect the high point of the urban-industrial revolution. Three full generations had passed since the city's overall murder rate had begun to fall in the 1870s—since public and parochial schools, factory and white-collar work, had combined to redirect the aggressive impulses of most of the population. Homicide was not then a major social problem for most of the population. The overall murder rate for Philadelphia, as counted by the best and highest method, the number of offenders known to the police, was 6.0 per 100,000 of population, very close to the big-city average of 6.8. By comparison with earlier years, and later, murder was almost domesticated. Over half of all killings, or 51 percent, occurred in the home and were confined largely within the circle of family, friends, and acquaintance. Only 14 percent of victims were strangers; less than 8 percent of them were robbed. The white murder rate stood at 1.8; the black at 24.6, or just fourteen times as high. Thus, for the first time in generations the officially recorded racial gap in this index of violence had not grown at all.[10]

The future had not looked so promising for decades, as greater opportunities continued to pull blacks out of the South and into northern cities. These in-migrants were by no means troublesome social problems on arrival. On the contrary, transplanted southerners were typically vigorous and ambitious young people, more of whom had graduated from high school—35 percent—than the 33 percent among the white population of the cities in which they settled. In Philadelphia specifically they were also much less prone to mental illness than those who had been longer exposed to the multiple problems that still afflicted people who had grown up in a metropolis.[11]

Many of the hopes, too, of these Afro-American migrants were apparently realized. The breakthroughs in civil rights helped create a new leverage in urban politics. Above all, the gains continued in factory and white-collar employment, matched by the steady but far smaller increases among professionals, managers, and other elite groups. The situation in Philadelphia was again typical. As of 1950, 8 percent of the black male work force had won white-collar jobs, fully 25 percent were classified as "operatives and kindred workers," and another 11 percent were called "craftsmen, foremen, etc." Over the next decade these figures crept up, the white-collar workers to 10.5 percent and the craftsmen to 12.5.[12]

The year 1960 marked three related and dramatic firsts. The census of that year, marking the climax to the long historic process of migration, recorded that the black population of the United States, once overwhelmingly rural, had reversed that situation and become more typically urban than the whites, by a margin of 73 to 70 percent. The end of an almost equally significant process was signaled by the black proportion of factory workers for the first time exceeding the white, or 28 percent to 21 percent in Philadelphia, 25 to 20 percent across the country. In a further development, the national death rate from homicide dropped for both whites and blacks—the white rate from 2.6 to 2.5 per 100,000 annually, the black from 28.8 to 23.1. As of 1960, which closed out three eventful and promising decades, the overall murder rate of 4.7 was the lowest in any decennial year since the F.B.I. began collecting statistics in 1933.[13]

PHILADELPHIA AND THE WIDER WORLD, 1960–

Yet the promise of the mid-century decades has not generally been realized, and in particular the condition of poorer blacks in cities is in many respects worse than it was a generation ago. Patterns of criminal behavior have intensified, exacerbating all other problems, as part of a wider national and even international increase in violent and illicit activity of all sorts. In other respects, too—some positive, many negative—the postindustrial era dating from the late 1950s has created a different world for Afro-Americans and indeed for everyone.

The central irony is that just as blacks were beginning to enter the urban industrial age, the economy and indeed the whole society shifted beneath them. The high point occurred toward the middle of the 1950s when the Afro-American unemployment rate reached a historic low of 4.5 percent. From then on, though migrants continued to move into the city, the city itself was increasingly not what it had been. Part of the reason that blacks had by 1960 become more characteristically urban than whites is that whites were leaving the city in large numbers. In the same year Philadelphia and other older cities suffered for the first time a net loss both in population and in jobs, a condition that has accelerated ever since.[14]

The result of this loss was that, as the nation moved out of the urban-industrial and into the postindustrial era, the hard-won gains of the war and postwar periods were easily eroded. Although the Afro-American middle class has become more firmly entrenched than ever and individual men and women have, as always, won success along many lines, those very facts have obscured the problems of other blacks. Those who were able to win factory jobs in the 1950s, for example, were never really rescued from insecurity, as earlier white immigrants had often been. Unions retained their "last-hired, first-fired" seniority rules, which threatened all blacks with layoffs. In other cases industries simply moved out of the city and into the racially segregated suburbs. As fewer jobs were available to the unskilled and the urban economy contracted, structural unemployment expanded. By 1960 the black unemployment rate had reached double digits, at 10.2 percent, and it has typically remained at twice the white rate, or worse, ever since. Among black women, meanwhile, the old jobs in domestic service were exchanged in many cases for nothing at all, or for welfare dependency. What the family had gained in terms of fertility it began to lose in growing rates of illegitimacy and of female-headed households.[15]

To complete the vicious cycle of problems for blacks, just at the point in the late 1950s when the promises of urban life were beginning to turn sour, the rate of violent crime began to escalate across the country. From that point on, the graphs used to illustrate the F.B.I.'s annual Uniform Crime Reports have, with a few zigs and zags, continued to move upward.

This is not a black problem exclusively, or even an American problem. All over the industrial world after World War II, the long drop in serious criminality that had begun in the previous century was dramatically reversed. The reason for this reversal is complex and not yet fully understood. Despite its enormous benefits, the matured industrial economy may have created the climate for a new surge in criminality and violence. This phenomenon may have resulted from a number of factors, such as social inequality, the breakdown of traditional standards, the temptations of affluence, the boredom of security, and the impatience, especially among young people, implicit in a consumer economy. These and other factors may account for the reversal for many citizens in the urban West of those changes in social psychology and habits which had been both the product and the condition of the urban industrial revolution.[16]

Whatever its explanation, much of the world has been involved in a massive crime wave for the past generation, and many of America's blacks have proven especially vulnerable to it. Never having experienced the forces that combined to push down the rate of homicide, they were left instead with a legacy of insecurity, weakened families, and violent behavior. During the 1960s the murder rate climbed around the Western world in general, but it climbed fastest among Afro-Americans. These rates differed by region in the United States, with urban blacks and southern whites having higher rates than those among rural blacks and northern whites, so that no one city can typify the whole of the national experience. But Philadelphia is a representative northern city, and in Philadelphia by the mid-1970s the white murder rate had gone up by over 50 percent since 1948–1952, from 1.8 homicides per 100,000 population to 2.8. The black rate, meanwhile, had shot up more than two and one-half times in the same period, to 64.2 per 100,000, or fully twenty-three times higher than the white rate.[17]

The year 1974 ended the period of fastest growth; rates since that time have climbed more slowly. But the patterns then established, both black and white, have been maintained across big cities generally. In many ways they resemble patterns established in the last great period of social dislocation in the United States, during the 1840s and 1850s, when rapid urban growth and Irish immigration proved a strain on public order too great for the institutions of a preindustrial society to handle effectively. Both the preindustrial and postindustrial periods, as compared with the era around 1950, were and are marked by higher rates of violence in general, and in particular violence associated with groups of underemployed young men, violence between races or ethnic groups, and violence wreaked on strangers and spread throughout the day and week.[18]

The underlying reason for these patterns among contemporary blacks, though related to the long history of economic discrimination, are not themselves simply or directly economic in nature. Culture, the product of history, is in this case more important than poverty or income. In many countries, as in the United States, rising rates of criminal behavior have accompanied rising affluence and involved many people who shared in that affluence. But economic activity covers more than the production of goods and services. A meaningful job is a source not simply of income but ideally of security and a sense of social participation. Over a long period the economic experience of a group helps to shape its culture. In the case of urban blacks it has specifically helped to shape the ways in which they deal with aggression. Recent Hispanic and Asian immigrants to the United States, though often statistically poorer than Afro-Americans, have markedly lower rates of interpersonal violence. These latest arrivals have known discrimination and hard times, but not the unique historical experience that made crime and violence a problem for blacks.[19]

For many blacks, the long tradition of coping with the lack of legitimate employment by turning to the illegitimate has now hardened into a kind of subculture within the wider culture of Afro-Americans generally. This hustling subculture has adjusted to the simultaneous contraction and expansion of opportunities that began in the 1960s, as new conditions have marked another round of joblessness. The civil rights earned by the hard work of some, such as the freedom to walk the streets and visit shops without harassment, has made burglary and shoplifting easier for others. Changing tastes have greatly accelerated the movement into drug sales. But in general, recent patterns of criminal activity continue strongly to resemble those already evident in the late nineteenth century. The abuse of alcohol remains a significant but not especially characteristic problem. During 1979–1981 black Americans, who are perhaps 12 percent of the population, contributed 16 percent of the total arrests for drunkenness, or little more than their proportionate share, and accounted for less than 7 percent of arrests for more serious offenses against the liquor laws. The most successful burglars, robbers, con men and fences remain overwhelmingly white, drawn from the blue-collar elite rather than the black ghetto.[20]

But black theft, if not so profitable as theft by other groups, remains disproportionately heavy. Afro-Americans in 1979–1981 accounted for 29 percent of arrests for burglary and nearly 31 percent of arrests for larceny. Beyond that, blacks were accused of 36 percent of all offenses against family and children. And the group's involvement in vice followed the same order of escalating importance as in the previous century, accounting for nearly a quarter, or 23 percent, of all drug-related arrests; over half, or 52 percent, of all gambling arrests; and two-thirds, or 67 percent, of all prostitution arrests.[21]

In terms of the history of race relations, the long continuance of these patterns of crime has served two important functions. First, it has helped whites to forget the origin of the patterns in a discrimination practiced against a nineteenth-century black population which had then an abundance of skills that it was simply not allowed to use, and which was otherwise as fully ready as any group of urban newcomers to participate in the new industrial economy from which it was barred. Second, like a self-fulfilling prophecy, the criminality created by racism has been used over time to justify racism, as the former black skills have been dissipated. The hustling subculture may represent a more or less successful adaptation to the special conditions of poverty in the ghetto, but it offers no way out and into the dominant economy. The late twentieth century, moreover, has greatly intensified not only the traditional white contempt for blacks but also the kind of racial fear first felt in Philadelphia during the late 1890s.

Today's demand for "law and order," which is an oversimplified response to conditions in the ghetto, results in part from the fact that, despite the similarities, current patterns of crime differ from those inherited from the nineteenth century in three ominous ways. One difference is that violence is now clearly more important than theft. Of the seven major offenses listed in the Uniform Crime Reports, blacks in 1979–1980 accounted for 29 percent of the burglaries, larcenies, and auto thefts, and 47 percent of the criminal homicides, forcible rapes, armed robberies, and aggravated assaults. The pattern has been evident for nearly a generation. It may reflect a loss or weakening of the verbal forms that traditionally provided some protection against aggression. Toasting and playing the dozens may perhaps be essentially healthy expressions of ego, assertions of the prowess of the individual in the face of a hostile world. They may thus offer opportunities for catharsis, or perhaps sublimation, channeling potentially violent impulses into harmless words and at the same time providing some training in verbal quickness and physical restraint. But the forms were never fully effective in the best of times. The game of insult and display has always been a risky one, ideally requiring not only self-restraint but the restraint of other actors, some of them strangers. Colorful descriptions of other people's mayhem, or mothers, may win points among students of cultural anthropology as well as peers and fellows on the street, but they may also cross the line between incitement and catharsis and lead to bloodshed. In any case, sometime during the 1960s the tradition itself lost its hold, the verbal forms were eroded, and the rage was no longer contained.[22]

The second difference in the patterns of crime is the rise in armed robbery. Except for simple larceny, the least important of the major crimes, the rate of armed robbery grew faster than any other during the 1960s, and it has continued to rise ever since. Armed robbery and its frequent end-point, felony-murder, were rare events in the nineteenth century, but they are not so now. The robbery rate around 1980 had reached 236 per 100,000 of population, and felony-murder, most commonly committed in the course of robbery, accounted for 17 percent of all criminal killings. This is the essential "street crime." Nothing has contributed more to the fears and tensions that cripple efforts to revive the urban economy. And nothing has been so heavily, and increasingly, associated with Afro-Americans, who by 1979–1981 accounted for 58 percent of all robbery arrests. Robbery is the point at which theft and violence meet. It is also a crime that combines verbal aggression with the real threat of physical violence, for a successful robbery depends upon words, the ability to manipulate victims, to give orders and directions to people often confused and even paralyzed with fear.[23]

The last difference between current and traditional patterns of crime is the closing of the black-white gap in murder rates. During 1969–1971, when the national murder rate averaged 7.8 per 100,000 of population, Afro-Americans accounted for well over half of all these arrests, or 61 percent. During 1979–1981, when the national rate had reached 9.8, the white share was 50 percent, although the white percentage of the population had declined over the previous decade. The Afro-American rate apparently stabilized around 1974, largely because of demographic change. Young men are always the most homicidal element in the population, and there have been proportionally fewer of these since the 1960s. But while the white population has aged more sharply still, its murder rate has continued slowly to climb, both here and abroad, in response to some social and economic malaise that no one has been able fully to diagnose or to cure.[24]

Among Afro-Americans, then, current rates of criminality are relatively simple projections out of the past, products of a subculture of violence long nurtured by exclusion and denial. The roots of black crime are threefold: a different social psychology resulting from blacks' exclusion from the dominant experience with factory, bureaucracy, and schooling; a heritage of economic and other insecurities; and a long and complex experience with criminal activity. Political subordination and dependence historically helped make the urban "vice district" largely congruent with its "black district." Residential segregation trapped large numbers into living in or near an underworld in which force was the predominant means of settling disputes. This condition aggravated the felt need to carry weapons, which was originally a kind of defense against white aggression and hostility. The effect of these three conditions over time has been an atmosphere in which violent behavior is not only accepted but often expected and even celebrated.

The rest of the developed world, including white America, has traveled a more complex path along a U-curve. The dominant experience is still quantitatively and qualitatively far different from that of the Afro-American minority. But in a sense we are now all together, both black and white. The hallmarks of our present uncertainty have long been familiar to the blacks among us: personal insecurity, fear for the family, and a weakened faith in the link between present effort and future reward.

The current situation is composed of new as well as familiar elements. A number of the problems that originally contributed to high black crime rates have eased in recent years. Afro-Americans have been for some time breaking out of the pattern of political dependence, a movement symbolized in Philadelphia by the election in 1983 of a black mayor. More fundamentally, the lessening intensity of racial prejudice and of direct economic discrimination have opened unprecedented economic and social opportunities to those qualified to benefit from them. But the question remains whether these developments, at this date, are in themselves enough to change the situation of the millions still caught in the cycle of poverty, dependence, and crime.

The most striking difference between the traditional and the present prospects of America's urban blacks is the nature of economic opportunity, with all that this implies for social behavior. The history of Irish and Italian immigrants demonstrates that under certain conditions a tradition of violence may settle out in a relatively short period of time. But both of these groups experienced dramatic changes in personal habits in reaction to a complex of processes associated with the urban industrial economy during the long period from the Civil War through World War II. Contemporary Afro-Americans are faced with an entirely different situation. The central paradox of the 1940s and 1950s still holds: the gradual conquest of racial prejudice, in its older forms, has been accompanied by changes that may have eliminated the ladder of opportunity in its old form. In the modern American economy, unlike the earlier one that welcomed unskilled white immigrants, it has grown difficult, perhaps impossible, for any large bloc of citizens to move up as a group. And it is hard to predict whether all this will change in ways that improve the position of the nation's impoverished blacks. The term *postindustrial* is itself tentative, a reminder that we know where we have been but not exactly where we are going, and that while history is our only real guide to the future, it remains an uncertain one.[25]

A BIBLIOGRAPHICAL NOTE
NOTES
INDEX

A BIBLIOGRAPHICAL NOTE

HISTORIANS of black Philadelphia are fortunate in having a number of unpublished primary materials for this period. The Leon Gardiner Collection of the American Negro Historical Society, now at the Historical Society of Pennsylvania, includes the papers of William Still, Isaiah Wears, Octavius Catto, and Jacob White, Jr.; the minutes of the Executive Committee of the Pennsylvania Equal Rights League; and the records of the Pythian Baseball Club. The 388 scrapbooks kept by William Dorsey, discovered in 1976 in the Leslie Pinckney Hill Library of Cheyney University, were committed to microfilm in 1983. These books of newspaper clippings, which extend from 1847 to 1920 and were consulted by W. E. B. Du Bois for *The Philadelphia Negro,* indicate Dorsey's wide curiosity about items dealing with blacks, Africans, native Americans, and other matters. A xeroxed guide, "Indices of the William H. Dorsey Collection," includes a brief biography, although much about both collection and collector remains unknown. But the most important sources, in addition to *The Philadelphia Negro,* are newspapers both black and white, records of the criminal justice system and other agencies, and the federal census.

THE CENSUS

The federal census is indispensable for historians of the Afro-American experience in this period. Since blacks left relatively few manuscript or other written records, historians have to use what others, including census takers, have written about them. But however necessary, the census is also a blunt instrument, which is not always trustworthy. Whereas urban politicians have today rightly complained that the 1970 and 1980 censuses undercounted the minority population and deprived blacks and others of congressional representation and federal funds, in Philadelphia during the previous century the mayors complained rather that any count conducted in the summertime overlooked those rich and distinguished citizens who spent the hot months at the shore or in the country. Although no one spoke for blacks, the group was then at least as likely to be suspicious of house-to-house enumerators as it is today. On July 26, 1860, the

Public Ledger reported that many blacks were afraid the purpose of the census was to locate Afro-Americans so that they might be shipped out to Liberia, by the millions, as a way of solving the crisis leading the country toward Civil War—a fear encouraged by the *Ledger*'s own editorial policy as expressed on January 9. Indeed, this was the official policy of the Commonwealth of Pennsylvania, embodied in a pair of resolutions passed during the previous decade. It is thus not hard to imagine the effect on South or Lombard Streets when a hireling of the federal government, then dominated by southern Democrats, came around to ask, "How may people live here? What is their color? What are their names?" The misadventures of the census takers, untrained political appointees, were a regular joke every ten years, especially as they lurched their way through immigrant and black districts. And in 1900 the count was conducted at precisely the time when the Municipal Leaguers were prosecuting black men for vote fraud. For two years previously the inhabitants of the downtown wards had been used to young men asking questions door-to-door and had developed a number of techniques not only of evasion but of confrontation, spilling things out of upper stories onto persistent callers.

The validity of the occupational census for any group in the city is suspect in view of the virtual absence of all those characters—boxers and madames, confidence men and thieves, keepers of opium dens and speakeasies, policy writers, professional gamblers, and prostitutes—who peopled the daily newspapers. It is not surprising that of the 71 black men and women named by the *Public Ledger* as arrested for theft between July and December 1880, 39, or more than half, are not listed in the manuscript census; only 18 are listed, and 14, with such common names as "George Washington," have two or more listings. But even people like Gil Ball and "Doc" Edwards, legitimate or quasi-legitimate entrepreneurs, are not included either, although Ball was willing to advertise his name and business in the city directory. Not only are the records distorted by omissions, the use of false names, and prostitutes listed as "keeping house" or doing "domestic work," but the problem of accuracy is not confined to the bottom of the social ladder and may in some respects be worse at the top.

Du Bois, when conducting his own occupational count, noted that he or his agents spent some time in each household of the Seventh Ward and tried gently to straighten out what they thought were misleading answers, such as separating entrepreneurs from ambitious wage earners. Census takers did not take these pains, with results that are illustrated by the professional category of "doctor" of "physician." One function of the Afro-American press was to record the achievements of the group, to list and describe those who had made it into prestigious occupations. On December 29, 1883, the New York *Globe* counted five black doctors in Philadelphia. The 1880 manuscript census, however, counted 11 black "physicians," four "doctors," and two "medical doctors," an apparent exaggeration of over 300 percent at least. This was in part a matter of definition, for those who answered the census takers were probably healers of some sort, people who took money or gifts in return for medical advice. But they were not doctors according to state law. The coroner often had to reprimand bogus or unlicensed practitioners who presumed to sign death certificates. And although the counts in the black press included osteopaths, the majority of the self-described professionals in the census should not be included with the city's genuine black doctors, most of whom were proud of their educations at the best of universities, here and abroad.

All counts, then, of professionals and businessmen given here are taken from black sources, such as Du Bois, Richard Wright, and the Afro-American journals. The census was used only to record the number of blacks in the city, the age-structure of the population, and the occupations among them, but with serious reservations, particularly about the accuracy of the last. The census was taken in part from a computer tape labeled "1880: Black Individuals," supplied by Henry Williams, director of the Center for Philadelphia Studies, formerly the Philadelphia Social History Project.

THE CRIMINAL RECORDS

The late nineteenth century was the golden age of state and local annual reports, a period in which public agencies sought to justify their work by describing it in great detail rather than merely publishing brief and uninformative pamphlets full of puffery. The criminal justice agencies of Philadelphia and Pennsylvania fit this description, although there are two main problems in using their records for statistical purposes. First, much of the information provided is of dubious accuracy. While police and jailers provided trustworthy figures about objective matters such as numbers of people dealt with, sex, offense charged, height, and weight, they also included more suspect material obtained from the accused themselves, such as occupation, age, and birthplace. The most elementary matters may be inaccurate, for men and women in the clutches of the law did not often give straight answers to such questions as "how many times have you been arrested before?" or even, if they could get away with it, "what is your name?" Second, changes in the content of the reports, some of which were published only irregularly or for short periods, often prevent the assembling of any long series of comparable figures.

The published records for the city and county of Philadelphia itself include the annual reports of the Police Department, the county jail at Moyamensing, and the House of Correction. These are included in the *Annual Reports* of the mayors of Philadelphia, and some are obtainable also in separately bound editions. A guide to these printed reports, as well as to the unpublished court and jail dockets appears in "Crime, Criminals, Law Enforcement, and Records," *Newsletter of the Philadelphia City Archives*, nos. 43–47 (June 1981–Oct. 1982).

The police reports are complete except for the year 1871, but they often change in format. Most years lead off with little essays of self-praise, and all go on to list expenses, number of men, arrests in all categories, and totals by race, sex, and nativity, although these arrest totals are not cross-tabulated. Beginning in the mid-1870s and continuing through the early 1880s, they list all property recovered, together with persons arrested for serious personal or property crimes in the various districts or divisions. Race is noted only erratically. Most years from 1870 to 1890 have separate reports for each division, including not only the several districts but specialized agencies such as the Harbor Police and the Vagrant Detective; these include "notable arrests." For a few earlier years and continuously during the reform-minded 1890s, there is a special report on the fate of those arrested for liquor or gambling offenses, the intent being to show that the general failure to crack down on these people did not belong to the police so much as the courts.

No other agency in Philadelphia's justice system has records as rich as these. The jail stopped publishing annual reports in the 1870s. Only a few of its reports, in the late 1860s and early 1870s, list all those "committed" after arrest, as distinct from those convicted and sentenced. All the annual reports, however, give totals by race, sex, and specific offense, as well as other matters such as occupation, birthplace, and education. After the annual reports stopped, the jail issued nothing directly except for a brief financial statement in the mayor's annual messages. The House of Correction, mostly for vagrants, alcoholics, and streetwalkers, published reports beginning with its founding in 1874. These list totals by race, sex, nativity, and offense, but are not cross-tabulated and are largely concerned with income from the House's "industrial" projects as balanced against its expenses.

The unpublished materials from the criminal courts and jails are housed in the city archives, except for bills of indictment kept in the office of the clerk of the court of quarter sessions. The court dockets are fairly simple, listing all indictments, whether or not returned as true, and the final legal disposition of cases. The only difficulty in using them is the widespread use of false names, compounded by the reporters' inability to spell foreign names. The jail dockets, in contrast, are interesting but complicated. For the years 1860–1929 there are "Convict Description Dockets" for Moyamensing and, beginning in the 1890s, for the second jail at Holmesburg. Separate books for males and females list name, height, weight, description, color, occupation, sentence, and previous convictions. There are also sets of "Sentence Description Dockets" which give somewhat less information about people sentenced for somewhat lesser offenses, although only at the extremes is there any consistency in terms of who got sent where, and a given larcenist might show up in either book.

The House of Refuge, or juvenile reformatory, published records throughout this period. They list boys and girls indentured or apprenticed out and their progress in school. The House was not technically a place of punishment but of reformation only. Most of its inmates were referred to it directly by parents or guardians, and it was in some respects a quasi-private agency, with a board appointed in part by the mayor and in part by the judges of the court of common pleas. Its reports are housed in the Historical Society of Pennsylvania, together with its manuscript records for the period beginning in 1898 when it was moved out of the city to Glen Mills in Delaware County.

The records of the Eastern State Penitentiary are considerably richer and fuller than those for the jails. There are published reports for all years from 1859 through 1898. In addition to essays about crime and prison management, these documents list not only totals for a great variety of matters but historical tables of varying interest, such as how many prisoners were treated in the hospital since its opening and how many died of what causes. Many of them list every admitted prisoner, by number, with race, age, sex, offense, sentence, court, birthplace, parental situation, education, occupation, and what the authorities believed was the underlying reason for incarceration, such as "intemperance" or "congenital depravity." After 1898 the totals may be taken from the manuscript dockets or "Convict Reception Registers," which were maintained through

1928. The Industrial Reformatory at Huntingdon, opened in 1889 for young male offenders thought to be good subjects for rehabilitation, published relatively thin biennial reports only, with no specific information about individuals. This information does appear in the manuscript dockets, which, like those for the prison, are located in the State Archives at Harrisburg.

A final source for the crimes of murder and abortion is the computerized record of all Philadelphia indictments and trials from 1839 to 1901, appearing in Roger Lane, *Violent Death in the City: Suicide, Accident, and Murder in Nineteenth Century Philadelphia* (Cambridge: Harvard University Press, 1979).

THE NEWSPAPERS

In the age of the computer it seems easy and tempting to find and analyze some numerical record in isolation, or in near-isolation, from anything else. But in contrast to the official numbers, the newspapers provide context, color, and the contemporary version of common sense. The *Christian Recorder* is the only one of several Philadelphia black weeklies in this period which has survived physically, except for the clippings in the Dorsey collection. Although this newspaper was the national organ of the A.M.E. Church, it was also concerned with the secular affairs of Afro-Americans everywhere, and since it was published in the city, much of the news and comment on its editorial page was concerned with events in Philadelphia. Occasionally, especially during the late 1870s and early 1880s, there was a lively column devoted entirely to local news and gossip, much of it political. Many issues are missing for the later years especially, and those that survive are sometimes missing pages.

The New York Papers edited by or inherited from T. Thomas Fortune are also full of Philadelphia news and comment. These are the New York *Globe,* which began in 1883 and became the *Freeman* late in 1884, and the *Age,* beginning in 1888. Both of these papers published some variant of "Letters from the Quaker City," although not as regularly as letters from other places. These columns are often witty accounts of religious, social, professional, and political life in Philadelphia. The editorial pages, too, comment on events in what was regarded as one of the most important and dstinguished centers of black population, and in the late 1880s and early 1890s there were special columns of comment by such black Philadelphians as Theodore Minton, John Stephen Durham, and Mrs. N. F. Mossell. There are few extent issues between 1892 and 1900, although other black journals, such as the Baltimore *Afro-American* and even the St. Paul. *Negro Word,* have some material on Philadelphia or Philadelphians.

Finally, Carl Bolivar wrote pieces for the Philadelphia *Tribune.* Although the *Tribune* has been publishing continuously since 1883, its earliest surviving issues date from 1912. Bolivar, the historian of black Philadelphia, contributed a column of reminiscence from then until his death in 1914. His memory stretched back to the early 1860s, and his column ranges from early business ventures through sports, politics, and music. His work is illuminated by the topical collection possessed by Harry C. Silcox.

At times during the late nineteenth century Philadelphia was home to nearly a dozen daily newspapers at once. The biggest and most prestigious was the nonpartisan *Public Ledger,* which dates from well before the Civil War. The *Inquirer* began publishing in late 1870 and boasted by the 1890s that it was the largest Republican paper in the city, perhaps in the country. It is the only paper from that period which is still in business.

The *Ledger* is in most respects the better journal, careful and conservative. Every issue from the years 1860, 1870, 1880, and 1900 was combed for this book. The somewhat breezier *Inquirer* for the years 1870, 1890, and 1895, was also read for the book. Both papers were consulted for notable political campaigns, all murder trials involving blacks, all "notable arrests" as listed in the police reports, and other significant events. Neither paper is indexed, but a guide appears in George Morgan, *The History of Philadelphia, The City of Firsts: Being a Complete History of the City from Its Founding, in 1682, to the Present Time* (Philadelphia: The Historical Publication Society, 1926). It gives a day-by-day chronology of newsworthy events listed in every issue of the *Public Ledger* from 1860 through 1925, and in some years adds a list of "necrology."

NOTES

INTRODUCTION

1. The most detailed surveys of the literature are Ted Robert Gurr, "On the History of Violent Crime in Europe and America," in Hugh Davis Graham and Ted Robert Gurr, *Violence in America: Historical and Comparative Perspectives*, rev. ed. (Beverly Hills and London: Saga Publications, 1979), pp. 353–374; Roger Lane, "Urban Police and Violence in Nineteenth Century America," in Norval Morris and Michael Tonry, *Crime and Justice: An Annual Review of Research*, vol. 2 (Chicago: University of Chicago Press, 1980), pp. 1–43.

2. The most ambitious surveys are Ted Robert Gurr, Peter N. Grabosky, and Richard C. Hula, *The Politics of Crime and Conflict: A Comparative History of Four Cities* (Beverly Hills and London: Saga Publications, 1977); Eric Monkkonen, *Police in Urban America, 1860–1920* (Cambridge: Cambridge University Press, 1981).

3. W. E. B. Du Bois, *The Philadelphia Negro: A Social Study* (Philadelphia, 1899). See also John W. Blassingame, *The Slave Community: Plantation Life in the Antebellum South*, rev. ed. (New York: Oxford University Press, 1979, orig. pub. 1972); Robert Fogel and Stanley Engerman, *Time on the Cross: The Economics of American Negro Slavery* (Boston and Toronto: Little, Brown, 1974); Eugene Genovese, *Roll, Jordan, Roll: The World the Slaves Made* (New York: Pantheon Books, 1976); Gilbert Osofsky, *Harlem: The Making of a Ghetto: Negro New York, 1890–1930* (New York, Harper and Row, 1963); Constance Green, *The Secret City: A History of Race Relations in the Nation's Capitol* (Princeton: Princeton University Press, 1967); Allan Spear, *Black Chicago: The Making of a Negro Ghetto, 1890–1920* (Chicago: Chicago University Press, 1967); John W. Blassingame, *Black New Orleans, 1860–1880* (Chicago: The University of Chicago Press, 1973); David M. Katzman, *Before the Ghetto: Black Detroit in the Nineteenth Century* (Urbana: University of Illinois Press, 1973); Kenneth Kusmer, *A Ghetto Takes Shape: Black Cleveland, 1879–1930* (Urbana: University of Illinois Press, 1976); Harold Rabinowitz, *Race Relations in the Urban South, 1865–1890* (New York: Oxford University Press, 1978); James Borchert, *Alley Life in Washington: Family, Community, Religion and*

Folklore in the City, 1850–1970 (Urbana: University of Illinois Press, 1980); Elizabeth Pleck, *Black Migration and Poverty: Boston, 1865–1900* (New York and London: Academic Press, 1980).

4. Comparative racial or ethnic statistics are hard to compile, as jurisdictions often do not maintain or publish summaries that distinguish Hispanics, and some, including Philadelphia, do not currently publish black-white differences, although they provide them to the Federal Bureau of Investigation. See Charles Silberman, *Criminal Justice, Criminal Violence* (New York: Random House, 1978), pp. 119–122; Department of Justice, Federal Bureau of Investigation, *Uniform Crime Reports for the United States, 1970* (Washington, D.C.: U.S. Government Printing Office, 1971), pp. 7, 131; *Uniform Crime Reports, 1981*, pp. 8, 179.

5. Roger Lane, *Violent Death in the City: Suicide, Accident, and Murder in Nineteenth Century Philadelphia* (Cambridge: Harvard University Press, 1979); David R. Johnson, *Policing the Urban Underworld: The Impact of Crime on the Development of American Police, 1800–1887* (Philadelphia: Temple University Press, 1981); Allan F. Davis and Mark H. Haller, *The Peoples of Philadelphia: A History of Ethnic Groups and Lower-Class Life, 1790–1940* (Philadelphia: Temple University Press, 1973); Theodore Hershberg, ed., *Philadelphia: Work, Space, Family, and Group Experience in the Nineteenth Century: Essays Towards an Interdisciplinary History of the City* (New York and Oxford: Oxford University Press, 1981); Russell F. Weigley, ed., *Philadelphia: A Three Hundred Year History* (New York: W. W. Norton, 1982).

1. A TALE OF TWO CITIES

1. See Dorothy Gondos Beers, "The Centennial City, 1865–1876," in Russell Weigley, ed., *Philadelphia: A Three Hundred Year History* (New York and London: W. W. Norton, 1982), pp. 417–470; Nathaniel Burt and Wallace E. Davies, "The Iron Age, 1876–1905," in Weigley, ed., *Philadelphia*, pp. 471–523.

2. See Russell Weigley, "The Border City in the Civil War, 1854–1865," in Weigley, ed., *Philadelphia*, pp. 363–416; William Dusinberre, *Civil War Issues in Philadelphia, 1856–1865* (Philadelphia: University of Pennsylvania Press, 1965).

3. David R. Johnson, *Policing the Urban Underworld: The Impact of Crime on the Development of American Police, 1800–1887* (Philadelphia: Temple University Press, 1979), pp. 26–35; Russell F. Weigley, ' "A Peaceful City': Public Order in Philadelphia from Consolidation Through the Civil War," in Allen F. Davis and Mark H. Haller, ed., *The Peoples of Philadelphia: A History of Ethnic Groups and Lower-Class Life, 1790–1940* (Philadelphia: Temple University Press, 1973), pp. 155–174; Roger Lane, *Violent Death in the City: Suicide, Accident, and Murder in Nineteenth Century Philadephia* (Cambridge: Harvard University Press, 1979), p. 63; Roger Lane, *Policing the City: Boston, 1822–1885* (Cambridge: Harvard University Press, 1967), pp. 26–38; James Richardson, *The New York Police, Colonial Times to 1901* (New York: Oxford University Press, 1970), pp. 23–81; Philadelphia *Public Ledger,* 7/14/60.

4. Lincoln Steffens, "Philadelphia: Corrupt and Contented," in Steffens, *The Shame of the Cities* (New York: McClure, Phillips, 1904), pp. 193–232.

5. George Morgan, *The City of Firsts: Being a Complete History of Philadelphia from Its Founding, in 1682, to the Present Time* (Philadelphia: Historical Publications Society, 1926), p. 243; Bruce Laurie, "Fire Companies and Gangs in Southwark: The 1840's," in Davis and Haller, ed., *Peoples of Philadelphia,* pp. 71–88; Johnson, *Policing the Urban Underworld,* pp. 95–100; Lane, *Policing the City,* p. 105; Richardson, *New York Police,* pp. 64–65; Howard O. Sprogle, *The Philadelphia Police, Past and Present* (Philadelphia, 1887), pp. 122–123.

6. Sprogle, *Philadelphia Police,* pp. 122–123, pp. 150–152.

7. Sprogle, *Philadelphia Police,* pp. 150–152.

8. Sprogle, *Philadelphia Police,* pp. 159–160; *Police Reports* contained in *Annual Address of Mayor William Stokley of Philadelphia* (Philadelphia, 1872), cited hereafter as *Annual Police Report.*

9. Sprogle, *Philadelphia Police,* pp. 189–191; *Public Ledger,* 2/7/70.

10. Beers, "The Centennial City"; Burt and Davies, "The Iron Age"; Gunther Barth, *City People: The Rise of Modern City Culture in Nineteenth Century America* (New York: Oxford University Press, 1982), p. 184.

11. Bureau of the Census, *Historical Statistics of the United States, Part I* (Washington: U. S. Government Printing Office, 1975), p. 165.

12. See Lane, *Violent Death in the City,* which also includes accident in the analysis; Martin Gold, "Suicide, Homicide, and the Socialization of Aggression," *American Journal of Sociology* 62 (May 1958): 651–661.

13. W. E. B. Du Bois, *The Philadelphia Negro: A Social Study* (Philadelphia, 1899), p. 127.

14. DuBois, *Philadelphia Negro,* pp. 411–418.

15. *Inquirer,* 12/12/89.

16. *Annual Reports* of Almshouse, House of Correction in *Annual Addresses of the Mayors; Annual Reports of the Superintendent to the Managers of the House of Refuge;* Negley K. Teeters, *They Were in Prison: A History of the Pennsylvania Prison Society, 1787–1937* (Chicago, Philadelphia, and Toronto: John C. Winston, 1937), pp. 331–344.

17. Elizabeth Geffen, "Violence in Philadelphia in the 1840's and 1850's," *Pennsylvania History* 36.4 (Oct. 1969): 38–410.

18. *Inquirer,* 3/3/90.

19. *Public Ledger,* 5/26/80.

20. Com. no. 491, April 1896, 10/21/96. All cases involving murder, unless directly quoted, are cited by Court of Oyer and Terminer Docket number (see A Bibliographical Note) and date of trial.

21. William Dusinberre, *Civil War Issues in Philadelphia, 1856–1865* (Philadelphia: University of Pennsylvania Press, 1965), pp. 137–139, 161–165, 169–170, 177–178, 182.

22. *Public Ledger,* 5/31/80.

23. Com. no. 354, Aug. 1892, 10/17/92.

24. U. S. Department of Commerce, Bureau of the Censu, *Twelfth Census of the United States* (1900), vol. I, pt. I, p. cxix; Du Bois, *Philadelphia Negro,* pp. 58–62.

25. Du Bois, *Philadelphia Negro,* p. 296.

26. Richard R. Wright, Jr., *The Negro in Pennsylvania: A Study in Economic History* (New York: Arno Press, 1967, orig. pub. 1912), pp. 75–76.

27. Wright, *Negro in Pennsylvania,* pp. 166–167; *Christian Recorder,* 10/25/83.

28. New York *Globe,* 5/31/84, 6/7/84; Wright, *Pennsylvania Negro,* pp. 167–168.

29. John T. Gillard, S.S.J., *The Catholic Church and the American Negro* (Baltimore: St. Joseph's Society Press, 1929), pp. 32–45; Baltimore *Afro-American,* 8/17/95; New York *Age,* 9/8/88; Du Bois, *Philadelphia Negro,* p. 220.

30. Philip S. Benjamin, *The Philadelphia Quakers in the Industrial Age, 1865–1920* (Philadelphia: Temple University Press, 1969), p. 137; *Annual Report of the Home for Destitute Colored Children; Annual Report of the Association for the Care of Colored Orphans.*

31. Benjamin, *Philadelphia Quakers,* pp. 3–25, 126–147; *Annual Report of the Association for the Care of Colored Orphans;* Alfred Cope to Octavius V. Catto, 4/23/69, in Catto Papers, Leon Gardiner Collection, American Negro Historical Society Papers, Historical Society of Pennsylvania (HSP hereafter); Mrs. N. F. Mossell, *The Work of the Afro-American Woman,* 2d ed. (Philadelphia: G. S. Ferguson, 1908), pp. 144–147; *Philadelphia Tribune,* 4/20/12; Microfilm minutes, Institute for Colored Youth, 1860–1914, Haverford College Library.

32. New York *Freeman,* 6/12/86, 11/7/86, 2/5/87.

33. Burt and Davies, "The Iron Age," p. 504; *Inquirer,* 1/14/90, 11/16/97.

34. Du Bois, *Philadelphia Negro,* p. 325.

35. Only two organizations in the city apparently had both blacks and whites on their boards, both of them founded by black leaders: the Home for Aged and Infirm Colored Persons, founded in 1865 by Stephen Smith and the Frederick Douglass Clinic, founded in 1895 by Nathan F. Mossell. Du Bois, *Philadelphia Negro,* pp. 355–357.

36. *Christian Recorder,* 4/30/76; Charles Fred White, Jr., *Who's Who in Philadelphia: . . . Biographical Sketches of Philadelphia's Leading Colored People . . .* (Philadelphia: A.M.E. Book Concern, 1912), pp. 18–19, 96; Herbert M. Morals, *The History of the Negro in Medicine* (New York: Publisher's, 1977), p. 80; New York *Age,* 5/11/89; White, *Who's Who,* pp. 70–73; William H. Dorsey Collection, microfilm of scrapbooks kept at Leslie Pinckney Hill Library, Cheyney University, Cheyney, Pennsylvania, scrapbook number 111, 1899, p. 3, clipping from Philadelphia Tribune, 1/28/99 (Dorsey Scrapbooks hereafter).

37. *Inquirer,* 6/27/90; Du Bois, *Philadelphia Negro,* pp. 114–115; Wright, *Negro in Pennsylvania,* p. 129; White, *Who's Who,* p. 42; Benjamin, *Philadelphia Quakers,* p. 146; Marjorie H. Dobkin, ed., *The Making of a Feminist: Early Journals and Letters of M. Carey Thomas* (Kent: Kent State University Press, 1980), p. 25.

38. Cf. David Katzman, *Before the Ghetto: Black Detroit in the Nineteenth Century* (Urbana: University of Illinois Press, 1973), pp. 81–103. Katzman argues that lower-class blacks were locked into an entirely separate or "caste" position, while upper-class blacks had greater social interaction with whites. See

also Kenneth Kusmer, *A Ghetto Takes Shape: Black Cleveland, 1870–1930* (Urbana: Black Cleveland, 1870–1930), pp. 91–122. This idea may have some basis in the social and professional lives of elite blacks in these two smaller and relatively integrated cities. Some elite blacks in them, as in Philadelphia, had white clients or customers. But the line between business and social relations was often a sharp one, and whereas the black press sometimes indicated that various doctors or lawyers had white clients, the white press explicitly denied this. See e.g. *Inquirer* 9/4/90.

39. Du Bois, *Philadelphia Negro,* pp. 322–367; Wright, *Negro in Pennsylvania,* pp. 167–174; Com. no. 168, Feb. 1989, 5/30/98; Com. no. 437, March 1899, 6/27/99.

40. Wright, *Negro in Pennsylvania;* conversation with Marjorie Merklin, middle school administrator, Lower Merion, Pennsylvania, Winter 1983.

41. Lane, *Violent Death,* pp. 72–73; *Inquirer,* 3/6/99.

42. Teeters, *They Were in Prison,* p. 170.

43. *Public Ledger,* 7/20/70; *Inquirer,* 6/8/90.

44. Edwin Bancroft Henderson, *The Negro in Sports,* rev. ed. (Washington D.C.: Associated Publishers, 1939), pp. 144–153; Octavius V. Catto to George F. S_____, Captain of Alerts Baseball Club, 6/30/67, in Pythian Baseball Club Papers, Leon Gardiner Collection, American Negro Historical Society, HSP; Philadelphia *Tribune,* 8/24/12.

45. Henderson, *Negro in Sports,* pp. 277–282.

46. Du Bois, *Philadelphia Negro,* pp. 277–282.

47. *Inquirer,* 1/12/80.

48. *Public Ledger,* 6/5/80; *Inquirer,* 9/21/80; 1880 casebook of Pennsylvania Society to Protect Children from Cruelty, Urban Archives, Temple University.

49. Du Bois, *Philadelphia Negro,* pp. 358–367.

50. *Inquirer,* 9/18/88, 9/21/88, 3/7/90.

51. Geffen, "Violence in Philadelphia," p. 388; *Inquirer,* 7/10/90; Com. no. 352, Jan. 1881, 1/31/81; Com. no. 390, Sept. 1881, 12/31/81; Com. no. 193, Sept. 1895, 10/16/95; Com. no. 757, Sept. 1897, 9/30/97; Com. no. 141, Jan. 1900, 1/25/1900.

52. Du Bois, *Philadelphia Negro,* 127.

53. Philadelphia *Tribune,* 5/25/12; *Christian Recorder,* 7/25/76; New York *Globe,* 10/13/83; New York *Freeman,* 8/8/85; Du Bois, *Philadelphia Negro,* 114–115; New York *Age,* 4/11/91.

54. New York *Freeman,* 11/6/87, 11/20/87; New York *Globe,* 8/23/83; Mossell, *Afro-American Woman,* p. 21; Du Bois, *Philadelphia Negro,* pp. 228–229.

55. Benjamin, *Philadelphia Quakers,* p. 137; Du Bois, *Philadelphia Negro,* p. 113.

56. Du Bois, *Philadelphia Negro,* pp. 112–113.

57. Du Bois, *Philadelphia Negro,* pp. 115–125.

58. William Still, "A Brief Narrative of the Struggle for the Rights of the Colored People of Philadelphia, in the City Railway Cars, and a Defense of William Still . . ." (Philadelphia, 1867), pp. 23–24; Baltimore *Afro-American,* 7/16/98; Du Bois, *Philadelphia Negro,* pp. 119–123.

59. Du Bois, *Philadelphia Negro,* pp. 32–35, 119–121.

60. Kusmer, *A Ghetto Takes Shape,* pp. 75–83, 114; August Meier, *Negro Thought in America, 1880–1915* (Ann Arbor: University of Michigan Press, 1964), pp. 121–160.

61. New York *Freeman,* 3/28/85; Theodore Hershberg et al., "A Tale of Three Cities: Blacks, Immigrants, and Opportunity in Philadelphia, 1850–1880, 1930, 1970," in Theodore Hershberg, ed. *Philadelphia: Work, Space, Family, and Group Experience in the Nineteenth Century: Essays Towards an Interdisciplinary History of the City* (New York and Oxford: Oxford University Press, 1981), pp. 461–491, p. 475; W. E. B. Dubois, *The Negro in Business: Report of a Social Study Made under the Direction of Atlanta University . . . 1899* (New York: A.M.S. Press, 1971, originally published 1899), p. 27; DuBois, *Philadelphia Negro,* pp. 115–126.

62. New York *Globe,* 10/27-12/29/83.

63. See Theodore Hershberg et al., "A Tale of Three Cities: Blacks, Immigrants, and Opportunity in Philadelphia, 1850–1880, 1930, 1970," in Hershberg, ed., *Philadelphia,* pp. 461–491; Stephen Thernstrom, *The Other Bostonians: Poverty and Progress in the American Metropolis, 1880–1970* (Cambridge: Harvard University Press, 1973), pp. 203–219; Lorenzo J. Greene and Carter G. Woodson, *The Negro Wage Earner* (New York: Russell and Russell, 1930); Charles H. Wesley, *Negro Labor in the United States, 1850–1925* (New York: Vanguard Press, 1927); Mary White Ovington, *Half a Man: The Status of the Negro in New York* (New York: Hill and Wang, 1969, originally published 1911).

64. Wright, *Negro in Pennsylvania,* p. 127; New York *Age,* 5/10/90; New York *Globe,* 12/15/83; Du Bois, *Philadelphia Negro,* pp. 326–347.

65. Theodore Hershberg and Henry Williams, "Mulattoes and Blacks: Intra-Group Color Differences and Social Stratification in Nineteenth-Century Philadelphia," in Hershberg, ed., *Philadelphia,* pp. 392–434; Hershberg et al., "A Tale of Three Cities," p. 475.

66. Hershberg and Williams, "Mulattoes and Blacks," pp. 410–413; Hershberg et al., "A Tale of Three Cities," p. 475; *Public Ledger,* 7/17/1900.

67. Philip Foner, *Organized Labor and the Black Worker, 1619–1973* (New York and Washington: Praeger, 1974); Foner, ed., *The Black Worker: A Documentary History,* vol. III, *The Black Worker During the Era of the Knights of Labor* (Philadelphia: Temple University Press, 1978).

68. Foner, *Organized Labor and the Black Worker,* pp. 17–120.

69. Du Bois, *Philadelphia Negro,* pp. 129–131; Wright, *Negro In Pennsylvania,* pp. 93–94.

70. Greene and Woodson, *Negro Wage Earner,* p. 108; John Stephen Durham, "Labor Unions and the Negro," *Atlantic Monthly* 81 (Jan. 1898): 222–231; Wright, *Negro in Pennsylvania,* p. 93; *Inquirer,* 8/3/97.

71. Green and Woodson, *Negro Wage Earner,* pp. 130–133.

72. *Inquirer,* 8/17/90.

73. *Inquirer,* 8/20/90, 8/26/90, 9/1/90, 10/18/90.

74. Greene and Woodson, *Negro Wage Earner,* p. 151.

75. Wright, *Negro in Pennsylvania,* p. 71; White, *Who's Who,* pp. 18–19; Mossell, *Afro-American Woman,* pp. 10, 21; Wright, *Negro in Pennsylvania,* p. 72.

76. Wright, *Negro in Pennsylvania,* p. 72; Eudice Glassberg, "Work, Wages,

and the Cost of Living: Ethnic Differences and the Poverty Line, Philadelphia 1880," in *Pennsylvania History* 66.1 (Jan. 1979): 17–58; Du Bois, *Philadelphia Negro,* pp. 170–171.

77. Du Bois, *Philadelphia Negro,* pp. 446–447, 139–140; pp. 446–447; *Inquirer,* 1/10/91.

78. Wright, *Negro in Pennsylvania,* p. 68.

79. Wright, *Negro in Pennsylvania,* 94; Herbert R. Northrup, *Organized Labor and the Negro* (New York and London: Harper, 1944), pp. 137–147; Leslie Robin, *Racial Policies and American Industry, Report Number 29: The Negro in the Longshore Industry* (Philadelphia: University of Pennsylvania Press, 1974), pp. 17–19; *Inquirer,* 6/21/98.

80. Katzman, *Before the Ghetto,* pp. 118–119; Du Bois, *Philadelphia Negro,* p. 135; Wright, *Negro in Pennsylvania,* p. 160.

81. See e.g. *Inquirer,* 3/17/90.

82. *Annual Reports;* White, *Who's Who,* p. 96; Glassberg, "Work, Wages, and the Cost of Living," p. 56; *A Directory of the Charitable, Educational, and Religious Associations and Churches of Philadelphia . . . Prepared by the Civic Club,* 2d ed. (Philadelphia, 1903).

83. *Public Ledger,* 6/15/60.

2. RACIAL AND URBAN POLITICS

1. *Inquirer,* 10/9-12/71.

2. *Inquirer,* 10/14/71, 10/15/71; Harry Silcox, "Nineteenth Century Black Militant: Octavius V. Catto, 1839–1871," *Pennsylvania History* 44 (Jan. 1977): 53–76.

3. *Philadelphia Annual Register of Deaths, 1890,* Dec. 1890; James Earle Miller, "The Negro in Pennsylvania Politics, with Special Reference to Philadelphia since 1933," Ph.D. diss. in Political Science, University of Pennsylvania, 1945, p. 85; *Inquirer,* 12/15/90.

4. Kenneth Kusmer, *A Ghetto Takes Shape: Black Cleveland, 1870–1930* (Urbana: University of Illinois Press, 1976), pp. 146–147; Allan H. Spear, *Black Chicago: The Making of a Negro Ghetto, 1890–1920* (Chicago: University of Chicago Press), pp. 75–76; *Inquirer,* 12/1/91.

5. *Inquirer,* 8/5/90; *Public Ledger,* 4/15/98.

6. *Public Ledger,* 1/31/1902; James N. Hardie to William Still, 2/4/65, and Sojourner Truth to Still 1/4/76, in William Still Papers, Leon Gardiner Collection, American Negro History Society Papers, HSP; *Christian Recorder,* 6/20/78, 5/16/89.

7. *Public Ledger,* 3/15/60, 4/23/60, 5/3/60.

8. Philip S. Foner, "The Battle to End Discrimination vs. Negroes on Philadelphia Streetcars," Part 1, "The Beginning of the Battle," and Part 2, "The Victory," *Pennsylvania History* 40.3 (July 1973): 261–290; 40.4 (Oct. 1973): 353–380.

9. William Still, "A Brief Narrative of the Struggle for the Rights of the Colored People of Philadelphia, in the City Railway Cars, and a Defense of William Still . . ." (Philadelphia, 1867).

10. *Public Ledger,* 3/28-31/60.

11. *Public Ledger*, 3/29/60; "Cross Tabulation of Population Sex by Age Controlling for Ethnicity," printout provided by Philadelphia Social History Project from 1860 census; John A. Saunders, *100 Years after Emancipation: History of the Philadelphia Negro, 1787 to 1963* (n.p., n.d.), p. 65; Com. no. 398, Feb. 1865, 11/21/65.

12. James M. McPherson, *The Struggle for Equality: Abolitionists and the Negro in the Civil War and Reconstruction* (Princeton: Princeton University Press, 1964), pp. 234–235; Pennsylvania State Equal Rights League, Minutes of Executive Board, 1864–1868, Gardner Collection, HSP.

13. Alexander McClure, *Old Time Notes of Pennsylvania*, vol. 1 (Philadelphia: John Winston, 1905), p. 596; *Why Colored People in Philadelphia Are Excluded from the Streetcars* (Philadelphia, 1867), p. 9; Pennsylvania State Equal Rights League, Minutes: *Christian Recorder*, 2/9/67, 6/30/66.

14. Foner, "Battle to End Discrimination," pt. 2, pp. 359–360.

15. Franklin W. Speirs, *The Street Railway System of Philadelphia* (Baltimore: Johns Hopkins University Press, 1897), p. 26.

16. *Christian Recorder*, 6/30/66.

17. Ira Brown, "Pennsylvania and the Rights of the Negro, 1865–1867," *Pennsylvania History* 37.1 (Jan. 1961): 49.

18. Still, "A Brief Narrative"; *Public Ledger*, 1/14/65; *Why Colored People are Excluded*," p. 5; Harry C. Silcox, "Philadelphia Negro Educator: Jacob C. White, Jr., 1837–1900," *Pennsylvania Magazine of History and Biography* 97.1 (Jan. 1973): 86.

19. Brown, "Pennsylvania and Rights," p. 50; *Christian Recorder*, 11/24/66; *Public Ledger*, 5/25/69; Alfred Cope to Catto, 4/23/69, in Catto Papers, Gardiner Collection, HSP.

20. Catto to Cornelia Saunders, 5/28/60, and bill from John Wanamaker's, 2/6/71, in Catto Papers; Silcox, "Octavius Catto," p. 58; lineup in Pythian Baseball Club Papers, Gardiner Collection, HSP, quoted in Silcox, "Jacob White, Jr.," p. 89.

21. John Hope Franklin, *Reconstruction after the Civil War* (Chicago: University of Chicago Press, 1961), pp. 127–173.

22. Brown, "Pennsylvania and Rights," *passim; ibid.*, p. 49.

23. McClure, *Old Time Notes*, II, 279–280; Brown, "Pennsylvania and Rights," p. 52.

24. Jacob White to Phillip S. Bell, Esq., corresponding secretary of Athletic Ball Club, 6/30/67, and Catto to Geo. F._____, 6/30/67, in Pythian Club Papers; Silcox, "Jacob White, Jr.," passim.

25. Conversation with Harry Silcox, winter 1983; John W. Johnson to Catto, 8/14/70, Catto Papers.

26. Franklin, *Reconstruction*, pp. 194–207.

27. *Inquirer*, 6/7-8/72.

28. Harry C. Silcox, "Philadelphia's First Black Politician: Isaiah C. Wears, 1822–1900," unpaginated paper in possession of the author.

29. *Christian Recorder*, 11/14/78; Brown, "Pennsylvania and Rights," pp. 54–55.

30. Brown, "Pennsylvania and Rights," p. 56.

31. *Christian Recorder*, 1/10/67; New York *Age*, 5/30/91.

32. Cf. W. E. B. Du Bois, "The Black Vote of Philadelphia," in Miriam Ershowitz and Joseph Zigmund, ed., *Black Politics in Philadelphia* (New York: Basic Books, 1973), pp. 31–39, originally published in *Charities* 78 (Oct. 1905).

33. *Inquirer*, 10/12/70; *Public Ledger*, 11/11/70, 10/12/70.

34. McClure, *Old Time Notes*, II, 283–285.

35. Brown, "Pennsylvania and Rights," p. 53; Clinton Rogers Woodruff, "Election Methods and Reforms in Philadelphia," *Annals of the American Academy of Political and Social Science* 17 (March 1901): 181–203; *Public Ledger*, 10/30/70.

36. *Public Ledger*, 2/18/70.

37. *Philadelphia City Directory*, 1879; *Inquirer*, 3/20/90, 10/20/81, 3/1/83, 5/11/87; *Public Ledger*, 2/8/83.

38. New York *Globe*, 11/17/83; New York *Freeman*, 2/6/86; *Inquirer*, 3/20/90; *Christian Recorder*, 2/7/84.

39. See e.g. Howard Frank Gillette, Jr., "Corrupt and Contented: Philadelphia's Political Machine, 1865–1887," Ph.D. diss. in History, Yale University, 1970.

40. *Inquirer*, 6/15-16/71.

41. William C. Quay, "Philadelphia Democrats: 1880–1910," Ph.D. diss., Lehigh University, 1969, p. 256; *Inquirer*, 11/6/78; *Public Ledger*, 10/14/70; Com. no. 170, Jan. 1880, 3/24/81; Com. no. 96, Feb. 1893, 4/6/93; Com. no. 346, Dec. 1901, 12/19/01; Elections and vote chart in Quay, "Philadelphia Democrats," pp. 263–264.

42. New York *Age*, 4/11/91; *Inquirer*, 6/26/90; *Christian Recorder*, 10/31/78.

43. *Inquirer*, 6/24/73, 10/15/73, 2/16/76.

44. *Inquirer*, 2/3/77.

45. *Inquirer*, 2/21/77.

46. *Inquirer*, 2/20/78; *Christian Recorder*, 2/21/78, 10/31/78, 11/14/78.

47. *Public Ledger*, 6/1/80, 11/3/80; Quay, "Philadelphia Democrats," p. 13; *Inquirer*, 9/19/80; *Public Ledger*, 11/3/80.

48. James Bryce, *The American Commonwealth*, vol. 2 (New York: Macmillan, 1927, orig. pub. 1888), pp. 365–384; George Vickers, *The Fall of Bossism: A History of the Committee of One Hundred and the Reform Movement in Philadelphia and Pennsylvania*, vol. 1 (Philadelphia, 1883); Gillette, "Corrupt and Contented," pp. 222–258, 344–350; Rudolph Blankenburg, "Forty Years in the Wilderness," a seven-part account of reform in the city appearing in *Arena* 33–34 (Jan. 1905–Aug. 1906), cited hereafter by part number only.

49. *Public Ledger*, 12/10/80.

50. *Public Ledger*, 12/10/80; *Inquirer*, 12/11/80.

51. *Public Ledger*, 1/5/81.

52. *Inquirer*, 12/16/80.

53. *Inquirer* and *Public Ledger*, 2/3/81; Vickers, *Fall of Bossism*, p. xxxiii; *Public Ledger*, 2/16/81.

54. Purvis name not on original list in Vickers, *Fall of Bossism*, p. xxxiii, but cf. Gillette, "Corrupt and Contented," p. 349; *Inquirer*, 8/6/81.

55. *Public Ledger*, 8/1-2/81; *Inquirer*, 8/6/81; *Christian Recorder*, 10/7/80.

56. *Public Ledger* and *Inquirer,* 8/10/81.
57. *Inquirer,* 8/23/81.
58. *Public Ledger* and *Inquirer,* 8/30/81.
59. *Inquirer,* 8/30/81.
60. New York *Age,* 4/11/91; William Still, *An Address on Voting and Voters, Delivered at Concert Hall, Tuesday Evening, March 10, 1874* (Philadelphia, 1874); *Christian Recorder,* 9/19/78; Raiford W. Logan, *The Negro in American Life and Thought: The Nadir, 1877–1901* (New York: Dial Press, 1954), p. 45.
61. *Christian Recorder,* 9/7/82; *Inquirer,* 9/5/82.
62. *Public Ledger,* 2/20/84; New York *Globe,* 3/15/84; Sprogle, *Philadelphia Police,* p. 173; *Inquirer,* 2/2/89; Saunders, *100 Years after Emancipation,* p. 102.
63. New York *Globe,* 4/12/84.
64. Edmund J. James, ed., *The City Government of Philadelphia: A Study in Municipal Administration* (Philadelphia, 1893), pp. 27–28; New York *Globe,* 1/13/83, 1/20/83; *Public Ledger,* 2/22/83; Miller, "Negro in Pennsylvania Politics"; John Hudley Strange, "The Negro in Philadelphia Politics, 1963–1965," Ph.D. diss. in Political Science, Princeton University, 1972, p. 203; New York *Age,* 11/28/91.
65. New York *Age,* 11/28/91.
66. New York *Freeman,* 8/8/85, 6/11/87; *Inquirer,* 8/30/81; New York *Age,* 3/7/91, 11/28/91; *Philadelphia Tribune,* 12/14/12.
67. New York *Globe,* 3/15/84; John Stephen Durham, "Labor Unions and the Negro," *Atlantic Monthly* 81 (Jan. 1989): 222–231.
68. *Inquirer,* 4/2/90; New York *Globe,* 5/10/84, 10/25/84; New York *Age,* 7/28/87; W. E. B. Du Bois, *The Philadelphia Negro: A Social Study* (Philadelphia, 1899), p. 119.
69. New York *Freeman,* 3/7/85; New York *Age,* 5/18/89.
70. James, ed., *City Government of Philadelphia,* pp. 49–73; Strange, "The Negro in Philadelphia Politics, 1963–1965," pp. 201–202.
71. *Christian Recorder,* 11/14/78, 9/26/78, 4/29/80.
72. *Christian Recorder,* 11/14/78, 5/20/80, 4/29/80.
73. New York *Age,* 11/28/91; *Public Ledger,* 8/13/97; John Trevor Custis, *The Public Schools of Philadelphia: Historical, Biographical, and Statistical* (Philadelphia, 1897), p. 267; Silcox, "Jacob White, Jr.," pp. 93–94; James, ed., *City Government,* p. 62.
74. *Inquirer,* 3/19/190, 10/17/90, 1/20/91.
75. *Inquirer,* 2/3/92, 2/11/91, 2/4/91.
76. *Inquirer,* 1/20/91; James, ed., *City Government,* 71–72; Du Bois, *Philadelphia Negro,* pp. 93–94; Charles Fred White, *Who's Who in Philadelphia: Biographical Sketches of Philadelphia's Leading Colored People . . .* (Philadelphia: A.M.E. Book Concern, 1912), passim.
77. W. E. B. Du Bois, "The Black Vote of Philadelphia."
78. Miller, "Negro in Pennsylvania Politics," p. 88.
79. New York *Age,* 7/28/88, 5/30/91, 5/10/90.

80. *Inquirer,* 11/29/90, 4/21/91; New York *Age,* 5/2/91.

81. Joseph S. Clark, Jr., and Dennis J. Clark, "Rally and Relapse, 1946–1968" in Russell Weigley, ed., *Philadelphia: A Three Hundred-Year History* (New York and London: W. W. Norton, 1982), pp. 649–703; *Inquirer,* 2/17/92.

82. Harold Zink, *City Bosses in the United States: A Study of Twenty Municipal Bosses* (Durham: Duke University Press, 1930), pp. 195–206, 208; Allen R. Steinberg, "The Criminal Courts and the Transformation of Criminal Justice in Philadelphia, 1815–1874," Ph.D. diss. in History, Columbia University, 1983, pp. 492–530; *Inquirer,* 3/17/90. Zink, *City Bosses,* p. 208.

83. James A. Kehl, *Boss Rule in the Gilded Age: Matt Quay of Pennsylvania* (Pittsburgh: University of Pittsburgh Press, 1981), pp. 84–85; Zink, *City Bosses,* p. 212; Walter Davenport, *Power and Glory: The Life of Boies Penrose* (New York: G. P. Putnam's, 1931), p. 108; New York *Freeman,* 6/11/87.

84. Kehl, *Matt Quay,* pp. 84–85, 188–189, 93–114, 128–129; George Morgan, *The City of Firsts: Being a Complete History . . . to the Present Time* (Philadelphia: Historical Publications Society, 1926), pp. 284–287.

85. *Inquirer,* 9/30/88; New York *Freeman,* 9/19/85.

86. *Inquirer,* 3/20/90, 4/15/90.

87. Logan, *Negro in American Life,* pp. 61–72.

88. Logan, *Negro in American Life,* pp. 65–66; Kehl, *Quay,* pp. 129–136.

89. Kehl, *Quay,* p. 135; New York *Age,* 8/9/90, 8/16/90, 8/23/90.

90. New York *Globe,* 11/17/83; New York *Freeman,* 2/6/86; Dorsey Scrapbooks, book number 89, p. 103, *Daily News,* 9/24/87; New York *Age,* 8/9/90; *Inquirer,* 12/11/90, 12/14/90.

91. Kehl, *Quay,* p. 136; Logan, *The Negro in American Life,* pp. 79–96.

92. *Inquirer,* 1/15/96, 9/16/96; Strange, "Negro in Philadelphia Politics," p. 203

93. *Quay,* "Philadelphia Democrats," p. 256; Blankenburg, *Forty Years in the Wilderness,* V.

94. Woodruff, "Election Methods and Reforms"; *Public Ledger,* 4/5/1900.

95. Woodruff, "Election Methods and Reforms"; *Public Ledger,* 11/17/99; Blankenburg, *Forty Years in the Wilderness,* V; McClure, *Old Time Notes,* II, 621; *Public Ledger,* 1/9/1900, 3/2/1900, 2/22/1900.

96. *Public Ledger,* 3/10/1900, 3/12/1900, 12/5/1900.

97. *Public Ledger,* 6/15-22/1900.

98. *Public Ledger,* 6/19/1900.

99. *Inquirer,* 1/25/91; *Public Ledger,* 6/20-21/70.

100. *Christian Recorder,* 9/25/90; Saunders, *100 Years after Emancipation,* p. 38; Mrs. N. F. Mossell, *The Work of the Afro-American Woman,* 2d ed. (Philadelphia, G. S. Ferguson, 1908), p. 10.

101. *Inquirer,* 8/5/90; *Public Ledger,* 4/19/98; Theodore Hershberg and Henry Williams, "Mulattoes and Blacks: Intra-group Differences and Social Stratification in 19th Century Philadelphia," in Theodore Hershberg, ed., *Philadelphia: Work, Space, Family and Group Experience in the Nineteenth Century: Essays Towards an Interdisciplinary History of the City* (New York: Oxford University Press, 1981), pp. 392–434.

102. Du Bois, *Philadelphia Negro,* pp. 197–221, 201.

103. Roger Lane, "James Jeffrey Roche and the Boston Pilot," *New England Quarterly* 33.3 (Sept. 1960): 341–363; *Christian Recorder,* passim.

104. *Public Ledger,* 4/4/1900; *Christian Recorder,* 7/20/76.

105. *Christian Recorder,* 9/9/80, 7/18/95.

106. Du Bois, *Philadelphia Negro,* p. 112; *Christian Recorder,* 10/17/78, 7/14/98, 10/21/97; New York *Globe,* 5/7/84; New York *Freeman,* 11/29/84, *Christian Recorder,* 10/21/97; New York *Freeman,* 12/27/84, 1/10/85.

107. *Christian Recorder,* 8/15/78, 9/19/78, 10/13/81; *Inquirer,* 8/23/81, 8/30/81; *Public Ledger,* 1/27/80; New York *Freeman,* 10/18/84.

108. *Christian Recorder,* 10/7/80; White, *Who's Who in Philadelphia,* pp. 74–76; *Christian Recorder,* 10/13/81.

109. New York *Age,* 4/11/91; New York *Freeman,* 1/3/85, 4/10/86; New York *Globe,* 1/13/83, 1/20/83.

110. *First Annual Report of the Board of Managers of the Frederick Douglass Memorial Hospital and Training School* (Philadelphia, 1896).

111. *Inquirer,* 11/29/90, 4/21/91, 8/30/81.

112. *Inquirer,* 11/3/75.

3. JUSTICE FOR ALL

1. Lawrence M. Friedman and Robert V. Percival, *The Roots of Justice: Crime and Punishment in Alameda County, California, 1870–1910* (Chapel Hill: University of North Carolina Press, 1981), p. 14 and passim; Edward J. James, ed., *The City Government of Philadelphia: A Study in Municipal Administration* (Philadelphia: Wharton School, 1893), pp. 27–28; Allen R. Steinberg, "The Criminal Courts and the Transformation of Criminal Justice in Philadelphia," Ph.D. diss. in History, Columbia University, 1983.

2. *Criminal Code of Pennsylvania,* revised by Public Law 402, March 31, 1860, rarely amended thereafter; cf. *A Digest of the Laws of Pennsylvania . . . Originally Compiled by John Purdon, Esq. . . . I* (Philadelphia, 1885), pp. 397–470.

3. See e.g. *Inquirer,* 1/26/80.

4. Roger Lane, *Violent Death in the City: Suicide, Accident, and Murder in Nineteenth Century Philadelphia* (Cambridge: Harvard University Press, 1979), pp. 106–107; *The Report of a Committee of One on the Office, Life, and Actions of the Honorable William S. Stokley, Mayor of the City of Philadelphia* (Philadelphia, 1880), p. 24.

5. *Annual Police Report,* 1898.

6. *Annual Police Report,* 1880; cf. *Inquirer* and *Public Ledger.*

7. *Inquirer,* 1/15/80; *Public Ledger,* 1/8/80.

8. *Public Ledger,* 9/15/1900.

9. Allen Steinberg, "The Spirit of Litigation: Private Prosecution and Criminal Justice in Nineteenth Century Philadelphia," paper presented at annual meeting of Social Science History Association, Nashville, Tenn., Oct. 23–25, 1981, p. 18; *Public Ledger,* 10/30/62.

10. W. E. B. Du Bois, *The Philadelphia Negro: A Social Study* (Philadelphia,

1899), p. 249; Mary Frances Berry and John W. Blassingame, *Long Memory: The Black Experience in America* (New York: Oxford University Press, 1982), p. 227.

11. *Public Ledger,* 10/7/81; *Inquirer,* 2/3/97.

12. Batsheba S. Epstein, "Patterns of Sentencing and Their Implementation in Philadelphia City and County, 1795–1829," Ph.D. diss. in Sociology, University of Pennsylvania, 1981, pp. 218–220; William Francis Kuntz II, "Criminal Sentencing in Three Nineteenth Century Cities: A Social History of Punishment in New York, Boston, and Philadelphia, 1830–1880," Ph.D. diss. in History, Harvard University, 1978, pp. 402–416; Timothy J. Naylor, "Crime, Criminals, and Punishment in Philadelphia, 1866–1916," Ph.D. diss. in History, University of Chicago, 1979, pp. 161–167; Steinberg, "The Criminal Courts," pp. 177–180.

13. Naylor, "Crime and Punishment," p. 166; Steinberg, "The Criminal Courts," pp. 179–180.

14. *Annual Police Reports,* 1877, 1887–1892.

15. *Inquirer,* 1870; *Public Ledger,* 1880, 1900.

16. Lane, *Violent Death,* chs. 4–5.

17. Cf. Lane, *Violent Death*, p. 108, from which this table differs because, among other reasons, the race of an accused or victimized person was not always noted properly in different papers. Thus, Sarah Washington, acquitted of hacking Maggie Neely to death, was the wife of a black man but was herself white. George Wilson, one of two police officers acquitted of shooting a young white man, was a black. Com. no. 548, Oct. 1880, 1/31/81; 520, Sept. 1900, 4/24/01.

18. *Inquirer,* 2/3/77; Com. no. 47 Oct. 1871, 5/4/77; Com. no. 383 Oct. 1871, 6/22/77.

19. Com. no. 392 Oct. 1871, 5/23/79; 587 Oct. 1871, 4/29/72; 475 Nov. 1871, 2/19/72; 181, Oct. 1886, 11/23/86.

20. A list of all executions appears in Negley K. Teeters, *Scaffold and Chair: A Compilation of Their Use in Pennsylvania, 1682–1962* (Philadelphia: Sponsored by Pennsylvania Prison Society, 1963); Lane, *Violent Death,* p. 68.

21. Com. no. 241 Jan. 1888, 2/3/88; 100 Aug. 1898, 11/3/98; 336 Dec. 1862, 4/10/63; 437 March 1899, 6/27/99; *Public Ledger,* 4/19/1900.

22. Com. no. 55, May 1885, 5/19/85; New York *Freeman,* 9/19/85.

23. Com. no. 1007 Sept. 1892, 10/28/92; *Inquirer,* 4/7/93.

24. Lane, *Violent Death,* pp. 105–106; Com. no. 218 April 1899, 6/20/99; 238 March 1899, 6/28/99; 63 March 1901, 10/4/01.

4. THE WAGES OF SIN

1. Thomas Jefferson, *Notes on the State of Virginia,* ed. William Peden (Chapel Hill: University of North Carolina Press, 1955), pp. 142–143; Eugene Genovese, *Roll, Jordan, Roll: The World the Slaves Made* (New York: Pantheon Books, 1974), pp. 599–612.

2. Genovese, *Roll, Jordan, Roll,* p. 602.

3. The ratio of imprisonment in the table was derived by dividing the white convict population / black convict population by the white population / black pop-

ulation of Philadelphia. According to the census, black population was: (1860) 20,630, or 3.7% of the total population; (1870) 19,550, or 3.0%; (1880) 30,413, or 3.6%; (1890) 39,371, or 3.8%; (1900) 62,613, or 4.8%. The age and sex structure of the black population differed substantially from the white in ways that cancel out the liability for criminal conviction. Blacks had proportionally fewer low-crime old people but fewer high-crime teenagers; there was a considerable excess of black females over males, but black females were more likely to be convicted of all crimes as compared with white females, than black males were as compared with white males. On the whole, the differences between arrest rates over time had more to do with what was happening among whites than among blacks, who were convicted at fairly constant rates, which ranged from a low of 40 per 10,000 around 1860 to a high of 52 around 1880. The 3.5% figure for "commitments" in 1869–1871 counts all those who were arrested for theft and did not make or were not given bail, including many who were later judged not guilty or otherwise freed. The jail reports for the late 1860s and early 1870s allow this distinction; the police reports do not break down arrests by race and category.

4. Roger Lane, *Policing the City: Boston, 1822–1885* (Cambridge: Harvard University Press, 1967), p. 147; Josiah Flynt (Willard), *The World of Graft* (New York, 1901), p. 150; Charles Silberman, *Criminal Violence, Criminal Justice* (New York, Random House, 1978), p. 78.

5. Edwin Crapsey, "Our Criminal Population," *Galaxy* 8 (Sept. 1869): 345–351, Crapsey, "Why Thieves Prosper," *Galaxy* 8 (Dec. 1869): 519–527; Crapsey, "The Nether Side of New York," *Galaxy* 11 (Feb. 1871): 188–199. See also Lane, *Policing the City*, pp. 142–156, 247.

6. *Inquirer*, 6/30/95; Benjamin Eldridge and William B. Watts, *Our Rival the Rascal: A Faithful Portrayal of the Conflict Between the Criminals of This Age and the Defenders of Society—The Police*, introduction by Roger Lane (Montclair: Patterson Smith, 1973, orig. pub. 1897), pp. v-xii and passim; Thomas Byrnes, *Professional Criminals of America* (New York, 1886), passim.

7. Byrnes, *Professional Criminals;* Eldridge and Watts, *Our Rival the Rascal,* pp. 109–111.

8. *Public Ledger*, 2/2/77, 2/14/77, 9/4/85, 2/26/90, 1/26/90, 10/18/99, 10/21/80, 11/15/80, 4/4/81, 6/14/81, 8/10/81, 1/11/81, 3/18/81, 4/4/00, 5/7/00, 6/4/00, 6/13/00, 12/15/00, 12/28/00; *Inquirer*, 2/2/77, 2/14/77, 9/4/85, 2/26/90, 1/26/90, 10/18/99, 12/7/95.

9. *Public Ledger*, 11/15/80, 4/11/81, 4/13/81, 9/8/00, 11/15/00, 2/8/00, 2/24/00; *Inquirer*, 6/30/95, 9/22/95.

10. *Annual Police Report*, 1880.

11. Brynes, *Professional Criminals*, p. 44.

12. Eric Monkkonen, *The Dangerous Class: Crime and Poverty in Columbus Ohio, 1860–1885* (Cambridge: Harvard University Press, 1975), pp. 101–103; Timothy Naylor, "Crime, Criminals, and Punishment in Philadelphia, 1866–1916," Ph.D. diss., University of Chicago, 1979, p. 197; Lawrence M. Friedman and Robert V. Percival, *The Roots of Justice: Crime and Punishment in Alameda County, California, 1870–1910* (Chapel Hill: University of North Carolina Press, 1980), pp. 210–211, find the proportion closer to five-sixths.

13. Eldridge and Watts, *Our Rival the Rascal,* pp. 109–111; *Public Ledger,* 4/24/74, 4/10/80, 4/16/80; *Inquirer,* 3/6/90, 11/21/99.

14. *Inquirer,* 4/11-22/92; *Annual Police Report,* 1892. The sentence for second-degree murder was twelve years, for first-degree was death; life was a commuted sentence only. One report of a thirty-year sentence for the rape of two twelve-year-old girls noted that the longest sentence ever was thiry-two years for a gang rape in 1870. *Inquirer,* 1/11/89.

15. *Inquirer,* 11/16-19/95.

16. W. E. B. Du Bois, *The Philadelphia Negro: A Social Study* (Philadelphia, 1899), p. 262. Allan Pinkerton of the detective agency warned in 1900 of a new class of criminals who would use guns. *Public Ledger,* 5/22/1900.

17. For professional or semiprofessional criminals, as in Jefferson Brown's case, a conviction every three years is assumed. Given about 200 black male convictions for property crimes each year, and assuming about 140 of these were repeaters and 60 were one-timers, three times 140 = 420, and giving 25 for life after 15, 25 times 60 = 1500. To lower the proportion of repeaters would lower the estimate for professionals or semiprofessionals and raise the number of one-timers. The economic impact of a theft was conditioned by who fenced the item and whether it went at the cheaper, second-hand rate to a white or a black.

18. *Public Ledger,* 11/14, 4/5, 9/24/70, 5/28/80, 8/31/00, 12/31/00, 10/17/00; *Inquirer,* 3/17/95, 3/2/95. Neither paper carried enough hard estimates to allow comparisons in 1860 or 1890.

19. *Public Ledger,* 1/6/00, 1/8/00.

20. Lane, *Policing the City,* p. 143; *Public Ledger,* 9/6/60, 5/30/00.

21. *Public Ledger,* 8/23/60, 5/20/81.

22. *Public Ledger,* 11/21/63, 3/23/80.

23. *Public Ledger,* 11/29/80, 12/3/80.

24. *Public Ledger,* 5/28/80, 6/20/81; *Annual Police Report,* 1880.

25. *A Digest of the Laws of Pennsylvania* (1885), pp. 413–414, 418–420, 424.

26. Cf. David T. Courtwright, *Dark Paradise: Opiate Addiction in America Before 1940* (Cambridge: Harvard University Press, 1982), pp. 35, 36–42, 100.

27. Mark Edward Lender and James Kirby Martin, *Drinking in America: A History* (New York: Free Press, 1982), p. 84; Lane, *Policing the City,* pp. 106–108.

28. Lender and Martin, *Drinking in America,* pp. 93–102, 109–114, 196.

29. Monkkonen, *Police in Urban America,* p. 73; *Annual Police Reports,* 1859–1901.

30. *A Digest of the Laws of Pennsylvania* (1885), pp. 1076–1087.

31. *Report of the Committee of One on the Official Life and Administration of Honorable William S. Stokley, Mayor of the City of Philadelphia* (Philadelphia, 1880), pp. 28–29.

32. *Annual Report of the County Prison,* 1869–1871.

33. Naylor, "Crime, Criminals, and Punishment in Philadelphia," pp. 85–87. Naylor divided number of arrests by number of convictions for each of several groups in order to construct a "discrimination ratio," suggesting the

chances of, for example, a given black, Irish, or native white arrested person being convicted after arrest. He concluded that blacks were the most likely victims of discrimination, while the Irish-born were heavily favored by the justice system. Yet he overlooked the fact that most arrests were for drunkenness and its variants. Thus, his figures really show that blacks had proportionally fewer arrests for drunkenness in comparison to other and more serious crimes than any other group; the Irish had the most. *The Annual Reports of the House of Correction,* begun in 1874, did not break down the reasons for commitment, overwhelmingly chronic drunkenness or vagrancy. During 1879–1881 blacks had an annual average of 172 commitments, or a little less than 3% of the total and less than their proportionate share. This increased over the years to 319 in 1889–1891, or 5% of the total, and 552 during 1899–1901, or 9% of the total.

34. *Annual Health Report,* 1899–1901.

35. Allen Davis and John F. Sutherland, "Reform and Uplift among Philadelphia Negroes: The Diary of Helen Parrish, 1888," *Pennsylvania Magazine of History and Biography* 94 (Oct. 1970): 496–517.

36. *A Digest of the Laws of Pennsylvania, Supplementary to the Eleventh Edition,* pp. 2229–2233.

37. *Inquirer,* 1/20/90, 4/1/90.

38. Alexander C. McClure, *Old Time Notes of Pennsylvania,* vol. 2 (Philadelphia: John C. Winston, 1905), pp. 286, 621; Blankenburg, *Forty Years in the Wilderness,* V, 465; *Public Ledger,* 11/30/1900.

39. *A Digest of the Laws of Pennsylvania, Supplementary to the Eleventh Edition,* pp. 2229–2233; *Inquirer,* 5/23/88.

40. *Inquirer,* 3/20/88, 3/23/88, 2/11/91.

41. *Inquirer,* 5/8/87.

42. *Inquirer,* 3/16-20/88.

43. *Inquirer,* 3/16–20/88.

44. *Inquirer,* 4/15/90, 3/20/90; *Public Ledger,* 3/18/96, 5/4/00; Charles Fred White, *Who's Who in Philadelphia: . . . Biographical Sketches of Philadelphia's Leading Colored People . . .* (Philadelphia: A.M.E. Book Concern, 1912), p. 140.

45. *Inquirer,* 3/3/90, 2/11/90, 4/15/90; *Public Ledger,* 3/14/96.

46. *Inquirer,* 7/29/95; *Public Ledger,* 12/28/98; Annual Report of the County Prison, 1889–1890.

47. Robert Obojski, *Bush League: A History of Minor League Baseball* (New York: Macmillan, 1975), pp. 3–13.

48. Edwin Bancroft Henderson, *The Negro in Sports,* rev. ed. (Washington: Associated Publishers, 1939), p. 226; Baltimore *Afro-American,* 8/17/95; New York *Age,* 5/17/90.

49. *Inquirer,* 7/29/95, 8/5/95, 7/28/90; *Public Ledger,* 3/3/1900.

50. *Inquirer,* 7/21/90, 11/1-2/93, 11/8/93, 2/17/95; *Public Ledger,* 3/3/00, 2/17/95.

51. Frank G. Martin, *The Encyclopedia of Sports,* 3d ed. (New York: A. S. Barnes, 1963), p. 244; Howard O. Sprogle, *The Philadelphia Police, Past and*

Present (Philadelphia, 1887), pp. 171–172; *Public Ledger,* 12/24-25/1900, 7/7/60; *Inquirer,* 8/11/95.

52. John Saunders, *100 Years after Emancipation, History of the Philadelphia Negro, 1787 to 1963* (Philadelphia, n.d.), pp. 200–201; *Inquirer,* 6/22/93, 4/27/95.

53. *Inquirer,* 5/17/88.

54. *Inquirer,* 1/22/90, 1/25/90.

55. *Inquirer,* 1/25/90, 1/22/90; *Public Ledger,* 12/18/00, 5/15/00, 11/17/00, 2/8/83.

56. Conversation with Mark Haller, spring 1983; *Public Ledger,* 8/25/00, 7/2/00.

57. *Christian Recorder,* 11/2/99.

58. *Public Ledger,* 5/30/60, 7/18/1900; Du Bois *Philadelphia Negro,* p. 265.

59. *Inquirer,* 11/19/90, 1/25/90.

60. *Public Ledger,* 4/11/00, 2/1/83, 12/18/1900, 7/14/81, 6/26/1900, 3/29/1900, 7/17/1900; *Inquirer,* 6/4/95.

61. *Public Ledger,* 1/1/1900; conversation with Mark Haller, spring 1983; David Johnson, *Policing the Urban Underworld: The Impact of Crime on the Development of the American Police, 1800–1887* (Philadelphia: Temple University Press, 1979, p. 162; *Annual Report of the County Prison,* 1889–1891, 1899–1901.

62. Lane, *Policing the City,* p. 99; Kenneth Kusmer, *A Ghetto Takes Shape: Black Cleveland, 1870–1930* (Urbana: University of Illinois Press, 1969), pp. 48–49; David M. Katzman, *Before the Ghetto: Black Detroit in the Nineteenth Century* (Urbana: University of Illinois Press, 1975), pp. 171–172; Allen H. Spear, *Black Chicago. The Making of a Negro Ghetto, 1890–1920* (Chicago: University of Chicago Press, 1967), p. 24–25; Gilbert Osofsky, *Harlem, The Making of a Ghetto: Negro New York, 1890–1930* (New York: Harper and Row), p. 14.

63. Claudia D. Johnson, "That Guilty Third Tier: Prostitution in 19th Century American Theaters," *American Quarterly* 27.5 (1975): 575–584.

64. *Inquirer,* 3/17/95.

65. *Inquirer,* 3/9/95, 5/1/95, 10/7/95.

66. *Inquirer,* 3/1/83, 4/24/95; New York *Globe,* 3/21/85.

67. *Inquirer,* 3/17/95, 2/21/95, 3/21/95, 7/30/95, 9/100/95.

68. *Inquirer,* 3/21/95; Richard R. Wright, *The Negro in Pennsylvania: A Study in Economic History* (New York: Arno Press, 1969, orig. pub. 1912), pp. 178–179; *Inquirer,* 3/28-29/95.

69. Rev. Frank M. Goodchild, "The Social Evil in Philadelphia," *Arena* 15 (Jan. 1896): 574–586.

70. Ruth Rosen, *The Lost Sisterhood: Prostitution in America, 1900–1918* (Baltimore: Johns Hopkins University Press, 1982), p. 3; William Sanger, *History of Prostitution: Its Extent, Causes, and Effects Throughout the World* (New York: Eugenics, 1939, orig. pub. 1858), pp. 677–679.

71. Walter Davenport, *Power and Glory: The Life of Boies Penrose* (New York: G. P. Putnam's, 1931), p. 109: *Inquirer,* 1/11/95, 1/10/95, 11/12/95.

72. *Inquirer,* 12/14/95, 12/19/95, 12/20/95, 1/11/96, 1/9/96.

73. *Inquirer,* 12/13/95, 1/5/96; Blankenburg, *Forty Years in the Wilderness,* IV, 355; Goodchild, "Social Evil in Philadelphia," pp. 575–576.

74. Goodchild, "Social Evil in Philadelphia," pp. 575–576; Rosen, *Prostitution in America,* p. 87 n8. Philadelphia Vice Commission, *A Report of Existing Conditions with Recommendations to the Honorable Rudolph Blankenburg, Mayor* (Philadelphia, 1913), found that about half of all prostitutes worked outside of houses, p. 6.

75. Harriet Beecher Stowe, *Uncle Tom's Cabin, or, Life among the Lowly,* ed. Kenneth Lynn (Cambridge: Harvard University Press, 1967), p. 377.

76. Goodchild, "The Social Evil in Philadelphia," p. 585; *Public Ledger,* 3/12/00, 3/3/00, 4/26/00, 3/12/00; *Philadelphia Tribune,* 5/9/14; Blankenburg, "Forty Years in the Wilderness," VII, 132–133; IV, p. 467.

77. *Annual Report of the County Prison,* 1889–1891, 1899–1901.

78. James Mohr, *Abortion in America: The Origins and Evolution of National Policy, 1800–1900* (New York: Oxford University Press, 1978), pp. 50, 73–85; Lane, *Violent Death,* pp. 90–94.

79. Lane, *Violent Death,* p. 177n41; *Public Ledger,* 3/8/60, 4/18/80, 7/12/80, 2/9/00, 6/15/00, 8/14/00; *Inquirer,* 7/13/87, 2/24/88, 7/2-3/90, 9/4/90, 1/24/93, 12/6/94, 1/14/95, 3/4/95, 7/9/95, 7/18/95, 4/30/96. The listings under "abortion" in the health records did not begin until late in the period and covered only a few deaths, not including those for peritonitis, for example, or septicemia.

80. Mohr, *Abortion in America,* pp. 95–98.

81. *Inquirer,* 5/27/81, 5/28/81, 6/3–4/81; *Public Ledger,* 5/30/81.

82. Lane, *Violent Death,* pp. 154–159, 97–98, 111. This is an undercount of the blacks involved, as are several in this discussion, since it assumes that a person was white unless identified otherwise. Given the little information available about most cases, some black women are sure to be mislabeled.

83. *Annual Register of Deaths,* 1866–1869; Lane, *Violent Death,* pp. 99–100, 110–111, 144–145.

84. Lane, *Violent Death,* pp. 95–96; *Public Ledger,* 1/24/70, 2/5/83, 7/13/00, 7/14/00; *Inquirer,* 9/21/80, 6/20/93, 11/27/95; Harvey Levinstein, ' "Best for Babies' or 'Preventable Infanticide,' " *Journal of American History* 70.1 (June 1983): 75–94. The Dorsey scrapbooks contain some accounts of baby farming, but as all are black, they allow no numerical comparison with white.

85. *Health Department Annual Reports,* 1890–1901.

86. Philadelphia Vice Commission, *Report,* p. 17 and passim.

87. See e.g. Rosen, *Prostitution in America.*

88. Isobel Eaton, "Special Report on Negro Domestic Service in the Seventh Ward," in Du Bois, *Philadelphia Negro,* pp. 467–468.

89. Rosen, *Prostitution in America,* p. 80; conversations with Mark Haller, spring 1983; *Inquirer,* 9/21/80, 1/5/96, 1/9/96; *Public Ledger,* 11/9/00; Com. no. 186, Nov. 1900, 12/7/1900.

90. *Public Ledger,* 3/4/70; *Inquirer,* 1/12-13/95, 1/18/95, 1/20/95, 1/24/95.

91. *Inquirer,* 12/19/95, 5/20/96.

92. Goodchild, "Social Evil in Philadelphia," p. 567; Johnson, *Policing the*

Urban Underworld, p. 157; Philadelphia Vice Commission, *Report,* p. 35; Rosen, *Prostitution in America,* pp. 96, 147–148, 205.

5. THE PRICE OF CRIME

1. Roger Lane, *Violent Death in the City: Suicide, Accident, and Murder in Nineteenth Century Philadelphia* (Cambridge: Harvard University Press, 1979), p. 113, App. B. The rates given here were calculated from the study of all indictments in the city; the actual years covered are 1860–1869 and 1890–1901. The total of 66 trials for the last years was increased by five to make up for eight months missing from the indictment docket books during 1892 and represents an average from the equivalent months of 1891 and 1893.

2. Lane, *Violent Death,* p. 71, App. B.

3. *Public Ledger,* 4/1/80-9/30/80. Injuries from fights accounted for 28 percent of all admissions in these months.

4. Lane, *Violent Death,* pp. 104–114, App. B.

5. Com. no. 491, April 1896, 10/21/96; 168, Feb. 1898, 5/31/98; 432, April 1898, 6/20/98.

6. *Inquirer,* 7/18/95, 3/25/95, 12/19/95; *Public Ledger,* 5/19-20/96, 3/3/00, 3/7/00, 3/27/00; Dorsey Scrapbooks, no. 110, p. 103, undated clipping evidently late in 1898.

7. *Public Ledger,* 12/27/98, 1/6/99; *Inquirer,* 12/27/98, 2/2/99, 6/29/99.

8. Lee Kennett and James LaVerne Anderson, *The Gun in America: The Origins of a National Dilemna* (Westport, Conn.: Greenwood Press), p. 156.

9. Com. no. 256, March 1872, 3/28/72; *Inquirer,* 1/1/72.

10. Lane, *Violent Death,* pp. 103–104, App. B.

11. Dennis Clark, *The Irish in Philadelphia: Ten Generations of Urban Experience* (Philadelphia: Temple University Press), pp. 74–76, 88–105; Lane, *Violent Death,* pp. 103–104, App. B.

12. W. E. B. Du Bois, *The Philadelphia Negro: A Social Study* (Philadelphia, 1899), p. 351.

13. Lane, *Violent Death,* pp. 28–29, 11–12.

14. The number of blacks indicted for murder was: during the 1860s, 13; the 1870s, 26; the 1880s, 25; the 1890s, 66.

15. Lane, *Violent Death,* p. 71, App. B.

16. U.S. Department of Justice, Federal Bureau of Investigation, *Uniform Crime Reports for the United States, 1981* (Washington, D.C.: U.S. Government Printing Office, 1982), p. 8, gives figures for 1979–1981.

6. CRIME AND CULTURE

1. E. Franklin Frazer, *Black Bourgeoisie: The Rise of a New Middle Class* (New York: Free Press, 1957), passim; Gunnar Myrdal, *An American Dilemna: The Negro Problem and Modern Democracy,* rev. ed. (New York: Harper, 1962), pt. 8 and passim; W. E. B. Du Bois, *The Philadelphia Negro: A Social Study* (Philadelphia, 1899), pp. 316–319.

2. *Inquirer*, 4/1/79.

3. *Public Ledger*, 5/19/96, 1/26/00; *Inquirer*, 6/28/79, 12/20/95; Dorsey Scrapbooks, no. 125, p. 85, undated and unidentified clipping from 1899.

4. Lawrence W. Levine, *Black Culture and Black Consciousness: Afro-American Folk Thought from Slavery to Freedom* (New York: Oxford University Press, 1977), pp. 407–408.

5. Levine, *Black Culture*, pp. 417, 418.

6. Booker T. Washington, *Up from Slavery: An Autobiography* (New York: Dodd, Mead, 1965, originally published 1901); *Public Ledger*, 10/31/00, 9/18/00.

7. Elliot Rudwick. *W. E. B. Du Bois: Propagandist of the Negro Protest*, 2d ed. (Philadelphia: University of Pennsylvania Press, 1968), ch. 1; Du Bois, *Philadelphia Negro*, pp. 126, 127, 390, 313.

8. Du Bois, *Philadelphia Negro*, p. 313; *Inquirer*, 12/3/95, 6/17/95.

9. *Inquirer*, 8/23/81.

10. Du Bois, *Philadelphia Negro*, pp. 257, 235, 242–259. Du Bois undercounted the relative extent of black crime in the city, first by counting all arrests, the great majority of which were for drunkenness, an offense for which blacks tended to be arrested far less than for other crimes, and second by counting all commitments to Eastern State Penitentiary, whose inmates were drawn not only from Philadelphia but from much of the eastern half of the state, an area with proportionally fewer blacks than the city proper.

11. Of the 388 Dorsey scrapbooks, the majority are devoted to special topics, some of them notable crimes and scandals. Those numbered 48–123, however, are chronological and deal largely with crime in the years 1883–1903. *Christian Recorder*, 7/29/97.

12. *Public Ledger*, 10/21/70, 10/24/70; *Inquirer*, 2/26/90; *Annual Police Report*, 1879. The Dorsey Scrapbooks contain a few interracial incidents from Philadelphia, most of them alleged "attempts" only, none involving legal convictions or headlines, in strong contrast to similar events as reported from the South. However, Dorsey Scrapbook no. 97, p. 51, includes an incident reported in an unnamed Philadelphia paper, 11/22/99, in which a mob of men from both races beat a white man accused of raping a black girl.

13. *Public Ledger*, 8/22/60, *Christian Recorder*, 4/6/82, 9/15/81, 8/22/78.

14. Du Bois, *Philadelphia Negro*, pp. 139–140; *Inquirer*, 9/10/90, 1/10/91, 5/20/90, 11/9/90.

15. Du Bois, *Philadelphia Negro*, preface, pp. 34–35; Harry C. Silcox, "Philadelphia Negro Educator: Jacob C. White, Jr., 1837–1900," *Pennsylvania Magazine of History and Biography* 97.1 (Jan. 1973): 82–97; *Inquirer*, 9/21/80, 5/17/89, 3/4/95; *Philadelphia City Directory*, 1896.

16. Elizabeth Pleck, *Black Migration and Poverty: Boston, 1865–1900* (New York and London: Academic Press, 1980), p. 76; Frank J. Furstenberg, Jr., John Modell, and Theodore Hershberg, "The Origins of the Female-Headed Black Family: The Impact of the Urban Experience," in Theodore Hershberg, ed., *Philadelphia: Work, Space, Family and Group Experience in the Nineteenth Century: Essays Towards an Interdisciplinary History of the City* (New York: Oxford University Press, 1981), pp. 435–545; Stephan Thernstrom, *The Other Bostonians: Poverty and Progress in the American Metropolis* (Cambridge: Har-

vard University Press, 1973), pp. 184–185; Charles Fred White, Jr., *Who's Who in Philadelphia . . . Biographical Sketches of Philadelphia's Leading Colored People . . .* (Philadelphia: A.M.E. Book Concern, 1912).

17. Du Bois, *Philadelphia Negro*, pp. 61–62, 178; Philadelphia *Tribune*, 6/25/13.

18. Philadelphia *Tribune*, 4/20/1912.

19. Names of lawyers are obtainable through original bills of indictment, kept in the office of the clerk of the court of quarter sessions, although a few accused killers had no counsel at this stage. *Public Ledger*, 3/12/00, 4/14/99, 11/21/99, *Inquirer*, 8/26/97, 5/1/96; Roger Lane, *Violent Death in the City: Suicide, Accident, and Murder in Nineteenth Century Philadelphia* (Cambridge: Harvard University Press, 1979), p. 186; Dorsey Scrapbooks, no. 94, p. 73, unnamed Philadelphia newspaper dated 11/4/97, and no. 101, p. 61, unnamed Philadelphia newspaper dated 7/6/98.

20. *Inquirer*, 9/4/90, 9/19/90.

21. New York *Globe*, 12/29/83, 5/8/85; White, Jr., *Who's Who in Philadelphia*, pp. 37–38, 58; *Inquirer*, 9/4/90, 7/18/95, 4/28/96; Baltimore *Afro-America*, 8/10/95; *Public Ledger*, 8/17/80; Com. no. 72, Oct. 1896, 1/21/97; 236, 7/2/96.

22. Quotation from Mrs. John Frederick Lewis, who worked in hospitals of the era, as recalled by her son Alfred Baker Lewis.

23. Allan Davis and John K. Sutherland, "Reform and Uplift among Philadelphia Negroes: The Diary of Helen Parrish, 1888," *Pennsylvania Magazine of History and Biography* 94.4 (Oct. 1970): 490–517; New York *Freeman*, 7/10/86; Du Bois, *The Philadelphia Negro*, p. 390.

24. John Blassingame, *The Slave Community: Plantation Life in the Antebellum South*, rev. ed. (New York: Oxford University Press, 1979), ch. 4; Robert Fogel and Stanley Engerman, *Time on the Cross: The Economics of American Negro Slavery* (Boston and Toronto: Little, Brown, 1974), pp. 78–86, 126–144; Eugene Genovese, *Roll, Jordon, Roll: The World the Slaves Made* (New York: Pantheon Books, 1976), Bk. 3, pt. 2; Herbert Gutman, *The Black Family in Slavery and Freedom, 1750–1925* (New York: Vintage Books, 1977).

25. Pleck, *Black Migration and Poverty*, pp. 167–178.

26. "1880 Grid Tally: Crosstabulation of Sex by Age," printout provided by Philadelphia Social History Project; Lane, *Violent Death*, App. B.

27. New York *Freeman*, 1/9/86; Lane, *Violent Death*, pp. 43–47; Du Bois, *Philadelphia Negro*, pp. 111, 194.

28. *Annual Report of the Superintendent to the Managers of the House of Refuge*, 1859–1861, 1869–1871, 1879–1881, 1889–1891. The House drew children from several counties; most figures are given separately for Philadelphia, but not information as to who committed them. In the 1890s the House stopped publishing figures by race.

29. Michael R. Haines, "Why Were Nineteenth Century U.S. Urban Black Fertility Rates So Low? Evidence from Philadelphia, 1850–1880," unpub. ms., pp. 32–33; Stewart Tolnay, "Black Fertility in Decline: Urban Differentials in 1900," *Social Biology* 27.4 (Winter 1980): 249–260. None of these demographers has used prostitution and venereal disease as primary explanations for urban black fertility patterns.

30. Ruth Rosen, *The Lost Sisterhood: Prostitution in America, 1900-1918* (Baltimore: Johns Hopkins University Press), p. 144; Du Bois, *Philadelphia Negro*, p. 313; *Public Ledger*, 11/21/63, 3/24/80.

31. Christian *Recorder*, 4/6/81, 11/18/89; *Inquirer*, 12/13/95.

32. *Inquirer*, 4/29/93; Du Bois, *Philadelphia Negro*, p. 241; Philadelphia *Tribune*, 6/28/13.

33. *Inquirer*, 4/29/93.

34. Com. no. 1007, Sept. 1892, 10/28/92; 218, April 1899, 6/20/99; 238, March 1899, 6/28/99; 63, March 1901, 10/4/01.

35. *Inquirer*, 8/26/97; Com. no. 437, March 1899, 6/27/99; 531, June 1901, 12/7/01; Lane, *Violent Death*, pp. 105-106.

EPILOGUE

1. The convict counts come from the "Convicts' Description Dockets" of Moyamensing Jail (killers were not then sent to Holmesburg) and the "Convict Reception Registers" (title varies) of the Eastern State Penitentiary. Convictions instead of indictments were used to establish relative murder rates because in this period the relevant court docket books for indictments did not run as far into the twentieth century as the convict dockets. The last penitentiary dockets are for 1928. Population figures from United States Department of Commerce, Bureau of the Census, *Twelfth Census of the United States, Taken in the Year 1900*, vol. 1, p. cxxi, p. 802, are: blacks 62,613, Italian-born 17,830, Philadelphia 1,294,387; from U.S. *Census* (1910), vol. 3, p. 588: black 84,859, Italian 45,308, Philadelphia 1,549,008; from U.S. *Census* (1920), vol. 3, p. 896: black 134,229, Italian 63,723, Philadelphia 1,823,779; from U.S. *Census* (1930), vol. 3, pt. 2, p. 671: black 219,599, Italian 68,156, Philadelphia 1,950,901.

2. Eric Monkkonen, *Police in Urban America, 1860-1920* (Cambridge: Cambridge University Press, 1981), p. 77, finds an upturn in homicide arrests in the 23 largest U.S. cities in the late nineteenth and early twentieth centuries, in contrast to the declining rates found in foreign jurisdictions by measures other than arrests. Arrests as a measure of the actual incidence of murder may be distorted by factors other than in-migration. A single episode may have generated either no arrests or a dragnet operation that resulted in twenty. Other factors that might push the statistics upward, without reflecting any real increase in homicidal behavior in the period, include larger and more efficient police forces, departmental use of fingerprints, automobiles and radios, and the classification of auto accidents as manslaughter. When the F.B.I. began to collect figures for murder rates based on "crimes known to the police" in 1933, when Italian and other immigration had slowed or even reversed, those rates turned down immediately and continued down for several decades. U.S. Department of Commerce, Buruea of the Census, *Historical Statistics of the United States, Colonial Times to 1970*, pt 1, pp. 407, 414.

3. There were 42 Italian-born convicts in 1901-1907, 44 in 1908-1915, 71 in 1915-1921, 24 in 1922-1928. Arthur P. Dudden, "The City Embraces 'Normalcy': 1919-1929," in Russell Weigley, ed., *Philadelphia: A Three Hundred Year History* (New York, W. W. Norton, 1982), pp. 566-600. Murder rates

based on convictions are not directly comparable with those based on episodes leading to indictment, since a single episode may result in no convictions or in several.

4. Frederick Miller, "Black Migration to Philadelphia," *Pennsylvania Magazine of History and Biography* 108.3 (July 1984): 315–350; W. E. B. Du Bois, *The Philadelphia Negro: A Social Study* (Philadelphia, 1899), p. 78.

5. John Dollard, *Caste and Class in a Southern Town*, 2d ed. (New York: Harper, 1949), ch. 13.

6. Dudden, "The City Embraces 'Normalcy,' " pp. 592–593, 588; Theodore Hershberg et al., "A Tale of Three Cities: Blacks, Immigrants, and Opportunity in Philadelphia, 1850–1880, 1900, 1970," in Theodore Hershberg, ed. *Philadelphia: Work, Space, Family and Group Experience in the Nineteenth Century: Essays Towards an Interdisciplinary History of the City* (New York: Oxford University Press, 1981), pp. 461–491; David T. Courtwright, *Dark Paradise: Opiate Addiction in America Before 1940* (Cambridge: Harvard University Press, 1982), pp. 97–98.

7. Philadelphia *Tribune*, 12/14/12; *Twenty-Fifth Annual Report of the Board of Managers of the Frederick Douglas Memorial Hospital*, 1920; Dudden, "The City Embraces 'Normalcy,' " p. 589.

8. Negley K. Teeters, *Scaffold and Chair: A Compilation of Their Use in Pennsylvania, 1682–1962* (Philadelphia: Pennsylvania Prison Society, 1963), pp. 177–184.

9. Joseph S. Clark, Jr., and Dennis J. Clark, "Rally and Relapse: 1946–1968," and Margaret B. Tinkham, "Depression and War, 1929–1946," in Russell Weigley, ed., *Philadelphia*, pp. 649–703, 601–648; Stephen Thernstrom, *The Other Bostonians: Poverty and Progress in the American Metropolis, 1880–1970* (Cambridge: Harvard University Press, 1973), pp. 197–202; Michael Haines, "Why Were Nineteenth Century U.S. Urban Black Rates So Low? Evidence from Philadelphia, 1850–1880," unpub. ms.

10. Marvin E. Wolfgang, *Patterns in Criminal Homicide* (New York: John Wiley, 1966, orig. pub. 1958), pp. 27, 69.

11. Karl E. Taeuber and Alma F. Taeuber, *Negroes in Cities: Residential Segregation and Neighborhood Change* (Chicago: Aldine, 1965), pp. 138–139; Seymour Parker and Robert J. Kleiner, *Mental Illness in the Urban Negro Community* (New York: Free Press, 1966), ch. 8.

12. *U.S. Census, 1950*, vol. 38, pp. 397–398; *1960*, vol. 40, pp. 749–750.

13. *U.S. Census, 1960*, vol. 40, pp. 749–750; Philip M. Hauser, "Demographic Factors in the Migration of the Negro," in Talcott Parsons and Kenneth B. Clark, ed. *The Negro in America* (Boston: Houghton Mifflin, 1965), pp. 71–101; U.S. Bureau of the Census, *The Social and Economic Status of the Black Population in the United States: An Historical View, 1790–1978* (Washington, D.C.: U.S. Government Printing Office, 1979), p. 75; U.S. Bureau of the Census, *Statistical Abstract of the United States, 1982–1983* (Washington, D.C.: U.S. Government Printing Office, 1983), p. 178.

14. *U.S. Census, 1960*, vol. 40, p. 103; *1970*, vol. 40, p. 16.

15. *Social and Economic Status of the Black Population*, pp. 67, 69, 98, 130.

16. Ted Robert Gurr, "On the History of Violent Crime in Europe and

America," in Hugh Davis Graham and Ted Robert Gurr, *Violence in America: Historical and Comparative Perspectives,* rev. ed. (Beverly Hills: Sage, 1979), pp. 353–374.

17.   U.S. Department of Justice, Federal Bureau of Investigation, *Uniform Crime Reports for the United States, 1970* (Washington, D.C.: U.S. Government Printing Office, 1971), pp. 7, 131; Lane, *Violent Death,* p. 113.

18.   Lane, *Violent Death,* pp. 137–138.

19.   Charles Silberman, *Criminal Violence, Criminal Justice* (New York: Random House, 1978), pp. 119–122.

20.   *Uniform Crime Reports, 1979,* p. 200; *1980,* p. 204; *1981,* p. 179. Some arrests that are made on the initiative of the police themselves, such as gambling, prostitution, drunkenness, and similar morals offenses, are open to the charge of prejudicial policing. However, blacks are less likely than whites to be arrested for some of these offenses, such as drunk driving. Many other offenses, such as robbery, murder, and family offenses, are based either on descriptions, hard evidence, or complaints by other blacks. Silberman, *Criminal Justice,* pp. 152–153.

21.   *Uniform Crime Reports, 1979,* p. 200; *1980,* p. 204; *1981,* p. 179.

22.   Silberman, *Criminal Justice,* pp. 141–160.

23.   *Uniform Crime Reports, 1970,* pp. 5–30; *1979,* p. 15; *1980,* pp. 13, 17, *1981,* p. 6.

24.   *Uniform Crime Reports, 1969,* pp. 6, 118; *1970,* p. 131; *1971,* pp. 8, 127; *1979,* p. 6, 200; *1980,* pp. 13, 204; *1981,* pp. 8, 179. The black-white gap in Philadelphia has also been closing with respect to death rates. During 1969–1971, when the overall murder rate was 17 per 100,000, the white rate was 5.0 and the nonwhite 42.6. In 1979–1981 the overall rate was 22.5, again very close to the big city average, with the white rate 9.3 and the nonwhite, somewhat lowered by the influx of new Asians, 40.9. *Philadelphia Department of Health Annual Statistical Report, 1969,* tables A–E; *1970,* table 7; *1971,* table 21; *1979,* table 27; *1980,* table 25; *1981,* table 27.

25.   Thernstrom, *The Other Bostonians,* pp. 260–261.

INDEX